The Arc of War

The Arc of War

Origins, Escalation, and Transformation

JACK S. LEVY AND
WILLIAM R. THOMPSON

THE UNIVERSITY OF CHICAGO PRESS   CHICAGO AND LONDON

JACK S. LEVY is the Board of Governors' Professor of Political Science at Rutgers University and former president of the International Studies Association (2007–8).

WILLIAM R. THOMPSON is Distinguished Professor and the Donald A. Rogers Professor of Political Science at Indiana University and former president of the International Studies Association (2005–6).

The University of Chicago Press, Chicago 60637
The University of Chicago Press, Ltd., London
© 2011 by The University of Chicago
All rights reserved. Published 2011.
Printed in the United States of America

20 19 18 17 16 15 14 13 12 11   1 2 3 4 5

ISBN-13: 978-0-226-47628-5 (cloth)
ISBN-13: 978-0-226-47629-2 (paper)

ISBN-10: 0-226-47628-6 (cloth)
ISBN-10: 0-226-47629-4 (paper)

Library of Congress Cataloging-in-Publication Data

Levy, Jack S., 1948–
  The arc of war : origins, escalation, and transformation / Jack S. Levy and William R. Thompson.
      p. cm.
  Includes bibliographical references and index.
  ISBN-13: 978-0-226-47628-5 (cloth : alk. paper)
  ISBN-10: 0-226-47628-6 (cloth : alk. paper)
  ISBN-13: 978-0-226-47629-2 (pbk. : alk. paper)
  ISBN-10: 0-226-47629-4 (pbk. : alk. paper) 1. War and civilization. 2. War—History. 3. War—Sociological aspects. 4. Social evolution. I. Thompson, William R. II. Title.
  CB481.L48 2011
  909—dc23

2011020001

♾ The paper used in this publication meets the minimum requirements of the American National Standard for Information Sciences—Permanence of Paper for Printed Library Materials, ANSI Z39.48-1992.

TO KIM, PARTNER IN FRIENDSHIP, LOVE, AND LIFE — JSL

AND

TO KAREN, DESPITE ALL THE CELERY CRUNCHING
AND THE TACHOPHOBIA ON THE SLOPES — WRT

Contents

List of Tables and Figures   ix

Acknowledgments   xiii

CHAPTER 1.   The Evolution of War   1

CHAPTER 2.   The Origins of War   19

CHAPTER 3.   Evolutionary and Coevolutionary Processes   54

CHAPTER 4.   The First Two Agrarian Warfare Accelerations   87

CHAPTER 5.   The Third Evolutionary Acceleration   126

CHAPTER 6.   The Coevolution of the Western Military Trajectory   155

CHAPTER 7.   Nonwestern Military Trajectories   186

CHAPTER 8.   The Coevolution of War, Past and Future   207

Notes   219

References   243

Index   273

Tables and Figures

FIGURES

Figure 1.1 Our argument / 2
Figure 1.2 Estimated battle deaths by century since 3000 BCE / 7
Figure 1.3 Frequency of great power war by decade, 1490–2010 / 8
Figure 1.4 Severity of great power war by quarter century / 8
Figure 1.5 Frequency of types of war, 1820s–2000s / 9
Figure 2.1 The origins of war / 52
Figure 3.1 The coevolution of war, threat environment, military organization, weaponry, political organization, and political economy / 56
Figure 3.2 Coevolutionary process / 63
Figure 3.3 Organizational/weaponry complexity and the costs of war between industrialized states / 71
Figure 3.4 The evolution of war / 76
Figure 8.1 Another look at the coevolutionary complex / 213

TABLES

Table 1.1 Selected major battle attributes / 6
Table 2.1 Cioffi-Revilla's evidence for early warfare / 21
Table 2.2 Ferguson's evidence for early warfare / 22
Table 2.3 Segmentation and warfare among foraging groups / 32
Table 2.4 Marriage payments and warfare among foraging groups / 33
Table 2.5 Carneiro's single versus multiple village chiefdoms distinctions / 35

Table 2.6   Stages of early political organization / 40
Table 2.7   The size of the warrior aristocracy and the frequency of warfare / 41
Table 2.8   Otterbein's evolutionary trajectories for pristine states, stratification, and conflict / 42
Table 2.9   Otterbein's evolutionary trajectories for pristine states, military organization, and war / 43
Table 2.10 Haas's overview of North American conflict propensities / 45
Table 2.11 Political centralization and economic subsistence / 48
Table 2.12 Subsistence, political centralization, war frequency, and rationale for war / 48
Table 2.13 Subsistence, political centralization, and military organization / 49
Table 2.14 Subsistence, political centralization, and weaponry / 50
Table 3.1   Six coevolutionary factors and their definitions / 55
Table 3.2   Warfare and political development from Cioffi-Revilla's perspective / 64
Table 3.3   Cioffi-Revilla's model recast / 65
Table 3.4   Main types of political economy / 66
Table 3.5   Political-economic influences / 66
Table 3.6   Stratification in 2005 military expenditures / 68
Table 3.7   Political-economic evolution and war / 70
Table 3.8   The western Eurasian military-war trajectory / 81
Table 3.9   Interstate warfare duration for less developed states, 1945–2007 / 84
Table 3.10 Three accelerations in coevolution / 85
Table 4.1   Energy (in footpounds) necessary to penetrate ancient armor / 91
Table 4.2   Empire and army size / 91
Table 4.3   Evolution and coevolution in ancient Egypt / 94
Table 4.4   Evolution and coevolution in ancient Greece and Rome / 106
Table 4.5   Evolution and coevolution in ancient China / 114

Table 4.6	Evolution and coevolution in ancient Mesoamerica / 118
Table 5.1	The timing of hypothesized military revolutions / 129
Table 6.1	Lynn's abbreviated matrix of core military style / 161
Table 6.2	The coevolution of organizations, technology, warfare, and political-economic context / 170
Table 6.3	The western military trajectory / 178
Table 6.4	Nonwestern influences on the western military trajectory / 180
Table 7.1	A comparison of external environments then and now / 189
Table 7.2	Implications of differences in external environments / 191
Table 7.3	Kaldor's evolution of old wars / 195
Table 7.4	Kaldor's main distinctions between old and new wars / 197
Table 7.5	Kalyvas's types of warfare in civil war / 202
Table 7.6	Sources of different types of warfare / 202

Acknowledgments

We want to thank numerous scholars who provided helpful comments on various sections of the manuscript: Jeremy Black, Christopher Chase-Dunn, Claudio Cioffi-Revilla, Brian Ferguson, Edward Ingram, Tim Knievel, John Lynn, Charles Tilly, Joyce Marcus, Jean-Bertrand Ribat, Randy Schweller, and two anonymous reviewers for the University of Chicago Press. We also received useful feedback from audiences at seminars or lectures in which we presented material from the book. These include talks at the political science departments at George Washington University, the University of Washington, the University of Illinois, and Indiana University; the School of International Relations at the University of Southern California; the Mershon Center at Ohio State University; the "The Transformation of Warfare: Symmetry and Asymmetry of Political Violence" conference, Hamburg Institute for Social Research, Hamburg, Germany; and at the 2005 annual meetings of the International Studies Association (ISA)–Midwest and the International Studies Association–Northeast (Thompson's keynote addresses as ISA president).

Sections of chapter 5 were published in Jack S. Levy, Thomas C. Walker, and Martin S. Edwards, "Continuity and Change in the Evolution of War," in *War in a Changing World*, edited by Zeev Maoz and Azar Gat, 15–48 (Ann Arbor: University of Michigan Press, 2001). An earlier form of chapter 6 was in published in William R. Thompson, "A Test of a Theory of Co-evolution in War: Lengthening the Western Eurasian Military Trajectory," *International History Review* 28 (2006): 473–503.

We would also like to thank the team at the University of Chicago Press. David Pervin, our editor, provided substantive feedback, guidance, and encouragement, for which we are grateful. David's colleagues at the Press also played an important role in moving the process along in a relatively quick but seamless fashion. Dawn Hall did a fine job of copyediting.

CHAPTER ONE

The Evolution of War

War is a persistent feature of world politics, but it is not a constant. It varies over time and space in frequency, duration, severity, causes, consequences, and other dimensions. War is a social practice adopted to achieve specific purposes, but those practices vary with changing political, economic, and social environments and with the goals and constraints induced by those environments. A complete understanding of war requires an explanation of how it originated and how it has evolved. If war has changed in form over time, we need to identify when, how, and why it changed. We also need to know how war influenced, and was influenced by, other institutions and processes. If we find that the likelihood of war has diminished, at least in some regions or within some groups, we need to explain war's selective transformation as a social practice.

Our primary, and admittedly immodest, aim in this book is to explain the origins, escalation, and transformation of warfare.[1] Central to that aim is describing and explaining how war has coevolved with other factors such as political and military organization, threat environment, political economy, and weaponry. Thus the arc of war is the storyline of war traced over time and space. In elaborating and explaining the arc of war, we make six arguments.

1. War emerged in different places at different times depending on the presence and absence of critical factors, including the development of hunting/homicidal skills, group segmentation processes, and the interactions among increased organizational complexity, resource scarcity, and conflicts of interest.
2. War coevolved with other activities, including military and political organization, political economy, threat environment, and weaponry.
3. Major changes in politico-economic complexity, in particular, have led to occasional transformations in warfare. Weaponry has become more specialized

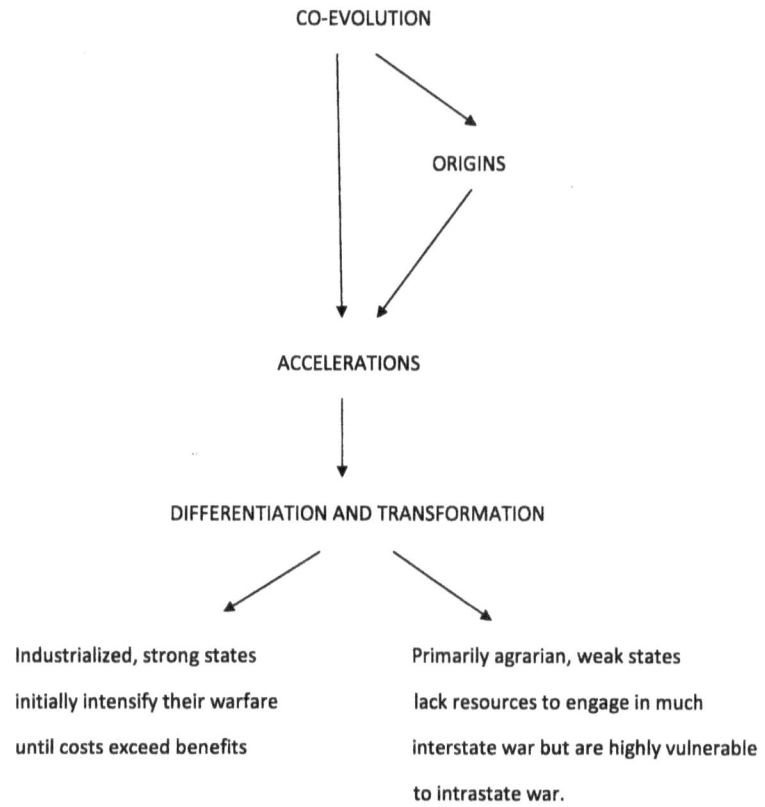

FIGURE 1.1. Our argument.

and lethal. Military organizations have expanded. Political organizations have expanded to manage larger and more deadly military forces and more intensified threat environments. The expansion of warfare, however, has not been inexorable. An important constraint is the escalating cost of warfare, which has especially impacted the probability of warfare between industrial states.
4. The pace of change/transformations in warfare and related processes has significantly accelerated three times—first in the late fourth to early third millennium BCE, then in the last half of the first millennium BCE, and again in the second half of the second millennium CE.
5. The attempt to centralize regional political-military power is one of the major drivers of periods of acceleration and transformation, especially in the third acceleration, which was concentrated in the western trajectory.

6. Much of the world did not experience the third acceleration directly (other than as targets), and it remains more agrarian than industrialized. As a consequence, states outside of the western trajectory tend to be weaker, vulnerable to internal warfare, and prone to fight fewer and shorter interstate wars.

Figure 1.1 provides a succinct summary of our argument. In brief, war originated and coevolves with other activities. The pace of evolution and coevolution has been characterized by three periods of acceleration. The contemporary outcomes of these changes and transformations are twofold: (1) strong, industrialized states for which warfare with other strong industrialized states has become very expensive and, therefore, less probable; and (2) weaker, agrarian states that have not experienced the third acceleration in the same way, and that are more likely to engage in internal warfare than in external warfare.

Our primary aim in this book is to elaborate and test these arguments about the arc of war. We must begin, however, by answering some preliminary questions. Does war in fact change over time? Are there major turning points? With what factors does war evolve and coevolve? What are the causal links among these processes?

Changes in Warfare over Time

Any discussion of the origins of war and any description of changes of warfare over time must begin with a discussion of what war is. All war involves violence, as Carl von Clausewitz reminds us,[2] but not all violence constitutes war. To say that war originated in a particular period of human history is not to say that life was entirely nonviolent prior to the advent of war.

We define war as *sustained, coordinated violence between political organizations*. We elaborate on this definition elsewhere (Levy and Thompson 2010b, 5–11), but a few points are worth mentioning here. For one thing, the actors who engage in war are political organizations, so that our definition is broad enough to include violent conflicts between states, empires, city-states, ethnic groups, chiefdoms, tribes, and hunter-gather groups, as well as many types of violent conflicts within those groups. In addition, for violence to constitute warfare it must be organized and it must have some threshold of magnitude or severity. This is standard in treatments of war in political science and in other social sciences.[3] We depart from some scholars, however, by not formally incorporating "political purpose" into the definition of war.[4] Our definition is behavioral. If two or more political units engage in the sustained and coordinated use of violence, it is a war regardless of the motivations for the violence.

Although we believe that most wars are driven by political motivations, we prefer to leave that as an empirical question rather than to assert it by definition. One issue is that the use of military force can be motivated by interests of actors other than the political organization itself. Political leaders may resort to military force for the primary purpose of bolstering their domestic political support, and bureaucratic organizations may advocate war to serve their own parochial needs. We do not want to imply that coercive force always aims to advance the interests of the organization in whose name force is used.

A second issue is that we can imagine instances in which military force is used not to influence others to act in a way to advance one's own interests, or to advance those ends by taking or destroying resources, but instead out of nihilistic or at least nonpolitical motivations. Although we think that most terrorist acts are politically driven, we concede that some might be more nihilistic. Note, however, that even if individual terrorists act out of nihilism, they almost always work for terrorist organizations for whom terror is a calculated political act. One exception might be the release of the nerve gas sarin in the Tokyo subways in 1995 by Aum Shinrikyo, a religious sect that was fixated on the impending end of the earth.[5]

Finally, we concede that some uses of military force may be driven by cultural rituals rather than by means-ends calculations to advance interests. This is one of the things that John Keegan (1993, 3) had in mind when he began chapter 1 of his *A History of Warfare* with the provocative anti-Clausewitzian statement that "war is not the continuation of policy by other means."

If war is defined as sustained, coordinated violence between political organizations, there is little evidence of war 50,000 years ago. Population sizes were small, political organization was restricted to the hierarchies of small bands, and their frequency of contact was limited. Weaponry was certainly available but its lethal effects were limited. Resource scarcity varied by location and by episodes of climate deterioration.

One caveat worth noting, however, is that the movement of the *Homo sapiens* species into areas earlier controlled by Neanderthals could well have generated incentives for something resembling interspecies warfare about 35,000 years ago (Otterbein 2004). We know only that the Neanderthals ultimately were extinguished and that our own hominid species triumphed.

It is certainly conceivable that this outcome involved bloodshed. Nicholas Wade (2006, 90–94) speculates that *Homo sapiens'* slow penetration of Europe, requiring some 15,000 years of "border skirmishes," was due in part to stubborn resistance on the part of Neanderthal groups unable to retreat without encroaching on neighboring Neanderthal territory.

Three assumptions underlie this speculation: (1) ancient hunter-gatherers tended to move into new territory to find new food sources and (2) to moderate overpopulation in their former habitats, and (3) the original occupants were fairly belligerent about defending home territories, given some fixed carrying capacity. None of these assumptions is implausible, and each is supported by much of what we do know about the interaction of hunting-gathering groups.

Note, however, that Wade emphasizes Neanderthal–*Homo sapiens* "border skirmishes" rather than "war." Just how sustained specific clashes might have been and whether they reflected the coordinated behavior of organized groups so as to satisfy our definition of war is anybody's guess. It is also possible that the two species had no or little contact and that Neanderthals disappeared because they could not cope with climate change and/or a shift in the nature of their customary food supply.[6]

Whatever the Neanderthal–*Homo sapiens* relationship, there is reason to believe that organized violence began to take place on a limited and sporadic basis long ago. The probability of some rival hunting groups occasionally coming to blows was moderately high, though evidence is scarce. Evidence of warfare begins to accumulate, if only slowly at first, for the last ten thousand years (Keegan 1993, chap. 2; Haas 1999; Cioffi-Revilla 2000; Gat 2006, chap. 2). Mass burials of bodies with projectile wounds, fortifications, burned walls, and pictures of armed combat and soldiers begin to appear.

For the last five thousand years, evidence becomes more plentiful and reliable. Full-fledged armies with armor-wearing soldiers in infantry formations begin to appear (Ferrill 1997). Gradually these armies became larger in size and more lethal in weaponry. States and empires emerged, grew in size, and built larger armies, and their wars became more lethal and began to claim more resources and lives.

As we indicate in table 1.1, which focuses on major battles, estimated deaths per war more than doubled between the fifth century BCE and the fourteenth century CE, more than doubled again between the fourteenth and early nineteenth centuries CE, and then increased by as much as a factor of ten between the early nineteenth and twentieth centuries. To

TABLE 1.1 **Selected major battle attributes**

Battle	Historical Significance	Primary Adversaries	Number of Armed Forces Involved	Casualties
Megiddo (1469 BCE)	sometimes referred to as the first recorded battle of history (even if it undoubtedly was not the first battle)*	Egypt vs. Palestinian rebel army	Possibly 10,000 Egyptians	Unknown
Marathon (490 BCE)	Greek defeat of the first Persian invasion of Greece	Persia vs. Athens	About 30,000	About 6,500
Crecy (August 1346)	Major defeat of heavy cavalry by much smaller force of infantry armed with the long bow	England vs. France	About 80,000	Between 10 & 20,000
Waterloo (June 1815)	Final defeat of Napoleon	France vs. Britain and Prussia	About 200,000	About 52,000 (including 7,000 French prisoners)
Battle of the Marne (September 1915)	Early Allied victory in World War I that halted German momentum in France.	Germany vs. France and Britain	Several million	500,000+
Operation Overlord (June–July 1944)	Allied cross-Channel invasion of Normandy (D-Day)	Allies vs. Germany	2 million+ (counting support units)	236,000 (including 41,000 German prisoners)

* The reference is to recorded history, but unambiguous battles between multiple bowmen are depicted on walls in Spanish caves that date back to sometime between the third and sixth millennium BCE. Third millennium Mesopotamian art also suggests quite strongly at least the immediate aftermath of battles.
Source: Extracted from multiple battle descriptions in Dupuy and Dupuy (1977, 6, 23–25, 355–57, 768, 938–39, 1105–07).

be sure, these battles are not necessarily representative of every battle occurring in that era, and substantial war-related deaths can result from many small engagements as well as from major battles (Pinker 2011, chap. 6), but these battles are probably roughly representative in terms of the increases in war-related deaths over time.

There are various ways to depict these trends graphically. Figure 1.2 sketches one individual's (Eckhardt 1992) estimated enumeration of battle deaths over several thousand years. The estimates are definitely unreli-

THE EVOLUTION OF WAR   7

able in the early part of the figure, but in general they correspond to the description advanced above.

Although the severity of warfare, defined in terms of the number of casualties, has increased dramatically over time throughout most of history, there is substantial evidence that the frequency of some types of war has declined. Admittedly, it is extraordinarily difficult to estimate long-term trends in the frequency of war (or most other events) spanning several millennia, given a certain historical myopia and a systematic tendency to undercount more temporally distant events (Payne 2004, 67–70; Pinker 2111, chap. 7). We have much greater confidence in identifying patterns involving wars between the most powerful states in the system in the more recent past, especially for the last five centuries of the modern era as defined by historians, because the prominence of those events means that they are less likely to be undercounted.

Figure 1.3 plots the frequency of wars between great or major powers per decade during the last five hundred years.[7] If we look at quarter-century periods, we find that the number of wars occurring every twenty-five years averaged around 5.5 in the sixteenth century and dropped to 1.25 in the twentieth century. A great power war has not occurred for over a half century, marking the longest period of great power peace for at least five centuries.[8] The trend in the severity of great power war, defined in terms of battle-related deaths, is precisely the opposite, as indicated

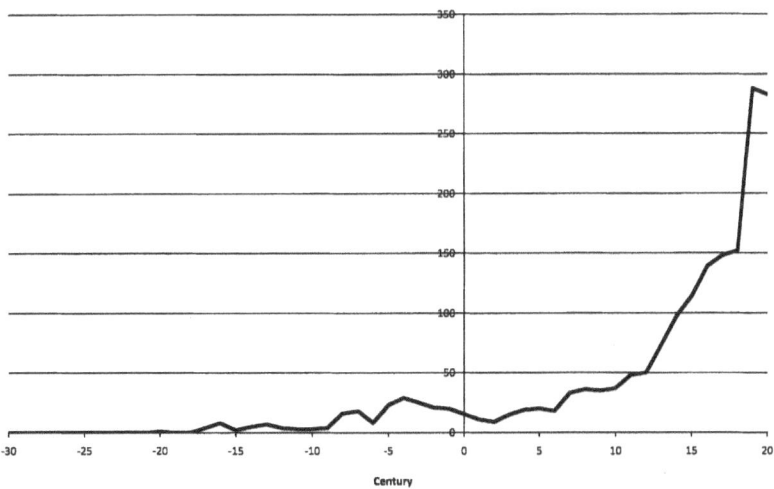

FIGURE 1.2. Estimated battle deaths by century since 3000 BCE.

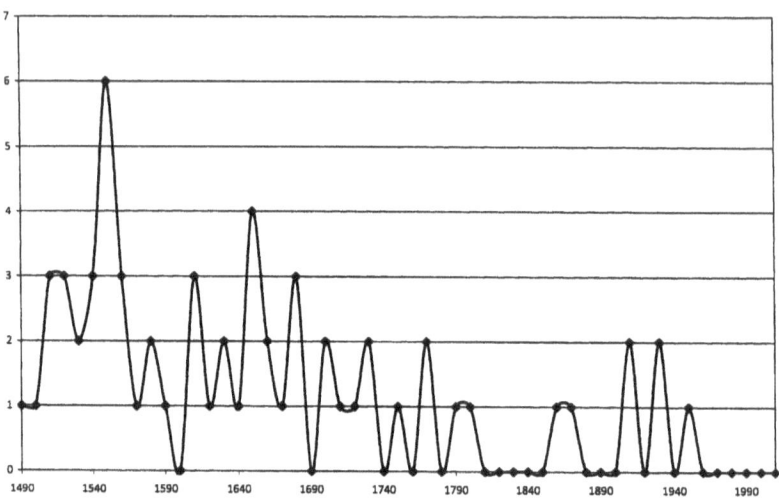

FIGURE 1.3. Frequency of great power war by decade, 1490–2010.

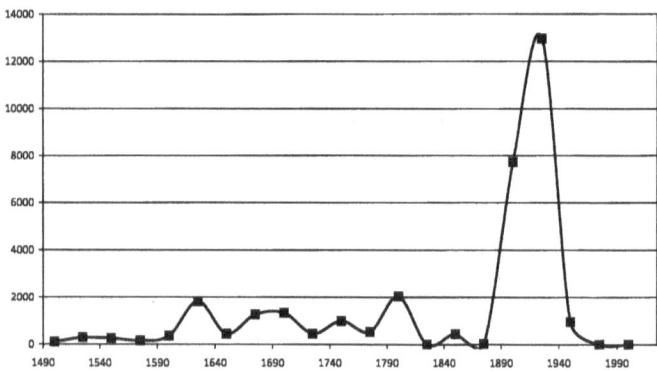

FIGURE 1.4. Severity of great power war by quarter century.

in figure 1.4.[9] Thus great power warfare has steadily increased in severity while declining in frequency.[10]

In the contemporary twenty-first century, a World War III, should it occur, has some potential for eliminating a substantial proportion of life from the planet. Yet in this same era there are significant parts of the planet in which, for the first time in thousands of years, most forms of warfare are highly unlikely to occur. Western Europe, for instance, certainly no stranger to warfare in the past thousand years, seems unlikely to experience anything resembling conventional interstate warfare in the near future. We could make the same argument about North America, and, perhaps with a little less confidence, about most of South America.[11] For some populations, then, warfare has become a more remote possibility than it once was.

At the same time warfare has been much more common in other parts of the world. Wars between states—in eastern Africa (Eritrea and Ethiopia), central Africa (Rwanda, Congo, Angola, among others), the Middle East (Arab-Israeli, Iran and Iraq, Iraq and the United States), and South Asia (India and Pakistan)—are all very recent events. Threats of war remain conspicuous in East Asia (Taiwan and the two Koreas).

Interstate war is only one form of warfare, however, and it is no longer the one that attracts the most attention. We also need to examine trends in intrastate war and "extrastate war" (defined as the colonial and imperial wars that were traditionally fought between European states and entities not formally recognized by the European powers). In figure 1.5 we plot the frequency of different kinds of wars during the last two centuries, with each data point indicating the number of wars in the following decade.[12]

The onset of interstate warfare follows an irregular wavelike pattern over the last two hundred years since the Congress of Vienna in 1815. After nearly two decades without an interstate war from the late 1820s

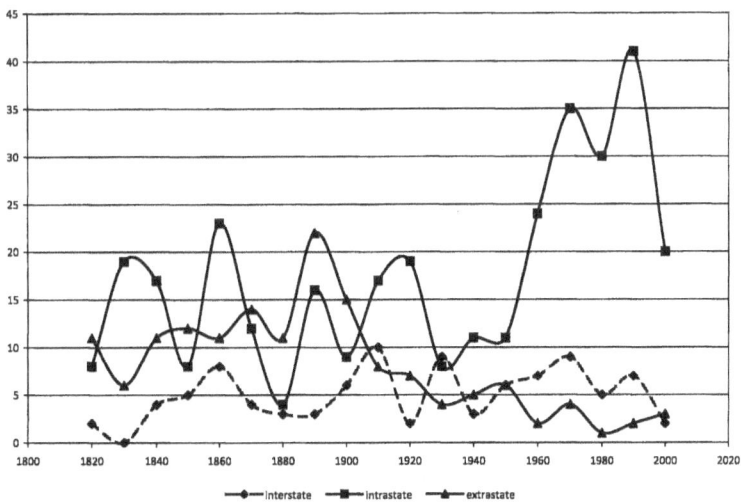

FIGURE 1.5. Frequency of types of war, 1820s–2000s.

to the late 1840s, the frequency of interstate war increased through the 1860s, declined briefly before increasing for another four decades through World War I, declined and peaked again around World War II, and rose again in the 1960s and 1970s before declining rather steadily through the end of the twentieth century. The phenomenon of extrastate war follows a somewhat similar pattern, though with different peaks and valleys. It peaked at the end of the nineteenth century at the height of European colonial expansion, persisted through much of the twentieth century at a low level, before ceasing altogether by the end of the 1970s, after the collapse of colonial empires following World War II.[13]

Intrastate warfare shares some of this rhythm, peaking in the 1860s, again around 1920, and again in the late 1980s after a sustained increase. What is different, however, is that while the number of new interstate wars declined precipitously after 1970 or so, the number of new intrastate wars increased or remained high in the last third of the twentieth century. Evidence suggests, however, that the frequency of intrastate war (and therefore all types of war, given the end of extrastate war and the relative infrequency of interstate war) began to decline in the 1990s (Hewitt, Wilkenfeld, and Gurr 2010; Human Security Centre 2005; Harbom and Sundberg 2009; Sarkees and Wayman 2010). Despite a more recent increase in intrastate war, the decline in the 1990s helped to trigger a lively debate about the possibility of a sustained decline in war and perhaps in other forms of violence as well (Gleditsch 2008; Pinker 2011).[14]

We save an explanation for some of these trends for later in this book. Our main point for now is that war is a multidimensional phenomenon that evolves over time. War expands or contracts and takes on alternative forms as a function of its appeal to actors as a strategy for advancing their interests and resolving conflicts of interest. Some behaviors, such as colonial wars, go out of existence. New behaviors, such as "modern" terrorism, become more prominent.[15] Our goal is to explain how and why these various forms of warfare evolve.

What Evolves and Coevolves?

What does it mean to look at war from an evolutionary and coevolutionary perspective? It means that we are interested in long-term changes in behavior and institutions associated with coordinated and sustained violence between competing political organizations. Groups seek a number of things. Three of the most important, at least for the questions we are asking, are security, wealth, and power. To obtain these ends people develop strategies and institutions. It is the evolution of these strategies and institutions—how they emerge, change, and, often, become obsolete over time and then decline—that are of most interest to us. These strategies emerge because individuals have problems to solve as they attempt to enhance their security, wealth, and power. These strategies change in response to a shifting internal and external environment that includes the changing strategies of others.

We will be giving particular attention to the interactions among threat environments, political organizations, military organizations, political economies, weaponry, and warfare. These factors evolve and coevolve as individuals develop new strategies and institutions to cope with problems or to exploit opportunities that arise. Our aim is to develop theoretical statements about *how* they evolve and coevolve over time.[16] We are not interested in tracing the history of conflict over many millennia—that is, in writing a military history—though we find others' military histories quite useful and we build upon them.

Our focus on evolution/coevolution will remain comparatively simple. People solve problems or exploit opportunities by choosing/developing strategies and institutions that serve the pursuit of security, wealth, and power (among other goals). The choices they make are neither inevitable nor random. They choose from a pool of possible alternatives (which, in evolutionary terms, constitutes *variety*), and the choices that result in the survival of the political organizations that select them, while perhaps not fully optimal, are good enough to be favored by the environments (which constitutes *selection*) in which the choices are made.

Thus evolution emphasizes environmental selection from variety. In selecting their strategies, individuals and organizations may not fully appreciate the implications of what they are doing, and it may take a long time for the consequences of their choices to emerge in full form. For instance, the classical Greek phalanx and modern infantry rifles both took some five hundred years to develop into fully competitive form. Neither was invented overnight. But whether they emerge quickly or slowly, the important thing is that individuals continue adapting to new problems and opportunities by experimenting with these strategies and institutions until they assume a recognizable shape and either do or do not supplant older strategies/institutions.

There are other approaches to evolutionary analysis. Some scholars (Falger 2001, for example) believe that evolutionary interpretations must adopt very strictly biological terminology and processes as their template. There is no reason, however, why biology should "own" the study of evolutionary processes, and biological evolution and political-military-economic evolution may work in slightly different ways. The biologists' emphasis on genetic variation, blind mutations, and very slow processes of change do not, we think, translate readily into what individuals do in developing strategies for war and related activities. There are no gene equivalents, the mutations are rarely blind, and the processes may be slow but not as slow as the many generations required to transform, say, dinosaurs into birds. When we use the term *coevolution* it is not the same type of process found in biology in which species evolve reciprocally (J. Thompson 1994). Instead of species coevolving, we see strategies, institutions, and processes coevolving. As long as changes in one sphere lead to changes in other spheres, that is coevolution as far as we are concerned.

Other international relations theorists and military historians offer evolutionary analyses of war. Bradley Thayer (2004) and Azar Gat (2006), for example, each adopts a Darwinian perspective and argues that individuals wish to survive and that those who survive are the ones that reproduce and secure resources to nurture their young in a competitive world defined by scarcity. We share much of the initial emphasis on survival, competition, and scarcity, but we emphasize that what is important is not individuals' intentions but rather the consequences of their actions. It does not much matter, for example, whether individuals are consciously interested in the survival and propagation of their genes. What matters is whether those individuals reproduce and whether their offspring receive the proper nurturing that facilitates their survival and further reproduction. When Genghis Khan noted that captured women were one of the perks of conquest he particularly enjoyed, we are prepared to take him literally at his word and doubt very much that his main interest was in ensuring the survival of his genes. Rape is hardly a trivial matter, but we think we can conduct an evolutionary analysis without worrying too much about reproductive urges as a primary source of motivation.

The Argument

Six interrelated arguments define the core of this book.

ARGUMENT 1: War originated and evolved as a practice over millennia. This implies that there was a time when evidence of war behavior is difficult to find. The evidence becomes clearer as we move forward in time, and we infer that the practice of warfare originated (or emerged or began) at some point. That the practice of war should have origins is not likely to be viewed as particularly controversial. The set of factors that are most responsible for the origins of warfare is a different matter.

In chapter 2, we advance a synthetic model of the origins of war that builds on a number of plausible hypotheses in the literature. This model suggests that war probably emerged in different ways in different places at different times, depending on the presence or absence of critical factors. The factors that we find most important include the development of hunting and homicide skills that made weaponry, tactics, and elementary military organization available. Another significant ingredient is group segmentation processes, which involved the construction of identities larger than immediate families, which facilitated the identification of enemies of the group, and which contributed to the development of political and military organization.

In addition, there are a slate of emergent processes—agrarian-induced population growth and density, circumscription, agrarian-pastoral divisions of labor, and resource scarcity—that came together to facilitate increased organizational complexity and conflict. Ultimately, it was the interaction between political-economic complexity and scarcities that generated warfare. As warfare became more common, political-economic complexity, military organization, and weapon lethality responded accordingly. But since different locales combined geography, threat environments, and political economies differently, warfare emerged earlier in some places and later in others and it did not always take the same form.

The second part of argument 1 implies that groups fought wars several thousand years ago and that the older forms do not look exactly like the more recent varieties. How wars are waged has changed over time. That observation is probably not hard to accept. Precisely what changes are most important and what the changes have meant are more contestable. The evolutionary changes and implications that we emphasize are taken up by our other arguments.

ARGUMENT 2: War coevolves with other activities, including military and political organization, political economy, threat environment, and weaponry. The basic thesis here is that a substantial change in one of the six spheres is likely to lead to major changes in some or all of the other spheres. A significant increase in external threat might lead to greater political centralization, an expanded military organization, new weapons, and new ways of raising money to pay for larger bureaucracies and armies and for new weapons systems. Similarly, a significant increase in political centralization might also lead to increased tax revenues, an expanded military organization, and new weapons, which contributes to a more threatening threat environment for other actors.

Every change need not "sweep the board" and dictate parallel changes in the other five spheres. Some changes might be relatively contained. An example is the monopolization of firearms in Japan by Toyotomi Hideyoshi after 1588, in which political centralization changed the domestic distribution of weaponry without altering the political economy or the threat environment (Lorge 2008, 62–63). Japanese political centralization did lead to attempts to expand into the Korean peninsula in the late sixteenth century, but once that effort failed the Japanese were not threatened by external enemies until the mid-nineteenth century. On the contrary, what became an unusually benign threat environment for several hundred years only reinforced the maintenance of a relatively isolated Tokugawa status quo.

There is nothing deterministic about coevolution. The theory is confined to heightened probabilities of change in one of the five other sectors as a consequence of major change in one of the six. While some of the six areas are less likely to lead to changes than some of the others, there is no compelling reason to privilege one of the six as a primary driver throughout time. In different times varying spheres of action are capable of stimulating changes elsewhere. We say more about evolution and coevolutionary change in chapter 2.

The coevolutionary theory does not suffice to handle all of our theoretical problems. We develop additional theories that we view as complementary to (rather than as rivals to) our emphasis on coevolution. While the coevolutionary thesis is neutral in giving permanent priority to one of the six spheres of activity, we will develop a second theory that gives priority to one of the six spheres, political-economic change, in explaining fundamental transitions in behavior over the very long term.

ARGUMENT 3: Major changes in political-economic complexity, as manifested in transitions to the predominance of hunting-gathering, agrarian, and industrial production strategies, led ultimately to major changes in warfare. Military organizations expand, weaponry becomes more specialized and lethal, and political organizations expand to manage the weaponry, the military organizations, and the intensified warfare that stems from bigger and more deadly armies clashing. Larger armies with more lethal weaponry create more hostile threat environments.

There is a catch, however, to this upward escalation in the coevolution of war and related factors. The escalation of war is constrained by the rapidly increasing costs of war. The industrialization of warfare radically increased its costs and led to the phenomenon of total war. At some point the perceived costs of war began to serve as a deterrent and reduce the probability of war—at least between equally industrialized states that are faced with the prospect of enormous losses even if they somehow "win" the war.[17] Note that we say "reduce the probability of war," not eliminate the possibility of war. That is far from the case. The escalation of war appears, however, to have diminished the probability of war on a very selective basis, that is, between industrialized states.

ARGUMENT 4: The evolutionary pace of changes in warfare (and associated processes) has accelerated three times in a revolutionary way.[18] The first acceleration took place in southern Mesopotamia predominately in the late fourth and early third millennium BCE, as urbanization, population density, and agriculture created new possibilities of scale and kind for intercity warfare. The second acceleration, focused on the eastern Mediterranean and China, occurred in the last half of the first millennium BCE. Near-constant warfare between competitive states created an escalatory spiral in warfare, army sizes, weaponry, and political economies.

The third escalation was centered in European developments in the second half of the second millennium CE. Between roughly 1500 and 1945, European warfare (which was not restricted to the continent), again predicated on the spiraling warfare of competitive states that managed to survive the half-millennium ordeal,[19] developed the application of gunpowder and its implications to the nth degree, culminating in the atomic bomb, which marked the presumed culmination of the period of total war.[20] The end of World War II marked the end of the Europe-centered world system, but the potential lethality of war continued to escalate.

If the first acceleration was a Bronze Age phenomenon and the second an early Iron Age event, the third acceleration was very much a product of the industrial era, even if it began prior to the British-led industrial revolution in the late eighteenth century.[21] Evolutionary accelerations significantly increase the number of soldiers killed in combat as well as trigger the other changes noted above.

ARGUMENT 5:   Whereas argument 3 is predicated on evolutionary shifts in the predominant political-economic production strategy, movement within regional evolutionary trajectories is fueled by a competition among states that is characterized by intermittent attempts to centralize political-military power in the region. Successful concentrations of power tend to be temporary and followed by periods of deconcentration of political-military power. The urge to subordinate rivals and to avoid being subordinated by rivals gives political units incentives to upgrade their military organizations and weaponry. Thus one of the major drivers for evolutionary acceleration is focused on what John Lynn (1996) calls "paradigmatic" armies that propel change within their regions. These paradigmatic armies do more than simply provide models for others to emulate. As organizations for aspiring regional hegemons, they also become a significant part of the threat environment for other units. This process was particularly salient in the third acceleration most manifest in the western trajectory. One of the consequences was establishing a foundation for the contemporary practice of distinguishing between strong and weak states with differential war-making tendencies.

ARGUMENT 6:   Much of the world did not experience the third acceleration in warfare firsthand. A good proportion of this very large chunk of humanity, not coincidentally, also retains economies that are still more agrarian than industrial. The interaction of these factors implies a different trajectory altogether for the nonindustrial world, which is largely a nonwestern world. States outside the western trajectory have largely agrarian economies. They tend to be weaker and markedly vulnerable to internal warfare, and they fight fewer and shorter interstate wars. Coevolution and the arc of war have worked differently in the global south than in the north.

The Plan of the Book

In subsequent chapters we expand on the coevolutionary model of the development of war over time. Chapter 2 explores the origins of warfare in prehistoric times. We trace those origins to a mixture of the availability of hunting skills, weaponry, and rudimentary military organization that was catalyzed by group segmentation. An imposing array of additional influences then created and maintained variable incentives to make war. Once war had emerged as a strategy, the expansion of political-economic and military organization, as well as weapon lethality, contributed to the expansion of warfare in terms of participation, scale, and impact. The coevolutionary processes, discussed in chapter 3, provide an armature for the expansion.

Evolution and coevolution do not necessarily proceed evenly and gradually. Chapter 4 examines what we view as the first two accelerations in the evolution of war. The first acceleration occurred when quarreling chiefdoms were supplanted by rival Mesopotamian city-states. The second acceleration was experienced more broadly in Eurasia during the second half of the first millennium BCE. In this period the intensification of competition among warring states and empires led to hastened coevolutionary consequences from the Mediterranean to China.

Chapter 5 looks more closely at the last five hundred years of development in the western trajectory—our third evolutionary acceleration. We highlight the military revolutions of early modern Europe and some of their consequences on the path to total war in the twentieth century. These same consequences have also contributed, somewhat ironically, to a diminished probability of war in some parts of the contemporary world. Which military changes were genuine revolutions and which changes had the most impact are subjects that are and will remain contested. We do not seek to resolve these debates. Our primary interest is drawing attention to how a series of changes in military organization, weaponry, political organization, political economy, and war—which is the way we think the military revolutions should be interpreted—led to major transformations in the landscape of warfare at the center of the world system. We also note how these transformations failed to take hold in more peripheral parts of the world.

Chapter 6 expands on coevolutionary change by linking it to intermittent attempts at regional predominance by paradigmatic armies. A long western trajectory encompassing Mesopotamian actors at the outset and the US armed forces in the current phase is examined as a focal point for these arguments. The nature of the western trajectory is particularly important to our arguments because it is this trajectory that to date has triumphed over others and that has contributed most to the current bifurcation in warfare propensities: a low probability of costly warfare between industrialized states while nonindustrialized states often lack the resources to fight interstate wars often or for long periods of time but do possess pronounced vulnerabilities to intrastate conflict.

Chapter 7 focuses on claims that contemporary interstate warfare has changed its format fundamentally (the "new wars" hypothesis) or that it is rapidly on its way to becoming obsolete. Some scholars claim that various types of novel forms of internal and asymmetrical warfare are on the rise. We are somewhat skeptical of the novelty. The present and immediate future is apt to be characterized by a complex mixture of major power tensions and continuing, but certainly not equal, probabilities of interstate, intrastate, and nonstate warfare. Warfare is not obsolete, but its manifestations have become more varied, just as the relative mix of different types of warfare is in the process of changing—but not for the first time.

Chapter 8 summarizes the complex relationships involving the coevolution of military organization, political organization, weaponry, political economy, threat environment, and war in the long term in the past, present, and future. That certainly does not mean we think we have expressed the last word on this subject. The perspective we advance invites considerable revision of existing interpretations of war and related processes. It also demands close scrutiny, elaboration, and empirical testing. The evolution of warfare is an old story but one with new chapters to be written.

CHAPTER TWO

The Origins of War

Anthropologists, archaeologists, military historians, and others debate the question of when and how war originated, but they have yet to reach a consensus. As one recent history of warfare put it, "the origins of warfare lie shrouded in mystery" (Archer et al. 2002, 1). Although data limitations may preclude us from ever knowing the precise origins of war with any certainty, we need to think about this question because it could have strong implications for our understanding of the subsequent evolution of war and its contemporary manifestations.[1]

The conduct of war has certainly evolved over the millennia—in terms of the nature and size of the political units, the number of combatants, and the nature and lethality of weaponry. But how much has it changed in other respects? And how quickly has it changed? Have transformations been relatively abrupt, as hypothesized in the extinction of dinosaurs due to catastrophic environmental change? Or have they been more gradual, as in the ways that giraffe necks were elongated or mammals lost their gills? To ask about evolutionary processes, we need some starting point to provide a basis for comparison with the contemporary period—which, alas, is not likely to be an ending point in the evolution of warfare.

There are three auxiliary problems that must be addressed or at least highlighted before we can expect to make much headway. One concerns the paucity of early evidence on the emergence of warfare, which forces us to speculate to some extent about the question of origins. A second is the question of whether warfare is instinctual or learned behavior. The significant variations in the practices of warfare suggest that war is unlikely to be purely instinctive behavior, but we cannot completely rule out the possibility that our genetic composition has shaped some aspects of aggression and war to a certain extent. The third problem is that our images of earlier warfare have been shaped by the assumptions and claims of previous scholars, and we constantly need to question the validity of those assumptions and interpretations in light of new information and better theories.

When Did War First Emerge?

Attempts to understand the origins of warfare are plagued by the fact that it is a prehistorical phenomenon. Whenever warfare began it did so prior to any observers writing about it. We have to search elsewhere for evidence. There are archaeological remains, and there are sometimes ambiguous paintings on rock that may depict human conflict in some form, just as there are some very clear pictures of men with weapons fighting other men with weapons. We have very old skeletons with wounds made by spears, clubs, and knives. Some of them may be the result of accidents, but multiple embedded arrowheads found in skeletons are not too likely to be there entirely by accident. We also have evidence of fortifications, walled settlements, burned buildings, and communities sited in places that were quite hard to get to and could only have been chosen for their defensive benefits. We have weapons that could have been used to kill, but the prey may have been either animals or humans.

We can speculate about the circumstances in which these weapons might have been used for human warfare. We can also examine the behavior of contemporary groups, such as foraging bands, who more closely resemble the way humans were organized thousands of years ago. This approach can provide an interesting basis for comparison, but it raises a potential methodological problem, often referred to as the "contact hypothesis." Contemporary foraging bands live in a world in which more complex societies coexist, and contact with representatives of those societies may change the nature of the less complex societies. The process of observing these societies may change them in certain ways. There is a small literature on the impact of European agents on New World Amerindians and consequent changes in warfare that cautions against assuming that postcontact groups behaved exactly as they did prior to contact (Whitehead 1990; Ferguson and Whitehead 1992). Thus complete analytical closure of this question of origins is unlikely. We can only try to put the pieces of the puzzle together in some reasonably coherent fashion, leaving open the possibility of refutation by future discoveries or better theorizing.

TABLE 2.1 **Cioffi-Revilla's evidence for early warfare**

Region	Earliest Locational, Structural, and Artifactual Evidence	Earliest Forensic Evidence
Levant	Major settlements founded with walls and defensive locations (Jericho, Ras Shamra, and Byblos), ca. 7500–6000 BCE	Anatolian burial probably caused by Halafian attack, ca. 5600–5000 BCE
Mesopotamia	Fortifications and concentrated weaponry remains at Tell es-Sawann, ca. 5600 BCE	Nothing before 2900 BCE and Early Dynastic warfare
East Asia	Fortifications at Yangshao, ca. 5000–3000 BCE	Scalped skulls in Longshan period sites, ca. 3000 BCE
Andes	Fortifications and weaponry concentrations at Salinas de Santa, ca. 3500 BCE	Headless skeletons, ca. 3000 BCE
Mesoamerica	Evident defensive locations of major settlements at San Jose Mogote, Oaxaca, and San Lorenzo, ca. 1900–1400 BCE	Cannibalized human remains, ca. 1200 BCE

Source: Based on Cioffi-Revilla (2000, 77–81).

A case in point is the evidence that we have for the earliest warfare. Tables 2.1 and 2.2 offer two compilations of indicators of early warfare, the first by a political scientist and the second by an anthropologist. The two tables are not fully in agreement, in part because of the two authors' different evidentiary demands. For table 2.1 Claudio Cioffi-Revilla (2000) requires very specific evidence in the form of walls, fortifications, or damaged skeletons. He suggests that warfare began roughly between 7500 and 3000 BCE in most parts of the world, with the earliest manifestations in the Near East. Brian Ferguson's (2002) list in table 2.2 begins about four thousand years earlier than Cioffi-Revilla's, with the earliest mass burial discovered to date in Sudan.[2] It also includes evidence of early warfare in Australia. Table 2.2 (Ferguson) also emphasizes western Europe and North America, in contrast to Cioffi-Revilla's (table 2.1) stress on Andean and Mesoamerican conflict.

The mass burial in Sudan to which Ferguson refers (first row in table 2.2) is particularly revealing. As Raymond Kelly (2000, 148–52) notes in his

TABLE 2.2 **Ferguson's evidence for early warfare**

Time	Place	Comments
Ca. 11,000 BCE	Jebel Sahaba, Nubian Desert	24 of 59 bodies have projectiles embedded in skeletons
8000–4000 BCE	N. Australia	Rock paintings portray initially individual and small group clashes, with large group confrontations beginning around 4000 BCE
6500–4500 BCE	Northern Iraq and Anatolia	Evidence of warfare in northern Iraq; weaponry and defensive fortification associated with Catal Huyuk (Anatolia); fortified Hacilar burned and reoccupied by new group
4300 BCE	Far western Europe	Frontier of spreading farming versus hunter/forager political economies—evidence of fortifications and arrow stockpiling
2600 BCE	Yellow River region, China	Although possible defensive ditches in fifth millennium, first clear signs of warfare in Longshan area
2500 BCE	North America	Intermittent warfare between Laurentian and Lamoka tribes in New York area
1500 BCE	North America	Spreading warfare in northwest Pacific area

Source: Based on the discussion in Ferguson (2002).

informative account, over two-fifths of the individuals in this burial ground show evidence of violent death; they include women and children, and most show multiple wounds. There is also evidence that many died at the same time. Kelly's interpretation of the evidence suggests that the violence involved group behavior, motivated by vengeance (the multiple wounds) and by the concepts of kin group responsibility and liability (the children).

Whether this clear evidence of group violence is enough to warrant its classification as warfare depends in part on one's definitions. With respect to our definition of war as sustained, coordinated violence between political organizations, there appears, based on Kelly's interpretation, to have been coordinated violence between groups with well-defined identities and presumably with some form of political organization. The question, however, is whether the violence was sustained or part of a campaign of sustained violence. A stronger case for sustained violence could be made if more than one burial site had been found in the area, but this was the only one. Thus the evidence as to whether this best case for early warfare is intriguing, but it is far from conclusive.

In contrast to ambiguous evidence of warfare ten to thirteen millennia ago, evidence is stronger as we move toward the less distant past, to the point that we have rather unambiguous evidence of warfare in most parts of the world by roughly five thousand years ago. William Hamblin (2006, 16–34) uses the criterion of a "military threshold"—the point at which warfare becomes sufficiently endemic in a region that most, if not all, groups need to militarize to some extent. Hamblin parallels Ferguson in tracing Anatolian warfare to the sixth millennium BCE. Iran may have crossed a military threshold in the late fifth millennium. Syria's military threshold transition is dated to around 4000 BCE, while Mesopotamia's was not reached prior to the last half of the fourth millennium (3500–3000 BCE).

Yet this evidentiary base may be conservative. The odds are that any armed clashes by foraging bands in Paleolithic times would not have left much trace unless the body count was relatively high. Since the probable size of Paleolithic foraging bands was not large, the casualties would likely have been limited in number.

Given these ambiguities there are a couple of general strategies for explaining the emergence of warfare. One could be conservative and begin with the indicators of fortifications and damaged skeletons. Or one could remain open to the possibility that warfare emerged on a very small scale at an earlier point, and that we only have traces of it after it subsequently attained some minimal scale of activity discernible by archaeologists thousands of years later.[3]

We prefer the latter strategy, keeping in mind that the first appearance of hard evidence varies from place to place. For instance, there is little evidence of violence in southeastern Europe prior to the beginning of the fourth millennium BCE, but there is ample skeletal evidence of extensive conflict in northern and western Europe several thousand years earlier, which Jane McIntosh (2006, 206) attributes as possibly due to greater pressure on resources. Tables 2.1 and 2.2 make a similar point in suggesting that different parts of the world experienced (or at least left evidence of) warlike behavior at different times.

This evidence that war appeared in different places at different times strongly suggests that the origins of warfare are related more to things such as population density, environmental scarcity, and organizational development than to innate instincts toward killing. If the latter were true we would expect evidence of warfare to appear everywhere groups of *Homo sapiens* had colonized. And between roughly 60,000 to 15,000 years ago, our ancestors had colonized the entire world.

We should acknowledge at the outset that some previous analytical forays into the origins of warfare question have probably only deepened the sense of mystery rather than dispelled questions about when warfare first emerged. One type of problem is quasi-mythological. European philosophers writing in the sixteenth to eighteenth centuries helped to create two contrasting images of ancient warfare. One is Thomas Hobbes's depiction of a "war of all against all" in the absence of some pacifying centralized government, and the other is Jean-Jacques Rousseau's image of the "Noble Savage" at peace with one and all. Although Hobbes's and Rousseau's philosophies have been enormously influential, their respective arguments that prior to the advent of civilization warfare was either constant or completely absent find little support in the archaeological record.[4] Ancient realities fell somewhere in between, and, as we have emphasized, varied from place to place. The interesting question is not whether human behavior fit Hobbes's image of a war of all against all in which life was solitary, poor, nasty, brutish, and short, or Rousseau's image of the Noble Savage, but instead how to explain the variation in the emergence of warfare in different places at different times.

A Genetic Basis for Aggression?

A second source of difficulty is the question of whether humans have aggressive instincts that help explain conflict. The question is certainly legitimate. Comparisons with various other animal species and their warfare are intriguing,[5] as are arguments that the human species is particularly aggressive relative to other species.[6] The problem with some arguments about the existence of aggressive instincts, however, is that they imply that aggression and/or war is a constant, for humans or for other species. Given the fact that war varies significantly over time and space, we must reject any line of argument that suggests that war should be a constant.[7]

This is not to suggest that all genetic explanations imply that aggressive behavior and violent conflict are constant. Richard Wrangham and Dale Peterson (1996) emphasize variation across species in arguing that only chimpanzees and humans, of some four thousand mammals and ten million plus animal species, engage in a repertoire of behavior encompassing intensive territorial defense, raiding, and attacks on vulnerable enemies (noted in Wade 2006, 149).[8] Frans DeWaal and Frans Lanting (1997) contrast chimpanzees with bonobos, another member of the great ape family.

Whereas chimpanzees are known for power politics and intergroup warfare, bonobos are "apes from Venus," "make-love-not-war" primates who live in matriarchal and egalitarian societies and who use sex as a conflict resolution strategy.

More aggressive chimpanzees do not always engage in aggression, however, and when and why they do so remains open to debate. Wrangham (2006) interprets the evidence to suggest that they are most likely to do so when they have a numerical advantage, possess territory to defend and expand, and have an opportunity to eliminate potential male rivals from adjacent communities that might stand in the way of future territorial defense or expansion. Stated in this fashion, chimpanzee behavior does not sound all that different from human behavior, especially human behavior at a time when hunting and gathering prevailed as the predominant economic production strategy. That behavior varies as a function of environmental conditions, and Wrangham provides an interesting explanation for that variation.

The argument that variation in conflict behavior across groups is genetically based implies that some groups possess different DNA structures than others, and that those differences explain differential warfare experiences. But a "war" (or "aggression") gene has yet to be isolated. Even if such a gene were eventually isolated, we would still need to relate its presence or absence to the known variation in political centralization, political-economic change, climate change, and a range of other nongenetic factors that appear to be correlated with fluctuations in warfare. Most analysts who prefer instinctual/genetic answers to warfare questions stop short of engaging the issues raised by observable variations in aggression and war. They aim to explain aggression and war as a constant or perhaps its variation across species. They cannot possibly explain the enormous variations in human war and peace over time and space that have been documented for at least the last seven millennia. Our preference is to remain agnostic on the gene issue and leave the question to others who are better equipped to explore genetic structures.

There is an alternative position, however, that also seems quite attractive. The question of whether *Homo sapiens* possess a warring gene presumes that our own species is more bellicose than others. Azar Gat (1999a, 2000a, 2000b, 2000c) vehemently denies this assumption and lays the blame on Konrad Lorenz's (1966) popularization of the notion that most species are characterized by ritualized and nondeadly fighting. Gat argues that the attempt to explain why humans are fairly unique in making war is simply the wrong question. Human violence does not demand a special explanation if, contrary to Lorenz, all or most species engage in serious killing, especially in reference to reactions to violations of territory.

For Gat there is nothing peculiar about this generalization about the pervasiveness of violence. Members of various species have at least two things very much in common. They inhabit the same ecological niches as do other members of the species, and they compete for the same resources and mates. Therefore, it should be hardly surprising that conflicts between these competitors have some propensity to escalate into violence. If all or most species behave similarly in this respect, there is no reason to single out humans as distinctive. Indeed, Gat (1999a, 2000a) notes that killing rates within the animal world are greater than those demonstrated by contemporary humans but are roughly similar to those exhibited by ancient hunting and gathering groups.[9]

Gat's position is anchored by a Malthusian perspective on growth dynamics. Species reproduce and tend to overpopulate their ecological niches unless they face constraints. As the population increases, carrying capacities become more strained and resources more scarce. As a consequence, even species that inhabit low-yield territories (such as deserts) share a desire to monopolize the resources encompassed by their respective niches and will fight other members of their own species or other species that interlope. Periods of heightened scarcity, moreover, are all the more likely to witness invasions from outside the home territory as others penetrate in search of resources for themselves.

Two points here are associated with this perspective. As noted, if all species engage in these processes, there is nothing especially distinctive about humans. Humans and other animals are prepared to defend territory and other resources (just as they are prepared to take resources from others). Equally important, these propensities were apt to be demonstrated from the very beginning of the human species. They did not depend on subsequent developments (such as agriculture or urbanized density) to develop a propensity toward violence. Later developments merely escalated the numbers of people, the frequencies of their frictions, and the increasingly specialized tools they employed to kill one another—all of which, of course, are likely to be important to the escalation of warfare.

We are not sufficiently familiar with all animal species to evaluate adequately Gat's generalization, but we find his general position that human killing behavior is not fundamentally distinctive a quite attractive starting point. It is certainly compatible with many of the observations we examine and advance in subsequent chapters. One difference is that we choose to put more emphasis on the escalation of fighting tendencies—as opposed to seeking basic root motivations for indulging in fighting. In other words, we cannot know for sure whether territorial defense is instinctual or learned behavior, as one can certainly construct a nongenetic explanation for the violent defense of home territory or of resources in times of scarcity. It suffices that quite a bit of territorial defense appears to have taken place in the past and is interwoven into the history of warfare.

Old Assumptions

The third source of problems created by analysts is twofold. The disciplines of anthropology and archaeology have not generally made warfare a priority question.[10] That bias has begun to change, but we do not have a long record of archaeological/anthropological analysis of conflict. The other side of that coin is that there has been an older tradition that assumes that ancient warfare was more ritualistic and less serious than contemporary warfare. An example is provided by Harry Turney-High's ([1949] 1991, 227) influential evaluation of "primitive warfare":

> Foregoing chapters have said the lack of tactical operations made primitive war "primitive." In the end, this means nothing more or less than saying the noncivilized fighter is no soldier, his warfare is not war, and his butchering is futile and primitive because his operations lack organization and because he has developed the functions of leadership and command so poorly.

We interpret Turney-High to be using his own experience in World War II as a reference point and arguing that because nonliterate warriors fought with less systematic training and command than he and his fellow soldiers did in World War II, earlier warfare had little in common with contemporary warfare, or that it did not attain the threshold required for genuine warfare. One might argue, however, that what is really at stake here is the question of efficiency and efficacy, not the presence or absence of warfare.[11]

If the question is whether the behavior that Turney-High describes as "primitive" war is really war, and if one accepts our definition of war as sustained, coordinated violence between political organizations, then the answer is clearly in the affirmative. Early warfare may have differed from modern warfare in various ways, but it still falls into the broad category of war. The questions then become, how does primitive war differ from latter forms of warfare? and how did primitive war evolve into later forms of warfare?

Our approach to explaining the evolution of warfare will focus in the next chapter on the coevolution of warfare with political and military organization, threat environment, weaponry, and political economy. By stressing coevolutionary developments, we hope to evade some fruitless pursuit of chicken-and-egg-type questions. Does military technology drive military organization? Is political organization a function of political economy or the other way around? Our position is that once these factors are in play it becomes difficult to assess the direction and order of causal influence. Significant changes in one of the six variables tend to lead to significant changes in one or more of the other five variables.

Given our present focus on the emergence of warfare, however, what came first cannot be totally evaded. We will propose a synthetic, causal ordering that appears to have characterized the emergence of warfare.[12] We argue that the origins of warfare can be reduced primarily to an interaction between political-economic scarcity and increasing complexity in political-military organization within various threatening environmental contexts. We make no claim, however, that this causal ordering has remained unchanged in subsequent millennia. While the interaction between political-economy concerns and organizational complexity is an arc of continuity across thousands of years, the way in which it is manifested has not been constant or linear.

Did Weapons Come First?

Arther Ferrill (1997) points out that weaponry and basic military formations emerged from hunting long before warfare became evident. The spear came first. Just when it emerged no one can say, but preserved artifacts date back 70,000 to 300,000 years ago. Hunting practices also were probably responsible for the two most basic military formations— the column and the line—and for enveloping tactics.[13] Once armed men begin using these formations and tactics under some kind of command structure, one has the beginnings of organized warfare from Ferrill's perspective. This could date warfare back to some unknown period in Paleolithic times.

More specifically, Ferrill (1997) argues that the first revolution in weapons technology occurred between 12,000 and 8000 BCE. During this time, bows, slings, daggers, and mace were introduced into the human weapons inventory. This period of time overlaps with the emergence of agriculture in the ancient Near East. In contrast to the conventional wisdom that increased conflict among sedentary cultivators led to the invention of new weaponry, Ferrill poses an intriguing alternative hypothesis. The earliest settlements in the ancient Near East were associated not only with agriculture but also with fortifications.[14] It is quite plausible that the new firepower linked to bows and slings increased the incentives to build protective walls. If so the need for defense may have preceded the emergence of agriculture.[15] If insecurity drove people into concentrated settlements for protection, it would have been difficult and even irrational to abandon the protecting walls when attackers appeared. Fortifications meant decreased mobility and an increased linkage to specified territory. Therefore, the incentives to invent new ways of feeding the inhabitants of these population centers would also have increased. Thus it is conceivable that warfare encouraged the emergence of sedentary agriculture—as much if not more than the other way around.[16]

Yet acknowledging that rudimentary weapons of some sort, even if they were only stones and sticks, had to precede coordinated warfare, leaves a great deal to be explained. Individuals and families can clash with weapons but we do not normally consider such conflict to be warfare. What are needed are processes that aggregate individuals and families into larger groups that require some form of political organization. The first step involves Raymond Kelly's (2000) emphasis on group segmentation.

Social Organization and Foraging Band Warfare

Kelly (2000) prefaces his argument with the observation that the earliest evidence for warfare is associated with urbanized states in the ancient Near East. Relatively large armies with armor, fortified cities, and clear signs of destruction on a significant scale were all present. But does that mean we need to equate warfare with the development of urbanization and the associated sedentary agriculture that fed increasingly large and dense populations? His answer is probably not, especially if there is reason to believe that warfare preceded the emergence of cities and states. Cave art, mass burials, and skeletons with embedded arrowheads that can be dated back some 10,000 to 30,000 years ago are suggestive of early warfare that preceded the advent of agriculture and cities.

Another clue is provided by the behavior of foraging societies, the types of social groupings that were most common up to about 10,000 years ago. If one examines a random sample of known societies and separates the foragers from the nonforagers, a group of twenty-five societies survives the cut. If then one asks to what extent these twenty-five foraging societies engaged in warfare activity, the answer turns out to be eighteen of the twenty-five or about 72 percent (Kelly 2000).[17]

This finding supports three or four generalizations about foraging band behavior. One is that it is quite possible that not all foraging groups experienced violent conflict with other groups. More than a fourth of the sample, after all, never or rarely engaged in warfare. The second generalization is that since nearly three-fourths of the sample had engaged in warlike activities, it is quite likely that most foraging groups have some experience with organized violent conflict. A corollary is that this same generalization probably applies to the Neolithic era.[18] Finally, it stands to reason that if some foraging bands are warlike and others are not, we should be able to explain why this is the case. What distinguishes the warring groups from the peaceful ones?

Kelly's (2000) answer is complicated but begins with the idea that groups, not unlike societies and states, have varying levels of social organization. "Unsegmented" groups consist of nuclear families that are not linked to other nuclear families. Some families of varying size may cohere for purposes of hunting or merely surviving. Such groups are mobile and have vague and nonpermanent identities. Seasonal change may lead to a breakup of the group into smaller sizes. Different families may come and go. The point is that membership in these unsegmented groups is unlikely to be recognized by the members of what is a highly transitory collectivity.

That changes with segmentation. Segmented groups also have nuclear families, but these families are linked through kinship ties to other nuclear families, thereby constituting clans. As D. J. Mattingly (1992, 32) notes: "Tribes are composed of a hierarchy of units: individual people make up households, several households form a kin group, several kin groups constitute a regional clan, a union of clans makes a small tribe, and these small tribes will on occasion . . . form larger confederations."

For our purposes, what changes with segmentation is the cognition of group membership, a sense of group identity. This is important for violence because in an unsegmented group an attack on one individual is merely that—an attack on one individual. If the individual dies, the immediate family may mourn, but the rest of the group is unlikely to sense a loss to their group. Therefore, there is much less basis for subsequent group vengeance. At best some members of the nuclear family may counterattack the killer. The critical question is whether the counterattack is viewed as vengeance on the perpetrator as an individual or as an attack on some larger, segmented group of which the perpetrator is considered a member.

In a segmented group, group membership is more meaningful, and, therefore, the loss of a member of the group is more likely to be felt as an attack on the group itself. Kin are then obligated to respond against the killer, but if the killer is also part of another segmented group, any member of the other group may suffice. Similarly, the other segmented group may feel obligated to view the response against the killer as an attack on the whole group.

The distinction between unsegmented and segmented groups is fundamental for the definition of war as violence between groups. The intergroup character of war distinguishes it from some other forms of violence. Whereas murder, duels, and capital punishment involve individual responsibility, war involves group responsibility for injury to another group. This means that collective punishment can be directed at any member of the offending group based on the principle of social substitutability of one member of the offending group for another. As Kelly (2000, 5) concludes, "War is thus cognitively and conceptually (as well as behaviorally) between groups."

Kelly (2000, 5) goes on to say that war should be analyzed as "meaningfully entailed social action (intelligible from the actor's point of view) rather than simply in behavioral terms." Similarly, Mead (1940) speaks of the importance of a group understanding the concept of war in addition to engaging in intergroup violence. In describing a traveling Eskimo who entered a settlement and who fought the strongest man in the settlement, with the aim of establishing his position, Mead argues that this is a test of strength and bravery, not war. She argues: "The idea of warfare, of one *group* organizing against another *group* to maim and wound and kill them was absent. And, without that idea, passions might rage but there was no war." Although this element of meaningful social action might need to be demonstrated in instances of organized violence between small groups, it can generally be assumed in cases of violence between the organized military forces of larger political units like states.

Thus in the process of moving from unsegmented group to segmented group, the basis for intergroup feuding is established in which a trespass against the group or any member of the group requires a group response.[19] Group responses, in turn, require coordination, decision-making, a plan of counterattack, and a group of people to carry out the plan.[20] Parallel conditions on the targeted side create an opportunity for conflict escalation and protracted violence, particularly if neither group is capable of dominating the other group.

Kelly (2000) presents strong evidence to support this thesis. Breaking down the twenty-five foraging groups into unsegmented and segmented yields the distribution of cases summarized in table 2.3. Almost all of the unsegmented foraging bands are less warlike. Almost all of the segmented groups are warlike.[21] Of course, the distribution might have worked out differently in prehistoric times, but since we have no information on group attributes in the distant past, the proxy behavior of known foraging group behavior may be as close as we can get to analyzing them in any systematic fashion.

Curiously perhaps, dowries are viewed as one of the major motors of this process. Whether marriage payments are a causal factor or a consequence, the redistribution of wealth between groups participating in the marriage signifies the recognition of intergroup/intragroup or interfamily linkages. The rituals and celebrations associated with marriages are also significant indicators because they are part of the process of creating bonds and social interactions between sets of people that tend to reduce intragroup conflict. Table 2.4 reports the distribution of marriage payments and warlike behavior among the twenty-five foraging groups. Most of the unsegmented-warless foraging groups fall into the upper left-hand corner cell in which dowries are not paid. Clearly, marriage payments are less than a perfect predictor of which groups are warlike, but all of the groups who engaged in this custom also engaged in warfare.

TABLE 2.3 **Segmentation and warfare among foraging groups**

	Less Warlike	More Warlike
Unsegmented	6 (86%)	2 (11%)
Segmented	1 (14%)	16 (89%)
TOTAL	7 (100%)	18 (100%)

Source: Based on information reported in Kelly (2000, 52).

TABLE 2.4 **Marriage payments and warfare among foraging groups**

	Less Warlike	More Warlike
Marriage payments absent	7 (100%)	8 (44%)
Marriage payments present	0 (0%)	10 (56%)
TOTAL	7 (100%)	18 (100%)

Source: Based on information reported in Kelly (2000, 61, 63).

What does this very early coevolution between social organization and warlike activity tell us about the history of warfare? If it is accurate to assume that most of the world's population consisted of unsegmented foraging bands for most of human existence, it is quite possible that there was little in the way of organized violence or war in Neolithic times up to as recently as 35,000 years ago. Occasional clashes are certainly conceivable in this context. Two transitory groups might collide unwittingly in pursuit of game or access to water, though with relatively very few people (by contemporary standards) the probability of chance collisions was probably fairly low. They might also fight, but such fights would be characterized by an absence of planning, organization, and specialized weaponry or warriors. The people who engaged in the fight would be those most proximate to the collision. The numbers would be small. Gender and age might not matter all that much in distinguishing between combatants and noncombatants. Once some outcome was obtained, the losing side might retreat if it could and leave the area to the winning side. The two bands of people would not necessarily anticipate a recurrence of combat. As long as resources were not too scarce, the bands would have little real incentive to pursue their conflict further. Whatever they had been looking for could just as easily be found somewhere else, and possibly in areas not already occupied by other humans. Why bother fighting in such circumstances?

Things began to change sometime in the past 35,000 years. Population growth led to higher densities of humans. Big game began to disappear (Otterbein 2004, 66–68).[22] Resource availability became scarcer, especially in areas from which people found it difficult to exit. Other areas became more difficult to find and move to and were increasingly likely to already be populated. Groups became more segmented. Intergroup collisions thus became more probable. Feuding and warfare also became more likely.[23] Or, as Ronald Cohen (1984, 333) puts it pithily: "the greater the competition for scarce resources . . . the greater the potential for and probability of disputes; the greater the number of disputes, the higher the likelihood of warfare in any particular region." Mass burials found in the Nile Valley suggest that this transition was already underway there some 12,000 years ago. Many other parts of the world had caught up by some 10,000 years ago.

Group segmentation is a first step toward the creation of larger groups that may find themselves faced with threats from other groups or opportunities to improve their welfare. But war requires more than the ability and willingness to identify with other people as belonging to the same extended group. Political organization, which often implies some type of military organization, is necessary to coordinate the defenses and attacks of the larger groups.

Chiefs, Circumscription, and Population Pressure

One of the best-known arguments about the origins of warfare is Robert Carneiro's (1970, 1990) "circumscription" thesis.[24] Carneiro contends that warfare occurred prior to the advent of agriculture but that it was not particularly significant at that time. Groups of people had begun settling into isolated villages, and as long as they remained relatively isolated, warfare remained sporadic and limited. The adoption of agriculture, however, led to a major population increase within a context of a finite supply of arable land. As arable land became more scarce—especially in areas that were circumscribed by natural features such as mountains, seashores, swamps, jungles, and the like, thereby discouraging movement away from territories with fairly definite boundaries—the incentives to take territory from neighboring settlements increased. The men who successfully led these efforts to conquer adjacent territories became paramount chiefs with political power over multiple villages—as opposed to the leader of a single isolated village.[25]

Isolated villages were unlikely to surrender their land and autonomy voluntarily. Success in amalgamating several villages rested on the application of sufficient coercion to defeat the resistance. Warfare intensified. It also became more frequent and more important because it changed the incentives of political entrepreneurs and the size and scale of military and political power, as delineated in table 2.5.

Once an isolated village was confronted with a situation demanding or encouraging some form of militant response, chiefs did not necessarily have any ability to command followers to engage in combat. They were

TABLE 2.5 **Carneiro's single versus multiple village chiefdoms distinctions**

	Single Village	Multiple Village
War motivation	Revenge and opportunistic plunder	Revenge and opportunistic plunder; territorial conquest; responses to offenses to prestige of leaders
Warriors	Voluntary	Potentially all able-bodied adults
Army size	Tens	Hundreds/thousands
Military leadership	Variable	Paramount chief
Weaponry	Medium range projectiles	Close range projectiles and shock
Battle casualties	Limited	Higher
Consequences	Limited	Successful chiefdoms expand in size and complexity, ultimately becoming states

Source: Based on Carneiro (1990) discussion.

not necessarily military leaders themselves. The number of combatants had to have been small. As a consequence, bows and arrows would have been the preferred weaponry because the enemy could be engaged at a distance and in a way that might compensate for small numbers. The small sizes involved literally guaranteed that the number of casualties would be limited. Most importantly, the isolated villages were most likely to remain isolated villages.

Leaders who could capture control of multiple villages found themselves in much different circumstances. The stakes had increased and so had the resources available to engage in conquest. If chiefs could punish "no-shows," potentially all adult males capable of bearing arms could be enlisted for the purposes of war. With some men becoming full-time warriors, depending on the nature of the demands for their services, greater specialization was possible. Expanded numbers and specialization encouraged closer-range fighting and a preference for shock tactics and weaponry. The size of the armies expanded from the tens into the hundreds and thousands.

The basic idea here is that mass leads to shock tactics. Small bands of soldiers should prefer to engage in ambushes or to use projectiles at some distance—at least until they are sure their opponents are as small or smaller in size and/or number. A lack of mass, therefore, encourages people to avoid hand-to-hand encounters if possible and especially to avoid being outnumbered by the opposition. An expanding population, however, creates the possibility of creating larger armies than previously thought feasible.

Given that the resultant conquests were at least partially the product of entrepreneurship, the successful military leaders were also the ones most likely to become the paramount chiefs whose power was bolstered and reinforced by the expanded armies. Expanded armies also meant more casualties would ensue in close-range battles. Thus warfare became more significant, and more complex chiefdoms ultimately became states, thereby leading to further escalation in matters related to warfare.

There can be little doubt that warfare sometimes in some (probably many) places followed this pattern. For instance, Spanish observers interviewed Wanka leaders in the late sixteenth century to obtain a better idea about how Peruvian society in the Mantaro Valley functioned prior to the Inca and Spanish conquests. One individual said that when "a local community multiplied to many people, they would eventually fight with others to seize their fields and food and their women." Leaders were former military commanders who had to demonstrate their prowess in battle to gain political legitimacy in peacetime. As one theorist of chiefdom politics put it, the sixteenth-century Wanka interviewees "could have been writing a section for Carneiro's paper" (Earle 1997, 114).

Yet there was variation. Intensified warfare did not necessarily follow population growth, and population growth did not necessarily lead to intensified warfare, with or without circumscription. Earle (1997, 129–31) discusses a second case involving Denmark in the early Bronze Age. Warfare was about cattle raiding, in which chiefs were content to expand their wealth but not territorial control. As a consequence, warfare was preceded by a decline in population rather than by population pressures.[26] Ronald Cohen (1984, 334–36) describes the behavior of Nigerian Chibboks as circumscribed predators who failed to develop increased political centralization prior to the advent of British rule, though he describes the Chibbok case as atypical. The point here is not that Carneiro's theory is often repudiated by case histories, but merely that some cases do not conform. The frequency of violations of the circumscription/population pressure hypothesis remains unclear.

On the other hand, there are plenty of examples of increased tribal complexity due to conquest. Herbert Lewis (1981, 208) suggests an expanded set of motivations that might lead to conquest/war behavior, including population pressure, recreation, land, glory, honors, plunder, controlling trade routes, protecting water sources, obtaining new pasturage, capturing slaves, rebelling against oppressors, or replenishing herds and flocks. He suggests that the specific motivation for war is not as important as the essential cost-benefit calculus of going to war. If the threat of potential loss or the promise of possible gain that can be won from war are sufficiently great, people perceive it as worthwhile to organize, fight, and accept risks (Lewis 1981, 211).

In a related vein, John Chapman (1999, 140) stresses frontier contexts as particularly susceptible to increasing the probability of severe warfare because they represent zones in which new groups are most likely to come into contact with already established groups. A second context especially susceptible to the escalation of warfare is one in which resources are distributed differentially. People located in more limited resource areas are encouraged to raid areas with less limited resources.

The advent of sedentary agriculture (and geographical circumscription) was important to these multiple motivations in enhancing the incentives to attack and to defend territorially fixed targets. Ross Hassig (1992, 12) elaborates this point by arguing that warfare expanded in Mesoamerica with the development of "fixed assets that could be seized, destroyed, or defended." Prior to this development, raiders would have lacked suitably attractive targets. Kelly (2000, 68) further establishes this point by listing a number of the consequences of food storage that might precede sedentary agriculture but that certainly became more likely after its successful adoption.[27] We list these below.

1. Limits the mobility of food cultivators
2. Stimulates population increase
3. Lays the groundwork for wealth accumulation and economic inequality
4. Increases vulnerability to raids in times of scarcity
5. Increases incentives for plundering by neighboring social groups
6. Increases incentives for defensive preparations to protect targets of value
7. Losing stored food may compel population migration and loss of territory

Although sedentary agriculture was not responsible for the origins of war, it did increase the incentives for aggressive behavior and in doing so contributed significantly to the escalation of warfare. The surplus resources supplied by sedentary agriculture also facilitated the development of larger and more professional armies, which also contributed to the escalation of warfare.

Moreover, the greater the gain or avoidance of potential loss and the greater the need for coordination of war efforts, the greater is the stature of the successful leader (Cohen 1984). Successful military leaders acquire armed followers who must be rewarded by gains from war but who can be used for other political and police purposes at home. Therefore, if the scope and intensity of warfare escalates, war leaders are likely to benefit in terms of political tenure, prominence, and power. The most successful war leaders would expand the territorial scope of their domain and, no doubt, in the process of doing so, create more complex political systems with which to rule their expanded domains.

Hunting, Agriculture, and Political Centralization

One of the more ambitious and distinctive interpretations of the origins of war brings together information on several topics—hunting, agriculture, political centralization, and military organization. In a number of ways it encompasses and synthesizes many of the arguments we have already looked at while at the same time advancing an original and appealing interpretation. Keith Otterbein (2004) notes that one school of thought sees mankind as inherently belligerent. Warfare, from this perspective, can be seen as an outgrowth of hunting activities dating back one or two million years. Another school of thought sees man as inherently peaceful until the advent of agriculture, increasingly dense settlements, and expansionary states. Otterbein offers an intriguing resolution of this debate by contending that both interpretations are correct. War originated twice—first, two million years ago in conjunction with hunting large animals more or less to extinction in many parts of the world, and then again several thousand years after the advent of agriculture.[28]

The linkages between hunting and warfare have already been highlighted. The weapons for one type of activity serve the other purpose just as well.[29] The tactics and coordinated activity employed in hunting large animals can be translated into attacks on other human groups. Hunting also forces hunters to roam over large areas that become even larger as the game becomes scarcer. Presumably, the probability of clashes with other hunters increased as the scope of movement expanded. The intensity of these clashes may also have increased as large animals became increasingly rare.[30] Warfare thus could have first ensued over violations of group conceptions of private hunting territories—not unlike much later disputes over political sovereignty in Kashmir, the Chaco desert, or Alsace-Lorraine.

The gradual disappearance of large game may have contributed to conflict in the short term, but, as Otterbein (2004) argues, it also created incentives for people to develop alternative ways of acquiring food, which dampened motivations for conflict over the long term. Warfare, always of a relatively limited scale given the numbers of hunters involved, died out as people developed alternative approaches to feeding themselves. A reliance on a combination of small game and grains gradually supplanted the tradition of hunting large game. Where soil and water resources facilitated it, a dependence on cultivated plants developed into sedentary agriculture.

The transition to agriculture, in Otterbein's view, also depended on another ingredient—the absence of warfare. If early groups attempting to develop sedentary agriculture came under attack, they were usually forced to move to defensive positions that would move them away from the most desirable soil-water locations. Successful agriculture required many years of relatively peaceful development so that people could stay in one place and learn to domesticate animals and plants. Otherwise, the attempts to move from one type of political economy to another would have been much less likely to succeed.[31]

Sedentary agriculture creates an environment conducive to increasing complexity in political organization. Table 2.6 lists Otterbein's stage sequence, beginning with small agricultural villages and culminating in mature states. The principal focus is on increasing political concentration and its implications for stratification and behavior. First, a leader, supported by some faction of followers, becomes a chief. Chiefs eliminate their rivals coercively and utilize coercion to solidify their rule. In the process the chief and his followers tend to become an upper class. The rest of the population assumes a subordinated position, willingly or unwillingly. The lower class may be forced to support the upper class by contributing labor and food. A warrior aristocracy emerges within the upper class initially to maintain the political-economic stratification of the chiefdom. Some portion of the forthcoming agricultural surplus diverted to maintain the upper class can then be utilized to provide resources for specialized weapons training and an increasingly professionalized warrior group or military organization.

Sedentary agriculture encouraged population increases but political centralization was essential to agricultural intensification. Public works— walls, irrigation, temples—implied forced labor that in turn relied on political coercion controlled by the ruler and his military resources. Ironically, then, part of Otterbein's thesis is that agricultural intensification,

TABLE 2.6 **Stages of early political organization**

Political Organization	Characteristics
Agricultural village	One leader and faction may emerge as dominant
Minimal chiefdom	The leader becomes chief and dominates with followers employing coercion
Typical chiefdom	The chief and his followers govern their community
Maximal chiefdoms/ inchoate early state	Increasing political centralization and coercion; state idea increasingly prevalent
Early state	Lower class subordinated, possibly providing labor for upper class; chief's followers and upper class constitute a military organization
Typical early state	Chief becomes king as territorial conquests in immediate area begin
Transitional early state	Increased centralization and conquests farther afield; more specialization in complexity, military organization, and political economy
Mature state	Kingdom increasingly subject to bureaucratic control

Note: The political organization scale represents a merger of Carneiro's (1990) chiefdom scale and Claessen and Skalnik's (1978, 22–23) early state typology. This table represents a major simplification of Otterbein (2004, 112).

with all of its implications for population densities, urbanization, and military power, awaited the earlier emergence of sufficient political centralization to bring it about, and not the other way around. Although elite warriors emerged initially to support the chief's political control, conflicts with other chiefs and their ruling classes in the immediate vicinity gradually became more probable around the "maximal chiefdom/inchoate early state/early state" phases of development specified in table 2.6. Warfare, thereafter, increasingly became a more routine behavior.

Still another part of Otterbein's extended thesis is that the upper class, and especially the warrior aristocracy, responds in predictable ways to the amount of warfare that occurs. If warfare is infrequent, the warrior group is likely to remain small and to retain its monopoly of weapons and weapons training. If warfare is frequent, there are two basic choices. Either one can expand the size of the warrior class and retain the weapons monopoly, or one can arm some portion of the lower class via conscription, thereby taking some risk of domestic rebellion. In this respect the size and nature of the military organization is very much a function of the threat environment. Table 2.7 summarizes this particular argument.

There is, however, one major caveat to Otterbein's interpretation. He restricts its application to processes that emerged in pristine areas or areas for the most part not subject to influences from developments in other areas. Once the earliest developers emerged (Mesopotamia in the Near East, China in East Asia, Mexico in Central America, Peru in South America), other groups were often influenced by either their example or their expansionary depredations. The capability and propensity to engage in interstate warfare thus emerged as a by-product of internal conflict in the pristine developers, but secondary developers created states and military organizations to emulate and/or to defend themselves against the pristine developers.

Otterbein proceeds to test his arguments by examining the evolutionary patterns found in the pristine areas. Tables 2.8 and 2.9 summarize his findings that tend to provide strong support for his arguments. Table 2.8 focuses on the evolution of political centralization, stratification, and conflict. In each of the four cases, there is little evidence of internal or external conflict in the early stages. Chiefs, wealth differences, and social classes gradually emerged, with increasing tendencies to abuse lower classes in terms of executions and human sacrifices. Rulers became more powerful and more despotic. Chiefs became kings and, later, emperors.

Military organization, weaponry, and warfare kept pace with the evolutionary pace summarized in table 2.8. Table 2.9 charts the changes in the military sphere. Initially, there were no military organizations and no warfare. Military organizations, fortifications, and specialized warriors in armor, along with internal and external warfare, begin to appear in the transition between the "typical chiefdom" and "inchoate early state" phases. In the "typical early state" phase and afterward, the weaponry became increasingly more lethal. Developments in Mesopotamia and China led to infantry formations, chariot warfare, and cavalry, while American warfare remained more elite-focused and also lacked the horses necessary for chariots and cavalry.

It is important to note that limitations on information about these early developments sometimes make it difficult to differentiate between external

TABLE 2.7 **The size of the warrior aristocracy and the frequency of warfare**

Warrior Class Size	Infrequent Warfare	Frequent Warfare
Small	Weapons restricted to elites	Conscription
Large	Unlikely	Weapons restricted to elites

TABLE 2.8 **Otterbein's evolutionary trajectories for pristine states, stratification, and conflict**

Type of Political Organization	Mesopotamia	China	Peru* (Chavin/Moche)	Mexico (Zapotec)
Villages	5700–4750 BCE no wealth differences— minimal conflict	6500–5000 BCE farming communities— minimal conflict	4500–3000 BCE foragers— minimal conflict	1400–1150 BCE nonhereditary leaders— minimal conflict
Minimal chiefdom	4750–4350 BCE minimal wealth differences— minimal conflict	5000–3200 BCE chiefs—minimal conflict	3000–1800 BCE no classes— minimal conflict	1150–850 BCE chiefs and wealth differences- minimal conflict
Typical chiefdom	4350–3700 BCE chief-priests— some conflict?	3200–2500 BCE two-level polities— executions	1800–800 BCE no classes but wealth differences— minimal conflict	850–700 BCE rival chiefs and social classes- minimal conflict
Maximal chiefdom/ inchoate early state	3700–3000 BCE social classes– coercion	2500–2200 BCE wealth differences— human sacrifices/ decapitations/ burials alive	800–200 BCE classes and two/three level polities— minimal conflict	700–500 BCE chiefs—forced labor
Typical early state	3000–2600 BCE kings-slaves	2200–1750 BCE warrior nobility—human sacrifice	200 BCE– 600 CE four level polities and social classes— torture and sacrifices	500–100 BCE despotic chiefs—lower classes forced to relocate and produce food for upper classes
Transitional early state	2600–2350 BCE kings—human sacrifices	1750–1045 BCE king, royal nobility—war captives for labor and sacrifice	600–1000 CE large polities intensified internal tensions	100 BCE–200 CE empire— conquest, forced relocation, terror
Mature state	2350–2150 BCE empire	1045–221 BCE extensive kingdom—decline of sacrifices	1000–1450 CE empire	200–700 CE empire

* Otterbein (2004, 132–33) uses different evolutionary categories for the Peruvian trajectory but adheres to a seven-stage structure. He also distinguishes between highland and coastal developments. We have eliminated both distinctions primarily due to space considerations.
Source: Based on Otterbein (2004, 124, 132–33, 144, 160).

TABLE 2.9 **Otterbein's evolutionary trajectories for pristine states, military organization, and war**

Type of Political Organization	Mesopotamia	China	Peru* (Chavin/Moche)	Mexico (Zapotec)
Villages	5700–4750 BCE no military organization; no war	6500–5000 BCE no military organization; no war	4500–3000 BCE no military organization; no war	1400–1150 BCE no military organization; no war
Minimal chiefdom	4750–4350 BCE no military organization; no war	5000–3200 BCE no military organization; no war?	3000–1800 BCE club, spear, slings; internal war rare	1150–850 BCE no military organization; no war
Typical chiefdom	4350–3700 BCE no fortifications; some internal war?	3200–2500 BCE no military organization; no war?	1800–800 BCE no fortifications; warriors with helmets, shields, and darts; internal war	850–700 BCE no military organization; no war
Maximal chiefdom/inchoate early state	3700–3000 BCE walls; elite warriors with maces, bows, and spears; war	2500–2200 BCE wall; spears, bows; intervillage warfare?	800–200 BCE fortresses; internal and external war	700–500 BCE chiefs lead warriors on raids; clubs, atlatls; war
Typical early state	3000–2600 BCE fortifications, bronze weapons, copper helmets, capes, and spears; chariots supported by infantry; internal and external war	2200–1750 BCE walls; elite warriors; bows, halberds, knives; internal war	200 BCE–600 CE warriors with spears, clubs, shields, darts, and knives; external war	500–100 BCE chief's relatives lead military aristocracy on raids; spears; internal war
Transitional early state	2600–2350 BCE copper helmets, shields, pikes, socket axes; massed infantry in phalanx; ruler/officers use chariots; war	1750–1045 BCE many walls; chariots, infantry, composite bows, halberds, knives; external and internal war	600–1000 CE elite warriors from upper classes; external war	100 BCE–200 CE elite warriors with helmets, shields, clubs, and thrusting shields; commoners defend walls; external war

TABLE 2.9 *continued*

Type of Political Organization	Mesopotamia	China	Peru* (Chavin/Moche)	Mexico (Zapotec)
Mature state	2350–2150 BCE infantry, archers; composite bow; internal and external war	1045–221 BCE massed infantry, conscription, swords, crossbows, cavalry; external and internal war	1000–1450 CE king heads elite army of warriors; external war	200–700 CE military aristocracy; war

* Otterbein (2004, 132–33) uses different evolutionary categories for the Peruvian case but adheres to the seven-stage structure. He also distinguishes between highlands and coastal developments. We have eliminated these distinctions due primarily to space considerations.
Source: Otterbein (2004, 124, 132–33, 144, 160).

and internal warfare. Archaeologists find evidence of warfare, but that does not mean they can always specify the identity of the adversaries.

Environmental Stress

If the motivations for going to war are likely to be several, so are the circumstances that either encourage or discourage conflict. In addition to geographical circumscription, population density and growth, and resource scarcity, environmental stress or deterioration often contributes to an increase in warfare. If population growth can lead to conflict over land for agrarian cultivation purposes, an increased number of mouths to feed within a context of diminishing resources can also facilitate conflict. Jonathan Haas (1999) provides a thumbnail sketch of early North American prehistory that speaks very directly to this issue. When nomads first began filtering into the New World some 13,000 to 15,000 years ago, population density was small and game resources were quite plentiful; there is no surviving evidence of territoriality, ethnic-cultural differences, or warfare. This state of affairs began to change between 9000 BCE and 1000 CE. Population density increased, game became either extinct or scarcer, and regional cultural differentiation emerged. Yet warfare did not emerge uniformly.[32]

In the American southwest, again according to Haas (1999), there is no evidence of warfare up to about 1000 BCE. For the next two thousand years, there was further population growth, scarcity of wild food, the adoption of sedentary agriculture, ethnic cultural differentiation, and the occupation of the most inhabitable sites. Yet major warfare did not break out until around 1250 CE, after one hundred years of climate change and drought. Large populations were confronted with diminished resources and greater threat and chose, as a consequence, to cluster together in fortified or defendable villages. Only after 1300 and some climatic improvement did the amount of warfare decline.

In contrast, in the American east, group frictions over occupation of the best territories and warfare had become detectable by 5000 BCE. The advent of agriculture is credited with decreasing the incentives to fight between 2000 BCE and the early part of the first millennium CE, as indicated in table 2.10. Agrarian cultivation increased the amount of available nonmarginal territory (vis-à-vis the earlier emphasis on hunting and foraging grounds), at least for a time. By 1000 CE, fortification and warfare were once again on the rise and continued into the period of European intrusions.

Haas spends little time explaining the differences between the east and southwest, but it appears that neither area conformed to what might have been expected from an agrarian/population pressure perspective. Warfare was very slow in coming to the southwest and was intermittent in the east despite increasing population pressures and the introduction of sedentary agriculture. The earlier warfare in the east may have been related to relative resource abundance. Analysts tend to argue that warfare in situations characterized by very scarce resources tends to be less likely because the harshness of the environment favors (selects on) cooperation rather than conflict.

TABLE 2.10 **Haas's overview of North American conflict propensities**

Location and Time Period	Conflict Propensity
North America, 13,000–5000 BCE	No evidence of warfare
Southwest North America:	
6000–1000 BCE	No evidence of warfare
1250–1300 CE	Major outbreak of warfare
Post-1300 CE	Reduction in conflict
Eastern North America:	
5000–2000 BCE	Appearance of warfare; conflict relatively common
2000 BCE–50 CE	Decline in warfare
1000 CE – European intrusions	Escalation in warfare

Source: Based on the discussion in Haas (1999).

That expectation does not hold, however, when an environment abruptly becomes harsher, when the resource "rug" is abruptly pulled out from under populations that previously had expanded, suggesting that the relationship between resource availability and warfare is highly nonlinear. If people have nowhere to go to secure more resources, increased conflict is likely. Islands and areas already marginal to begin with (as in deserts) should be especially prone to this problem. Patrick Kirch (1984), for example, emphasizes this syndrome in the history of Polynesian island conflicts. Steven LeBlanc (1999) goes into considerable detail on the southwest American phenomenon.[33]

The conflict-facilitating role of environmental stress need not necessarily contradict the link between sedentary population pressures and conflict. A deteriorating resource base can increase the pressure on the carrying capacity of the land that is being cultivated. So, too, can an expanding population if the land resources are relatively fixed. The point is that introducing an environmental stress component expands the repertoire of conflict-inducing possibilities. Population growth and/or environmental deterioration can lead to a greater potential for conflict and warfare. Political entrepreneurs (military leaders, chiefs) can act in these circumstances to create larger political systems by coercion if they are successful. Presumably, they may also act similarly in the absence of population growth and/or environmental deterioration.

Another variant on this dimension is the early emergence of a division of labor between agrarian farmers and pastoral shepherds (Cohen 1984, 334; O'Connell 1995, 75). The latter specialize in animal husbandry and need to move their charges from one pasture and watering hole to another. The mobility of the flock/herd can be blocked or opposed by sedentary farmers who may control access to grass and water. In periods of environmental stress, grass and water become more scarce and therefore something to fight about. Then, too, the greater the division of labor, the greater is the need for pastoral specialists to have access to the sedentary economy that produces grain and metal tools. If agrarian groups choose to bar access to these commodities through trade, nomadic groups have little recourse but to engage in raids to secure the same objectives. In this case an early structural division of labor made conflict and war more probable, and especially in times of environmental stress.

O'Connell (1995, 75) adopts an especially extreme stand on this question when he credits "the origins of true human warfare in the initial confrontation between the sedentary and the nomadic." There are two problems in emphasizing this facet of early conflict propensities. Sedentary-nomadic divisions of labor were not evenly developed throughout the world. It also took some time for fully nomadic groups to come into existence and develop formidable military skills. For instance, sedentary-nomadic warfare in the ancient Near East and Egypt became more significant only after the development of intercity warfare in Mesopotamia and the conquest of Lower Egypt by Upper Egypt.

Greater Political-Economic Complexity in General

One thing that Cohen (1984), Cioffi-Revilla (2000), Kelly (2000), Carneiro (1970, 1990), and many other war origins analysts share is an emphasis on organizational complexity facilitating warfare. Complexity is neither necessary nor sufficient for war, but it is a powerful stimulant to what can be done on the battlefield, and, for that matter, why humans might end up on battlefields in the first place. The way this facet of warfare is sometimes raised is by asking whether political centralization or sedentary agriculture, both markers of greater political-economic complexity, are important to warfare and its escalation. Our coevolutionary reflex is to say that sedentary agriculture and political centralization tend to evolve in tandem.

Table 2.11 tests this hypothesis by examining warfare propensities of a random sample of fifty societies developed by Otterbein (1970) for other, albeit related purposes.[34] Here we contrast less political centralization (band and tribe) with more political centralization (chiefdom and state) and sedentary agriculture with nonsedentary forms of subsistence.[35] Ninety percent of the bands and tribes engaged in nonsedentary subsistence while nearly 60 percent of the more politically centralized depended on sedentary agriculture. Thus we might pursue the coevolutionary implications of political centralization and sedentary agriculture separately but are clearly justified in viewing them as tending to coevolve.

Our question is: if political centralization (political organization) and sedentary agriculture (political economy) tended to coevolve, what can we say about their implications for war, military organization, and weaponry? Thanks to Otterbein's (1970) sample, we can explore these questions empirically. Table 2.12 looks at the relationships among political centralization, agriculture, and the frequency of warfare. Greater political centralization in the absence of sedentary agriculture does not appear to

TABLE 2.11 **Political centralization and economic subsistence**

Type of Agriculture	Less Political Centralization	More Political Centralization
Not sedentary	27 (79%)	3 (23%)
Sedentary	7 (21%)	10 (77%)
TOTAL	34 (100%)	13 (100%)

TABLE 2.12 **Subsistence, political centralization, war frequency, and rationale for war**

	Less Political Centralization	More Political Centralization	Total
Not sedentary agriculture:			
Less warlike	8 (80%)	2 (20%)	10 (100%)
More warlike	15 (79%)	4 (21%)	19 (100%)
Sedentary agriculture:			
Less warlike	3 (75%)	1 (25%)	4 (100%)
More warlike	3 (33%)	6 (67%)	9 (100%)
Not sedentary agriculture:			
Less territorially oriented reasons for war	18 (78%)	5 (22%)	23 (100%)
More territorially oriented reasons for war	6 (86%)	1 (14%)	7 (100%)
Sedentary agriculture:			
Less territorially oriented reasons for war	5 (63%)	3 (37%)	8 (100%)
More territorially oriented reasons for war	2 (22%)	7 (78%)	9 (100%)

influence the frequency of warfare (compare 20% versus 21 percent). It is only in the presence of sedentary agriculture that political centralization makes a strong difference (67 percent versus 25 percent).

Why this might be the case is elaborated in the bottom half of table 2.12. This table breaks down the major reason for going to war into two clusters.[36] The less territorially inclined causes include defense, revenge, trophies, and plunder (including captives for slaves, hostages, or adoption). The more territorially inclined causes are subjugation, tribute, and land. As one might expect, the less territorially inclined causes predominate in nonsedentary situations, regardless of political centralization. The reverse outcome is found in settings of sedentary agriculture. Political centralization appears to be an important factor.

TABLE 2.13 **Subsistence, political centralization, and military organization**

	Less Political Centralization	More Political Centralization	Total
Not sedentary agriculture:			
Less professional military organization	19 (86%)	3 (14%)	22 (100%)
More professional military organization	8 (73%)	3 (27%)	11 (100%)
Sedentary agriculture:			
Less professional military organization	4 (33%)	8 (67%)	12 (100%)
More professional military organization	3 (27%)	8 (73%)	11 (100%)
Not Sedentary agriculture:			
Less sophisticated military formations	22 (79%)	6 (21%)	28 (100%)
More sophisticated military formations	5 (100%)	0 (0%)	5 (100%)
Sedentary agriculture:			
Less sophisticated military formations	5 (63%)	3 (37%)	8 (100%)
More sophisticated military formations	2 (22%)	7 (78%)	9 (100%)

Table 2.13 examines relationships involving military organization and formations. In the first contingency table, the question is whether political centralization influences the likelihood that a society will develop an army with specialized or professional warriors. Both political centralization and sedentary agriculture appear to make some difference. In nonfixed cultivation settings, political centralization encourages military specialization (the percentage of cases nearly doubles, from 14 percent to 27 percent). In sedentary settings the influence of political centralization is less evident (increasing from 67 percent to 73 percent). The bottom part of the table looks at the impact of military formations and distinguishes between societies that emphasize ambushes and/or the use of projectiles and those that develop shock tactics in lines and have specialized units and coordinated actions among the various units. Here the role of political centralization is more pronounced. In the nonsedentary agriculture situations, more sophisticated military formations appear only in less politically centralized systems. With sedentary agriculture, however, there is a strong positive

TABLE 2.14 **Subsistence, political centralization, and weaponry**

	Less Political Centralization	More Political Centralization	Total
Not sedentary agriculture:			
Projectiles	8 (89%)	1 (11%)	9 (100%)
Projectiles and shock	16 (76%)	5 (27%)	21 (100%)
Sedentary agriculture:			
Projectiles	3 (75%)	1 (25%)	4 (100%)
Projectiles and shock	3 (25%)	9 (75%)	12 (100%)
Not sedentary agriculture:			
Shields or no protection	16 (84%)	3 (16%)	19 (100%)
Body armor	4 (80%)	1 (20%)	5 (100%)
Sedentary agriculture:			
Shields or no protection	6 (75%)	2 (25 %)	8 (100%)
Body armor	0 (0%)	5 (100%)	5 (100%)
Not sedentary agriculture:			
No fortified defense	11 (100%)	0 (0%)	11 (100%)
Fortified defense	12 (67%)	6 (33%)	18 (100%)
Sedentary agriculture:			
No fortified defense	0 (0%)	1 (100%)	1 (100%)
Fortified defense	4 (33%)	8 (67%)	12 (100%)

relationship, with more sophisticated military formations associated with more politically centralized systems.

The outcomes associated with the utilization of various types of weaponry found in table 2.14 are mixed. The use of shock tactics, in contrast to relying primarily on projectiles launched at some distance, are assumed to be associated with larger populations, weapons training, and some coordination or military organization. If we contrast societies that use some shock tactics with those that depend on projectiles exclusively, political centralization, regardless of the nature of the economy, appears to make some difference. The second contingency table focuses on comparing societies that use body armor with societies that fight without protection or only with shields. In the nonsedentary situation, political centralization does not seem to matter much. Its influence is much more apparent in sedentary settings. In contrast, the third contingency table looks at the use of village fortifications. In this case, political centralization makes its strongest impact in the nonsedentary setting. Quite clearly, village fortifications are the norm in sedentary settings.

Thus the data examined provide strong support for coevolutionary interactions among political organization and political economy long before the emergence of the modern interstate system. In turn, changes in these spheres variably influence changes in military organization, weaponry, and war—a theme that we will elaborate in chapter 3. Reciprocal relations of war, military organization, and weaponry on political organization and political economy should never be ruled out, even though the simple type of data analysis done here cannot really pursue that more complicated causal question.

Recapitulation: The Origins of War

We have sought to put together a synthetic reconstruction of how war may have first emerged and then escalated. Drawing on a number of authors who suggest plausible arguments and who provide some empirical support, we find many of the contentions to be fairly compatible as long as one does not insist on any one component being the key to the emergence of war problem.

Although it is quite likely that warfare emerged in different ways in different places, we can still develop a model that encompasses the differences. We start with the observation that hunting and homicide skills made suitable weaponry, tactics, and rudimentary military organization available (Cioffi-Revilla 2000; Archer et al. 2002, 1; Otterbein 2004). Group segmentation (Kelly 2000) helped define group identities and enemies, thereby also facilitating the potential for organizing politically and militarily.

Given a variety of motivations for war, both offensive and defensive, a number of factors worked at different times and in different places, depending in part on the nature of the specific threat environment, to increase the probability of war and to expand political-economic and military organization and weapon lethality. These factors include circumscription; sedentary agriculture and its corollaries of population growth, density, and agrarian-pastoral divisions of labor as well as resource scarcities and environmental stress. We see these factors working in either of two categorical ways: (1) political entrepreneurs, circumscription, sedentary agriculture, and population growth/density contributed to increasingly centralized political organizations, or (2) population growth/density, resource scarcities, environmental stress, and agrarian-pastoral specialization accentuated scarcity.

FIGURE 2.1. The origins of war.

In the interactions among these various processes—especially between political-economic organizational complexity and scarcity—warfare first emerged and then escalated. The escalation of warfare then encouraged the further expansion of political-economic organization and weapon lethality. Figure 2.1 provides a sketch of how these factors might have come together.

We are endorsing, therefore, an early if infrequent start for warfare among hunter-gatherers. But it had to have been a fairly limited type of warfare given the few people potentially available as participants. Several factors, including population growth and circumscription, serve to increase the frequency of early warfare and to facilitate the escalation of warfare. In this very early stage, it is difficult to distinguish between emergence and escalation because they were occurring almost simultaneously. Where the first outbreak of war (as opposed to other forms of violence) took place— which depends on one's specific operationalization of war—we probably will never know. Even so, Kelly's (2000) argument that the period prior to about 10,000 to 8000 BCE was relatively war free seems plausible given the low population density of that era.[37]

It is not long after 8000 BCE that the surviving indicators of warfare emerged (tables 2.1 and 2.2). By this time the frequency and scale of warfare were already escalating. Yet we can also say that war was still emerging in two important respects. War did not suddenly emerge everywhere at the same time. Different regions had different mixtures of the ingredients that facilitated the occurrence of war. The emergence of warfare thus was a protracted and uneven affair. Moreover, as it escalated it continued to change its form—as in the movement from ambushes to clusters of bowmen to lines of warriors armed with shock weaponry. In Paleolithic and Neolithic times, the amorphous shape of warfare was still crystallizing. Hence the emergence and coevolutionary escalation of war went hand in hand at the outset of the history of warfare.

Once warfare emerged, it continued to evolve and coevolve. Warfare in the twenty-first century CE is a much different phenomenon from warfare of ten millennia ago. We think, however, that our basic coevolutionary model is quite capable of framing the types of changes that ensued. We now turn to a consideration of the coevolutionary model in chapter 3.

CHAPTER THREE

Evolutionary and Coevolutionary Processes

There are numerous military histories that describe the evolution of warfare in rich detail (Delbruck 1975; Jones 1987; Archer et al. 2002; Morillo, Black, and Lococo 2009). Our approach is more analytic. Rather than simply describe the changes in warfare over time, we construct a relatively simple and overarching theoretical framework. We specify six main factors that account for the evolution of warfare over the last ten millennia: military organization, political organization, weaponry, political economy, threat environment, and war. In the abstract, all six of these factors interact, and there is no single master variable. At various times one or more of the six may be a more significant driver of change than are the others, and any of the six factors retains some potential for bringing about change in the other five. Within this framework, however, we also propose a second, more specific theory: major contextual changes in political-economic complexity—the transitions from hunting-gathering to agrarian and then industrial production—have led to significant changes in military and political organization, weaponry, threat environment, and war. For this particular theory we do privilege one of the six factors as the primary, if highly macro, causal driver.

The Coevolutionary Framework: The Basic Variables

Political organizations resort to war for a wide variety of purposes. To make warfare more effective, however, specialized tools (military technology) and some organizational capability to mobilize resources (manpower,

TABLE 3.1 **Six coevolutionary factors and their definitions**

Coevolutionary Factor	Definition
Warfare	Sustained and coordinated combat between political organizations
Military weaponry	Technology employed to inflict damage in warfare
Military organization	Institutions specializing in the planning, coordination, and execution of combat
Political organization	Institutions specializing in authoritative decision-making for groups (bands, chiefdoms, states)
Threat environment	Distinctive characteristics of the operational milieu in which people are faced with the possibility of physical damage from enemies (e.g., the proximity of grassland plains sustaining horse-riding nomads, the presence and proximity of multiple strong states, or relative insulation from attack due to bodies of water that are difficult to cross)
Political economy	a. Strategies for organizing economic production (hunting-gathering, agrarian, industrial, postindustrial) b. Relative scarcity of resources

political support, military technology, and, after some time, the financial sinews of war), along with some further specialized organizational capability to apply coercive force, are necessary. Military technology, political organization, and military organization can make going to war more effective, but all three must operate according to constraints and opportunities made available by and within the prevailing threat environment and political-economic milieu.

The six key variables are defined in table 3.1 and sketched in figure 3.1. Political and military organizations refer to the institutions to which political systems of varying kinds allocate authoritative decision-making and armed combat, respectively. Weaponry refers to the tools employed in armed combat and in warfare in general. These behaviors and institutions perform in the larger contexts of the threat environment and the political economy.

The threat environment, which can be either internal or external (or both), captures significant differences in the attributes of the types of security threats confronting different groups in different locations. For instance, China, India, and the Near East were attacked by horsemen from Central Asia for about a millennia and a half. For the most part, western Europe was not exposed to many threats of this kind. Nor, for that

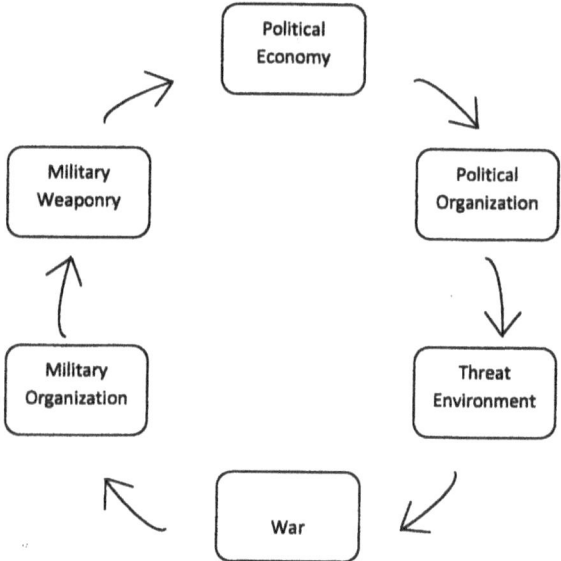

FIGURE 3.1. The coevolution of war, threat environment, military organization, weaponry, political organization, and political economy.

matter, did Mesoamerica have to deal with invading horsemen before the sixteenth century CE. The problem is that there are only so many ways of dealing with light cavalry raiders. Thus places adjacent to light cavalry raiders are more likely to develop similar military organizations and strategies than are places that face entirely different sorts of security risks (Chase 2003).

Finally, military, political, and martial activities are influenced strongly by prevailing political-economic contexts. These include two dimensions. One is the predominant economic strategy for production (hunting-gathering, agriculture, industry)—an extremely macro consideration that characterizes epochal eras, as opposed to year-to-year variation. The other is the level of resource scarcity that prevails at a given time. Whereas levels of scarcity may be quite persistent, this more micro consideration varies much more than the economic strategy context.

The predominant economic strategy influences a host of societal phenomena (as we explain in more detail later in this chapter), including the goals and incentives for warfare and the capabilities of the organizations that pursue warfare. The prevailing degree of resource scarcity, in contrast, influences the probability of military conflict between groups over control of resources.

All six factors interact, and one or more of the six may appear to be a more significant driver of change than the others at particular times. Although we do not believe that any one factor is always the main driver of change, we will argue that threat environment, political economy, and political organization are the three most important factors, at least most of the time. Shortly we will also stress the very long-term significance of one of the factors, political economy, in accounting for the "arc" of war—its general configuration over at least the past 10,000 years.

For immediate purposes, though, the core of our first theoretical argument contends only that the six factors or processes tend to coevolve. A major change in one or more factors is apt to lead to major changes in the other factors.[1] We may not be able to anticipate when an initial change will occur but we should be able to trace the consequent paths of change once they are underway with the aid of our six-factor framework. The framework also tells us where to look for the most probable consequences.

We recognize that there is more to evolving warfare than what can be encompassed in our six factors. From time to time we may note the utility of incorporating other factors into explanations of particular phenomena. We assume, however, that these six key variables encompass the main dimensions of change and evolution in warfare. This assumption applies both to our own interpretations and to those of others.[2] Keep in mind what we are seeking to do. We are making a forced march through thousands of years of history in order to theorize as explicitly as possible about war and its interaction with other social, economic, and political institutions. In other words, we want to tell a social science story about how one rather obtrusive part of our existence has changed over millennia.

One can imagine other possible influences on the evolution of war. One set of additional variables might include population and climate. Peter Turchin and Sergey Nefedov (2009) and Andrey Korotayev, Artemy Malkov, and Daria Khaltourina (2006), among others, have developed the idea of the "secular cycle." Essentially this is a Malthusian dynamic applicable to agrarian societies in which population growth eventually exceeds the carrying capacity of the resource base (Malthus [1798] 1992). In this view different types of warfare are associated with different phases of the cycle. External warfare is most probable before rising population growth exceeds the ecological carrying capacity (when some states are thought to be at their strongest). Internal warfare is more likely after that point is attained and there are too many mouths to feed, both literally and figuratively, unless or until the resource base can be expanded.

The secular cycle argument is quite plausible, and it draws considerable support from the evidence. We believe, however, that its two key variables of climate and population growth can be efficiently incorporated within our political-economy variable and linked to the resource scarcities dimension.[3] Imagine, for example, that our principal six factors lie on a circle (like figure 3.1), or put war in the middle surrounded by the other five factors. Then draw a larger circle, in which additional factors might be placed, each with influences on the six main variables. Population considerations are easily linkable to political economy and scarcity.[4]

Other analysts (Keegan 1993; Katzenstein 1996; Lynn 2003), no doubt, would wish to add political culture, religion, and other ideational variables to this six-variable ensemble. There is no question that political systems, military organizations, and political economies have important cultural dimensions and that these assemblies of norms, rituals, symbolic meanings, and expectations offer some explanatory value. Japanese samurai, Ottoman janissaries, or Zulu warriors did not engage in combat in identical ways, and their variations in behavior were to some extent propelled by specific beliefs held by the fighters and the organizations and rulers they served. Military organizations have distinctive traditions, customs, and histories. Armies, air forces, and navies do not always cooperate as well as they might because they have different doctrines on how things should be done. The same can be said about behavior within these military organizations—cavalry and infantry, bomber and fighter pilots, or submariners and naval aviators.

Imagine the variety of ideas and beliefs over the last ten thousand years about how political organizations and economies should function. Consider, for instance, the political-economic ideational conflicts among aristocrats, fascists, communists, liberals, and jihadis. The underlying ideas are difficult to disentangle from the preoccupations of the nineteenth through early twenty-first centuries and the warfare that has ensued in part to advance or defend the rightness of the various ideas.

Societal and organizational cultures may help to explain certain decisions for war and the way in which particular wars are fought. Strategic cultures also help to shape military doctrines.[5] We are reluctant, however, to bestow too much explanatory weight on culture and ideas as autonomous variables in a theory of the long-term evolution of war. Ideology and culture are always embedded in a complex system of interrelationships.

As Jack Snyder (2002) argues, "ideas and culture are best understood not as autonomous but as embedded in complex social systems shaped by the interaction of material circumstances, institutional arrangements, and strategic choices, as well as by ideas and culture." Ideas and culture are sometimes even endogenous to material factors.[6] In addition, strategic cultures that detract from efficient uses of existing resources and technologies in a given threat environment are weeded out of the system over the long term. Military technology and practices, once introduced, tend to diffuse among the leading powers in the system (Horowitz 2010).

Thus while we recognize that beliefs about combat vary, military organizations are not all alike, or that ideologies and culture can affect episodes of warfare, we push those considerations aside in our attempt to address our specific question of the evolution of war over ten thousand years. If by minimizing the impact the of cultural and ideational variables on the long sweep of warfare in the global system we fail to explain important long-term trends and patterns, we expect others will be quick to correct us. If we also stimulate others to pursue the same theoretical objectives with different strategies, we will all likely benefit.

Still other scholars might argue that key individuals have played a critical role in influencing organizations, weaponry, warfare, and their coevolution over time. We do not deny that some "captains" loom larger than others in the annals of warfare. Alexander the Great, Julius Caesar, and Napoleon are among the first that come to mind. Undoubtedly many wars would not have occurred but for the decisions of particular political leaders. We concede that individuals often play a key role in the causes of particular wars (Levy and Thompson 2010b) and undoubtedly in their outcomes as well. Our aim here, however, is not to explain the causes or outcomes of particular wars but rather to account for the evolution of warfare as a social practice over the last ten thousand years and beyond. For these purposes the judgments and actions of individuals are generally secondary to the threat environment, political economy, and institutional context in which they operate, and personalities are rather ephemeral in their long-term impact. Just as any long-term macroanalysis is usually forced to ignore or suppress the activities of prominent agents, our analytical wager is that we can tell our coevolution of war story reasonably well without incorporating the role of notorious individuals into our model. We are dismissing neither individuals nor political culture, but instead are giving them a lower priority within our framework.[7]

Coevolutionary Processes

The six variables in our model (warfare, military weaponry, political and military organizations, threat environment, and political economy) raise all sorts of interesting chicken-and-egg questions. What comes first, technology or organization? Did the expenses associated with gunpowder artillery lead to expanded state organizations, or was it only possible to contemplate those expenses once one had created expanded state organizations (Bean 1973)? Did war really make the state and then states made war, as Charles Tilly (1975) argues? Why does new military technology tend to emerge in the midst of warfare, as opposed to before or after warfare? Referring to these puzzles as chicken-and-egg-type questions hints strongly at one likely resolution of the causal conundrums raised: many of these relationships are highly reciprocal, so that it is difficult to say that one is always temporally prior to another.

Although some of these questions can be answered definitively for specific periods of time, the answers may be different at other times. For instance, the weapons technology to make war almost certainly preceded organizational developments in prehistorical times. As we have noted, spears and bows were available long before there were coordinated hunting groups, armies, or states (Ferrill 1997, 18–19). Yet it has also become abundantly clear in the twentieth and early twenty-first centuries CE that only some state organizations (so far) are capable of producing nuclear weapons. Similarly, there can be no question that warfare has expanded the power of some states while destroying others, but that other processes have also influenced state making. Whereas the centralization of power in the state was associated with war in early modern Europe, it is the decentralization of state power that is associated with war in the contemporary system (Levy, Walker, and Edwards 2001, 33). War makes states, but not exclusively so (Cohen 1984; Haas 2001).

Another way of conceptualizing these coevolutionary iterations is as part of a sequence of disequilibrating "military revolutions" in which radically novel organizational, weaponry, or tactical innovations are introduced (Rogers 1955). Williamson Murray and MacGregor Knox (2001, 6–7), for instance, attribute the following effects to military revolutions:

1. They recast military organizations;
2. They alter the capacity of states to create and project military power;

3. They fundamentally change the framework of war;
4. They bring about systemic changes in politics and society; and
5. They are additive in the sense that it is difficult to leap-frog over earlier military revolutions by merely adopting contemporary technology.

At the same time, however, military revolutions can be brought about by radical changes in military organizations, military doctrine, military tactics, the threat environment, and/or by the nature of war itself—all supported by synergistic changes in political organizations and the more general political-economic context. Conversely, the vested interests, organizational routines, and cultures of military organizations can impede the development of new technologies and doctrines.[8] Since any of these variables can be both cause and effect, it is rather difficult to anoint a primary driver that holds this position throughout all time.[9]

The pragmatic way out of these analytical quagmires involves a simple statement about coevolution. Warfare, threat environment, military technology, political and military organizations, and political economy tend to coevolve. A significant change in one subsystem is highly likely to lead to significant changes in some or all of the other subsystems. Sometimes one variable may assume the lead causal influence, while at other times another variable may lead. There is no compelling reason to privilege one as the principal mover in all historical systems. It suffices to say that changes in one of the six tend to lead to variable changes in the other five, subject to lags and dependent on various qualifications linked to spatial and temporal considerations.

War is critical to the process because it provides the incentive for innovation, change, and reform. As such, war represents an important selection mechanism for weeding out actors who fail to adapt to novelty on the battlefield. Defeat in one war can motivate decision-makers to change their strategies for the next one. The uncertainties and insecurities associated with expectations of the next war can also lead to the search for new or modified military organizational formats, tactics, and weaponry. The paths that such changes will take, as well as their pace and intensity, will often hinge on the nature of the threat environment. Limited threats slow down the pace of change. Some types of threats call for changes that are not likely to be associated with other types of threats. Political organizations must find ways to control and feed military demands, which, in turn, depend on the political-economic milieu in which the political organization is embedded.

The manner in which the figure is drawn in figure 3.1 greatly oversimplifies the process. The causal arrows do not go only in one direction. All of the arrows should probably be double-headed, indicating reciprocating influences. For example, military organizations choose specific weaponry and then find themselves adjusting organizational features to accommodate the new weaponry. Increased technological development in the economy is likely to make wars more intensive and extensive in their combat. Yet war usually creates incentives for developing new technology that is initially applied to military purposes but later to more civilian pursuits.

Then, too, the causal influences need not proceed only in the circular fashion shown in the figure. Tactical changes can lead directly to the need for the political organization to raise more money to pay for them by either penetrating more deeply into the state's economy (more taxes and tax collection) or even reconstructing the nature of the political economy (for instance, creating feudalism or state socialism). Alternatively, a highly technological economy will develop weapons of a similar ilk that can encourage military organizations to recruit different types of soldiers. One last illustration is the defeat in war that leads to military occupation, the imposition of new political institutions, and a radical downsizing of the military organization.[10]

Figure 3.2 offers a more complex view than the circular process of figure 3.1. Change proceeds, as we see it, as the set of interactions at time 1 give way to the set of interactions exhibited at time 2, and so on indefinitely. Thus figure 3.2 encompasses both coevolutionary and evolutionary processes. The coevolutionary clusters at successive points in time evolve from one clustered set to the set in the next time period. While figure 3.2 depicts a finite movement from time 1 to time 2, the potential number of movements from one set to another in the real world are infinite.[11] So, too, are the ways in which the six factors can come together from time period to time period and from place to place.

In adopting this perspective, we are following a lead established by Claudio Cioffi-Revilla's (2000) war and political development model, outlined in modified form in table 3.2. Cioffi-Revilla's starting point is the observation that humans utilized homicidal and coordinated hunting skills to attack other humans, which we have seen before in chapter 2. Prior to the development of increasingly complex political organizations, the bellicose outcome was something short of war. Only with the emergence of political organization could military skills, institutions, size, and weaponry be expanded to lead to something increasingly resembling warfare. Warfare, in turn, reinforced the increased complexity of political organization.

Time 1

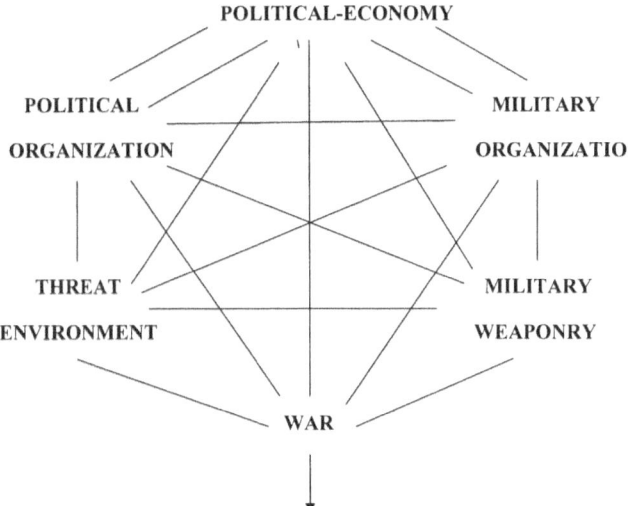

Time 2

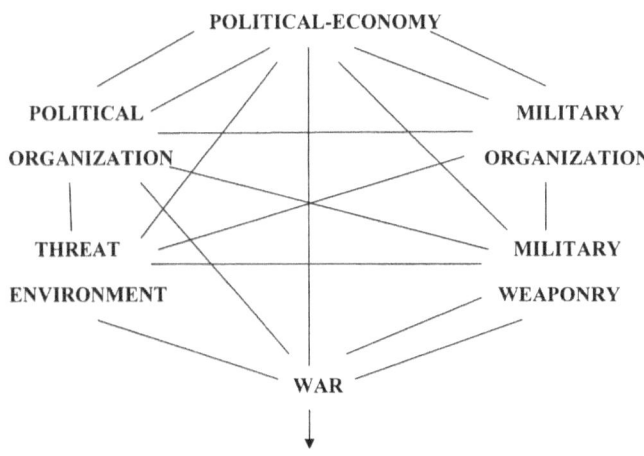

FIGURE 3.2. Coevolutionary process.

Cioffi-Revilla's (2000) model is inherently coevolutionary in form even though he does not use that term. His emphasis is on the interactions between the capability to kill humans and the capability to organize, coordinate, and supply expanding numbers of soldiers. Four of our six variables are present in this interpretation (see table 3.3). Only threat environment and political economy are missing. Moving as the model does from the absence of political organizations to empires, it is obviously focused on

TABLE 3.2 **Warfare and political development from Cioffi-Revilla's perspective**

Warfare	Complexity of Political Organization
Background Behavioral Skills: Homicidal skills: Humans learn how to kill other human individuals. Hunting skills: Command, coordination, formation, intelligence, stealth, navigation.	Negligible
Stage 0 Protowarfare: Coordinated killing by human groups applying homicidal and hunting skills; pictography with archery battles; ambiguous forensic evidence; no other evidence of indicators.	Chiefdom
Stage 1 Chiefly warfare: Spontaneous warfare, organized by chief; first specialized weapons; soft fortifications; sporadic ad hoc institutions of war; raiding; unstable territorial conquests, if any.	State
Stage 2 Interstate warfare: Full-time specialized warriors; full-time weapons industry; hard fortifications; permanent institutions of war; logistics now perfected; stable and frequent territorial conquests.	Empire
Stage 3 Imperial warfare: All previous features of state warfare, plus multi-ethnic composition of troops and leadership, major political role in governance of the empire, long distance logistics prevail.	

Source: Based on Cioffi-Revilla (2000, 87).

the origins of ancient warfare. Yet there is no reason to confine the utility of these observations to the distant past. The causal processes that began to operate thousands of years ago have continued to function into the present, and in all likelihood they will continue to operate into the future in some form.

We depart most evidently from Cioffi-Revilla's lead by emphasizing the role of political economy—as opposed to his focus on war and the development of political organizations—in order to develop a long-term perspective on warfare and the evolution of our coevolutionary clustered interactions. Our starting point is not that the development of political organization in our scheme is irrelevant. It is, after all, one of our six key factors. We think, however, that political-economic change tends to precede developments in political organization. That is, we "endogenize" political organization by taking one step back in order to explain it. Whereas Cioffi-Revilla's model posits that

> political organization → war,

TABLE 3.3 **Cioffi-Revilli's model recast**

Coevolutionary Variable	Stage 0	Stage 1	Stage 2	Stage 3
Warfare	Proto	Chiefly	Interstate	Imperial
Military organization	Coordinated groups	Ad hoc groups organized by chiefs	Specialized warriors	Multiethnic warriors
Weaponry	Hunting tools	Initial specialization	Advanced specialization	Advanced specialization
Political organization	Negligible	Chiefdoms	State	Empire

our model posits that

political economy → political organization → war,

along with some other relationships—including the threat environment factor that is also absent in the Cioffi-Revilla scheme.

We begin our third theoretical argument, following arguments about origins and coevolution, by suggesting that political-economic history and predominant economic strategy can be subdivided into three main, successive types: hunting and gathering, agrarian, and industrial.[12] As defined in table 3.4, hunting and gathering clearly came first and predominated until sometime after the emergence of agriculture around ten thousand years ago. Agrarian political economies then became dominant in most parts of the world over much of the last ten millennia. Industrial political economies only began to appear after the end of the eighteenth century CE and Britain's industrial revolution. Currently, all three types are practiced, but hunting and gathering has become increasingly rare. The elite states of the world economy are industrialized, and some may even be approaching a postindustrial status.[13] The vast majority of the states in the system at the beginning of the twenty-first century, however, remain agrarian—and many are likely to remain so for some time to come.

Privileging political economy in this fashion provides considerable explanatory power. The predominance of each main type of political economy is associated with a number of variables that have clear bearing on political organization and on warfare. The first four variables in table 3.5 encompass the extent to which groups are concentrated in ever-larger numbers (population size) in one place (population density, sedentarization,

TABLE 3.4 **Main types of political economy**

Type	Principal Strategy for Generating Income/Wealth or Subsistence
Hunting and gathering	Pursuit of animals and collection of wild grasses and seeds
Agrarian	Cultivation of food and fibers
Industrial	Machine production powered by inanimate energy sources

TABLE 3.5 **Political-economic influences**

Attribute	Hunting and Gathering	Agrarian	Industrial
Population size	Very small	Expanding	Large but leveling
Population density	Very low	Expanding	High
Sedentary settlements	Unlikely	Yes	Yes
Urbanization	No	Yes	Extensive
Division of labor/ occupational specialization	Limited	Expanding	Great
Economic productivity	Low	Expanding	High
Generation of economic surplus	Very limited	Increasing	Intensive
Technological innovation	Limited	Some	Great
Intercommunity interaction	Infrequent	Increasing	Extensive
Intercommunity interdependence	Unlikely	Variable but generally increasing	High
Political organization	Family/band	Tribe-state	Complex states
War	Limited	Expanding	Expanding with selective pacification

urbanization). Other things being equal, larger, more urbanized groups are more capable of constructing not only more complex political systems but also larger armed forces and wars than are smaller, more mobile groups.

The next four variables reflect wealth generation and technological development. Again, more affluent and more technologically developed groups are more capable of engaging in political complexity and intensive, highly lethal warfare than are poorer and less technologically developed groups. These four are followed by two more that highlight intergroup interaction. "Intercommunity interaction" emphasizes potential frictions that are likely to increase the probability of conflict and the need for political management. "Intercommunity interdependence" stresses interdependence, which generally works toward the voluntary suppression of some conflict-escalation propensities.[14] Therein lies the possibility of working against some of the implications of the upward trends in size and wealth for greater magnitudes of conflict and violence.

In general, though, the evolution toward more complex political-economic settings has three effects of particular importance to our analysis. Moving toward greater political-economic complexity generates greater incentives to go to war, at least up to a point. There are all sorts of reasons for going to war but at the core are desires for acquiring more resources and territory or defending what one already has in these areas. If one increases the presence of wealth and the political significance of turf, the incentives for warfare are expanded substantially.

Movement along the political-economic complexity continuum also implies greater resources with which to go to war. More men for armies and navies are available. Weaponry becomes increasingly more lethal. Governments learn how to extend their logistical reach to support military movement. They also learn how to mobilize more financial and labor contributions from their populations for war purposes. More interaction also leads to greater frictions or opportunities to escalate disagreements to full-fledged conflicts. In these three respects—expanded incentives, resources, frictions—the movement toward more of each facilitates the likelihood of more complex political organizations and expanded warfare.

In coevolutionary terms our third theory says that greater political-economic complexity leads to expanded military organizations and increasingly specialized and lethal weaponry. More complex political organizations are needed to manage and survive the expanded warfare and intensified threat environment that result.

The shift toward greater size, wealth, and interaction need not imply, however, an ever-upward movement in more frequent and deadlier warfare. There are implicit constraints on warfare that are built into escalating warfare in scope, expense, and lethality. As warfare becomes too expensive for most actors to afford and too costly in its human and economic consequences, the cost-benefit calculus inherent in political leaders' decisions for war reverses, and the incentives for war decline.[15] At some point

TABLE 3.6 **Stratification in 2005 military expenditures, constant 2005 US dollars**

US Dollars (billion)	Number of States	State
> 500	1	United States
50–100	2	China, United Kingdom
15–50	8	France, Germany, India, Italy, Japan, South Korea, Russia, Saudi Arabia
5–15	15	Australia, Brazil, Canada, Taiwan, Germany, Greece, Iran, Israel, North Korea, Netherlands, Poland, Singapore, Spain, Sweden, Syria, Turkey
1–5	38	Algeria, Angola, Argentina, Austria, Belgium, Chile, Colombia, Cuba, Czech Republic, Denmark, Ecuador, Egypt, Finland, Hungary, Indonesia, Iraq, Ireland, Kuwait, Kyrgyzstan, Malaysia, Mexico, Morocco, New Zealand, Norway, Oman, Pakistan, Peru, Portugal, Qatar, Rumania, South Africa, Switzerland, Thailand, Ukraine, UAE, Venezuela, Vietnam
< 1	99	Afghanistan, Albania, Armenia, Azerbaijan, Bahrain, Bangladesh, Barbados, Belarus, Belize, Benin, Bhutan, Bolivia, Bosnia and Herzegovina, Botswana, Brunei, Bulgaria, Burkina Faso, Burundi, Cambodia, Cameroon, Cape Verde, Central African Republic, Chad, Dem Rep. of Congo, Rep. of Congo, Costa Rica, Croatia, Cyprus, Djibouti, Dominican Rep., East Timor, El Salvador, Equatorial Guinea, Estonia, Ethiopia, Fiji, Gabon, Gambia, Georgia, Ghana, Guatemala, Guinea, Guinea-Bissau, Guyana, Hungary, Iceland, Ivory Coast, Jamaica, Jordan, Kazakhstan, Kenya, Latvia, Lebanon, Lesotho, Libya, Lithuania, Luxemburg, Macedonia, Madagascar, Malawi, Mali, Malta, Mauritania, Mauritius, Moldova, Mongolia, Mozambique, Namibia, Nepal, Nicaragua, Niger, Nigeria, Panama, Papua New Guinea, Paraguay, Philippines, Rwanda, Sao Tome and Principe, Senegal, Serbia, Sierra Leone, Slovakia, Slovenia, Sri Lanka, Sudan, Suriname, Swaziland, Tajikistan, Tanzania, Togo, Trinidad and Tobago, Tunisia, Turkmenistan, Uganda, Uruguay, Uzbekistan, Yemen, Zambia, Zimbabwe

Source: Extracted from information in US State Department (2005).

in the expansion of war, some potential for selective pacification tendencies begin to emerge. A number of actors (but not necessarily all) can be expected to essentially drop out of coercive competition that is perceived as becoming more costly than it is worth.

Dropping out of coercive competition does not mean that states beat their swords into plowshares. They maintain armies and often navies and air forces but their armed forces are simply not competitive with the states that have the resources and willingness to spend the most money on military concerns. This point can be made fairly easily by looking at the distribution of military spending for any year. Table 3.6 shows the distribution for 2005. One state, the United States, spent far more than any of the other states.[16] It did so because it has a highly sophisticated military, broad-ranging objectives, and expensive payrolls. It also has the most lethal and expensive weapons. One estimate (Schwarz 1998, 4) of the amount of money spent on US nuclear weapons, a good example of the heights of lethality reached by contemporary weapons evolution, between 1940 and 1996 is 5.48 trillion dollars (in constant 1996 dollars). That sum is at least five times all world military expenditure in 2005.[17] While the United States does not have a monopoly on nuclear weapons, there are some limitations on which states can and will go to the lengths necessary to pay for the most destructive arms.

Sixty percent of the states listed in table 3.6 spent less than 1 billion per year on their armed forces in 2005. Some of these states might be competitive with one another but they lack anything resembling strategic reach and cannot compete even with the states in the next echelon up the spending ladder. The military forces of the 1 to 5 billion dollars per year military spenders are not regarded as particularly impressive coercive instruments in their own right. They in turn are not particularly competitive with the twenty-six states above them in the 2005 stratification. More than half of those twenty-six states (the 5 to 15 billion dollar spenders) are not competitive with most of the eleven states at the top of the distribution. Within the biggest spending group of the top eleven states, six have no nuclear weapons and, so far, a limited force projection reach. France has a minimal force de frappe and the United Kingdom relies on borrowed US warheads for its small SLBM force. What all this means is that most states in the world system either cannot afford to be competitive or choose not to be competitive at the top of the system. More nuclear proliferation may increase military spending overall but is unlikely to alter the high degree of stratification demonstrated in table 3.6.

Table 3.7 situates the origins of warfare in an era in which hunting and gathering predominated. The increased predominance of agrarian cultivation led to the expansion of warfare over what had been possible in an era in which hunting and gathering predominated. Industrialization made weapons more lethal and war more total. Total warfare means that greater proportions of the population were mobilized for warfare purposes. It also means that more civilians had become vulnerable to attack from enemy forces. Alexander Downes (2008, 45–47), for instance, enumerates some 18.3 million estimated civilian deaths due to 1870–2003 interstate warfare. Sixty-nine percent of these deaths can be attributed to two total wars (World Wars I and II).[18] War's societal impacts became more total as well.

TABLE 3.7 **Political-economic evolution and war**

Political-Economic Evolution	War
Hunting and gathering	Origins
Agrarian	Expansion
Industrial	Expansion with selective pacification

All of this made warfare, at least between industrial powers, very costly. In turn, the possibility of selective pacification became more feasible.[19] At least some industrialized actors became less likely to solve their conflicts with other industrialized actors through coercive means.

Figure 3.3 illustrates this dynamic. The basic idea is that the benefits of warfare often exceeded its costs in the hunting-gathering and agricultural stages. In the industrial stage, however, the costs of war (at least between industrialized states) spiral upward faster than do the benefits. Adam Smith ([1776] 1991) recognized this over two centuries ago.[20] Smith, however, based his argument on a different premise. He proposed four stages: hunting, pastoral, agriculture, and manufacturing. In each stage, people had to make sacrifices to engage in warfare. Hunters could not search for food and fight at the same time. Shepherds might have to ignore their flocks. Some farmers would have to abandon their fields. Manufacturers ran the risk of watching their factories go idle if too many workers were sent to the front. As a result the nature of the opportunity costs of war varied by stage. From Smith's perspective, hunters could probably still wage war on occasion without starving. Shepherds could actually bring their flocks with them when they went to war. Farmers could reduce their opportunity costs if the fighting was restricted to nongrowing seasons. Some proportion of the population could be spared to become professional soldiers without losing maximal agricultural productivity. It is in the manufacturing stage that costs are likely to exceed what Smith termed the spoils of warfare. As weapons became more complex and more men were needed on the battlefront, it would be difficult to avoid serious productivity losses that would offset any returns from warfare.

Thus Smith would have drawn his version of figure 3.3 differently from ours. His y axis would demarcate the costs and spoils of war. For the purpose of simplification, imagine increasing levels of spoils associated with each of the four stages. The cost function would be close to the spoils line (but still below it) in the hunting stage. Costs would dip even lower in the pastoral and hunting stages. But in the manufacturing stage, costs would escalate upward quickly and exceed the spoils associated with this stage.

We reach a similar outcome but our argument is different. Our y axis captures increases in the complexity (and lethality) of political-military organization and weaponry. As one moves forward in political-economic complexity, the costs associated with the complexity and lethality of political-military organization and weaponry escalate rapidly in the industrial stage.

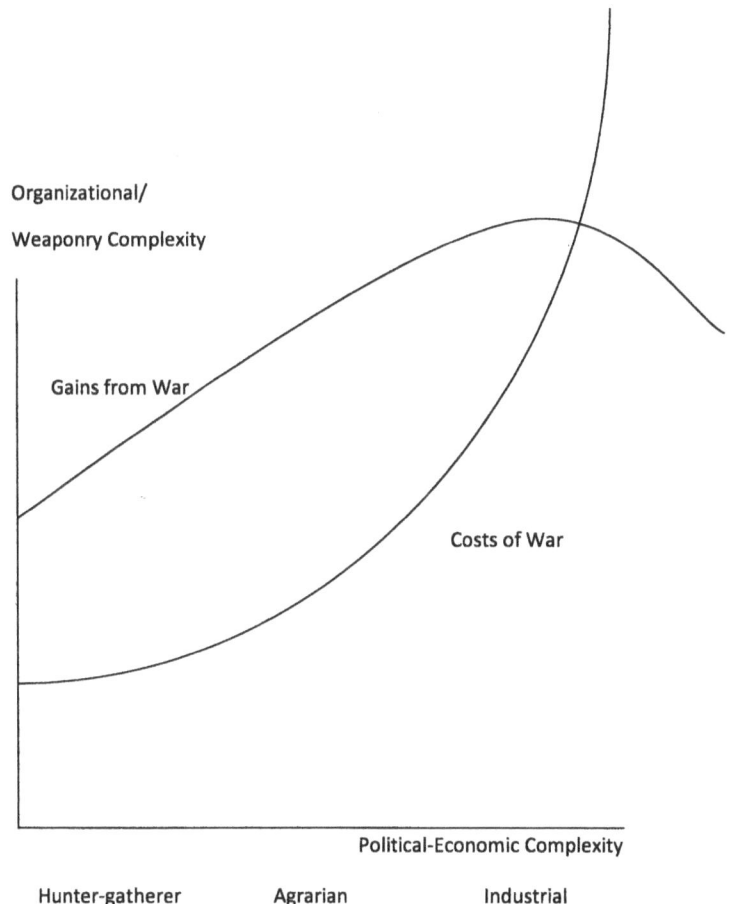

FIGURE 3.3. Organizational/weaponry complexity and the costs of war between industrialized states.

Despite the similarity in outcome, the arguments are not interchangeable. We prefer our argument to Smith's because we are not convinced that opportunity cost calculations by hunters, shepherds, farmers, and manufacturers have governed the probability and onset of warfare in their respective eras.

Carl Kaysen (1990) also argues that wars will end when actors no longer expect benefits to exceed costs. As in Smith's argument and our own, industrialization is the major transformer of wars' cost-benefit calculi. Kaysen's argument, which encompasses our own, attributes a large number of changes to industrialization that in turn alter the cost-benefit ratio. He draws attention to mechanical and electric power replacing animal power, factories and foundries replacing handicraft technology, urbanization, the industrialization of weapons and logistics, accelerations in transportation and communication, capital becoming more important than land, increases in the proportion of the population mobilized in wartime, losses of life in warfare, the hostility of conquered populations, increased popular participation in political systems and the expansion of welfare considerations, and nuclear weapons.

We do not disagree with Kaysen's (1990) argument, but we think the same point can be made more parsimoniously. We subsume the emphases on the replacement of animal power and handicraft technology plus accelerations in transportation and communications with industrialization. The industrialization of weapons and logistics increases the proportion of the population mobilized in wartime and the losses of life in combat. Other processes such as urbanization, political participation, and welfare considerations are not unrelated to industrialization, but they belong in their own theories.

Along somewhat similar lines, Azar Gat (2005, 2009) has argued that industrialization is responsible for what others have called the democratic peace—the increasing tendency for democratic states not to go to war with one another.[21] Contrary to our own thesis, however, Gat explicitly rejects the notion that selective pacification is related to the rising costs of war, which, he contends, the evidence suggests have not actually risen. On this point we think he is mistaken. Statistical studies of war intensity and severity dealing with trends in war frequency and military battle deaths are the only evidence he cites.[22] But in actuality no one has ever calculated the total costs of contemporary warfare. That would be a rather heroic undertaking. One would need, in addition to military battle deaths for which information is readily available, data on civilian deaths and casualties, demographic impacts, the impact of disease (Iqbal 2010), interest on national debt, veteran benefits, and economic productivity foregone. Preparations for warfare, especially on but not limited to weaponry, would have to be included as well.

Neither Gat nor we currently have access to this information. But we think we have some sense of the types of shifts at stake. We have already mentioned the great inequality in military spending, the tremendous costs associated with US nuclear weapons, and the number of civilian deaths thought to be linked to interstate and especially total warfare. We can add two other pieces of information. Downes's (2008) information on civilian deaths due to interstate warfare encompasses the 1870–2003 period. If we divide these years into two equal segments of about sixty-six years at 1936, 1.7 million people died in the first segment and 16.6 million died in the second segment. These numbers, which no doubt are underestimates, largely reflect the fact that World War I occurred between 1870 and 1936 while World War II took place in the second segment.

Even if we exclude the two total wars, however, the numbers are still similar in terms of direction. Without World War I, at least 744,384 civilians were killed in 1870–1936. Without World War II, at least 4,929,044 civilians were killed between 1937 and 2003. Of course, what we would really like to know is how many civilians were killed in interstate warfare before the nineteenth century and the advent of industrialized warfare. Yet even without that information it would appear that we are safe in concluding that the number of civilians dying in interstate warfare is increasing. We are also aware that population sizes have been increasing as well during this time period, but regardless of the proportional number of casualties, civilians in industrialized states have become more greatly involved in warfare preparations and in combat, as direct participants and as targets.

There is also one exception to the generalization that no one has calculated the economic costs of warfare. One estimate for the United States (Daggett 2010) claims the following estimated costs of warfare in 2011 constant US dollars: late eighteenth century (1775–83)—2.4 billion; nineteenth century (1812–15, 1846–49, 1861–65, 1898–99)—92.7 billion; twentieth century (1917–21, 1941–45, 1950–53, 1965–75, 1990–91)—5.6 trillion; twenty-first century (2001–10)—1.1 trillion.[23] If we control for the number of years involved in warfare, the average annual cost during the American Revolution was 0.267 billion. In the wars of the nineteenth century, the average annual cost was 6.18 billion. Annual war costs in the twentieth century averaged to 207 billion per year. In the first ten years of the twenty-first century, war costs have averaged 110 billion per year.

It is not easy to compare eighteenth-century military expenditures with twenty-first-century expenditures. If nothing else, the size of the US economy has expanded greatly as well, so that the proportion of the gross domestic product devoted to war needs to be considered. The War of 1812 consumed around 2.2 percent of the American economy at the time, while the Iraqi/Afghani warfare of the twenty-first century is consuming closer to 1 percent annually of the American economy. Total defense expenditures, however, may provide a better comparison. In the War of 1812, total defense expenditures matched war expenditures fairly closely (2.7 percent versus 2.2 percent). Total defense expenditures in the ongoing Iraq-Afghanistan conflict era range between 4 to 5 percent of GDP, or about double the case in the early nineteenth century.

Equally pertinent are Stephen Daggett's estimates for the larger American wars. In the nineteenth century, the most expensive war was the Civil War, the United States' first taste of industrialized warfare, which consumed about 11.7 percent of the Northern economy in its peak year. In the peak years of the two world wars total defense expenditures consumed 14.1 and 37.5 percent of the US economy. The United States' case is not typical, but even so it is fairly clear that the costs of warfare have increased in the last three centuries.

Thus we think Gat (2005) is wrong when he rejects the costs of war argument too quickly. But his argument that industrialization made the democratic peace possible has merit. Gat argues that industrialization made it possible to break free of agrarian subsistence production, which in turn made it possible to improve standards of living, expand trade, and create conditions that led to the expansion of liberalism and democracy. From his perspective it is these benefits of peace and not the costs of war that are most responsible for a decrease in warfare in comparison to preindustrial times.

We cannot dismiss this argument out of hand. It is quite conceivable that industrialization is responsible for multiple outcomes that contribute to selective decreases in warfare. Empirical tests of the relative explanatory powers of "benefits of peace" versus "costs of war" theories are needed. We doubt that they are mutually exclusive interpretations—that is, empirical support is likely to be forthcoming for both types of explanation. Our only preference is that we not bundle together all of the implications of industrialization as a single argument. Gat complicates his argument by adding that the greater pacificity of liberal democracies is also influenced by affluence, urbanization, sexual promiscuity, the proportional number of available young adult males, enfranchisement for women, and nuclear weapons. Whether all of these factors can be linked directly or indirectly to a decline in the probability of warfare between industrialized states remains to be seen. In this case, however, at least one of the additional Gat factors, the development of nuclear weapons, is part of our organizational and weaponry costs complex. That is still another reason to be cautious in categorizing the many implications of industrialization and their assorted and asserted effects.

Another Type of Transformation

Our identification of three types of political economy and warfare in table 3.7 and figure 3.3 is certainly parsimonious. While it may seem overly parsimonious to some, its real flaw is that the planet has only moved imperfectly from one main type of political economy to the next, with states with more complex strategies dominating places focused on less complex strategies. Currently, the world is definitely not hunting-and-gathering oriented but, then, neither is industrialization or agriculture universally predominant. We have a mixed situation in which most economies are either primarily industrial or primarily agrarian. That might not be a major analytical problem if the warfare of agrarian political economies was continuing to expand while industrial political economies waged very intensive warfare or engaged in little war. Presumably, that is what table 3.7 might be thought to predict. We know that is not quite the case. Industrial states have waged the most intensive wars (World Wars I and II) seen to date. Yet most industrial states, after surviving the exhausting world wars of the twentieth century, appear to be highly unlikely to go to war against each other again.[24]

Agrarian states are not exactly engaging in more and more warfare. Interstate warfare between nonindustrialized states is not becoming more common. Intrastate warfare in nonindustrialized states has increased in recent decades but not inexorably. Something else, presumably, must be at work (assuming that table 3.7 summarizes a useful, if imperfect, argument).

We see the evolutionary development trajectory implied by table 3.7 applying roughly to world history up to a point. That point is the great divergence in political-economic styles and behavior currently manifested. There are some industrial states that fit the expectations of table 3.7.

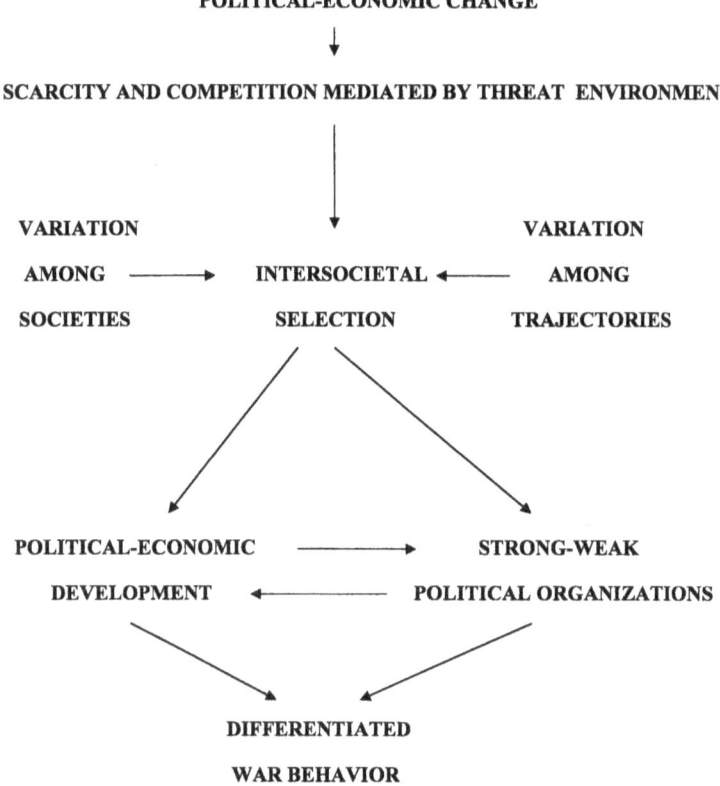

FIGURE 3.4. The evolution of war.

There are many agrarian states that are not participating in expanding warfare—either inside or outside the state. The world has not reached a point in which industrial political economies are widespread. They are among the most powerful states in the world system, but they remain relatively small in number. Primarily agrarian political economies remain quite common. Nor are they the large agrarian empires of yore (for example, Han, Ottoman, or Mogul) that fought nearly constantly. Instead, most agrarian political economies fight rarely because their resources for fighting remain quite limited. It is the many small agrarian states that by and large are not expanding their external warfare behavior.

To explain this divergence we need to introduce a fourth theoretical argument that remains consistent with our earlier arguments. This fourth theory is sketched in figure 3.4. Tendencies toward greater size feed into arenas characterized by scarcity and competition for resources and territory. Some societies do better than others in this competition thanks to the possession of attributes that favor success. This is what "selection" means in evolutionary terms. Some actors are more likely to do well in competition because they have advantages over other actors and are consequently selected in and by competition.[25]

Yet all societies and all times do not experience precisely the same levels of scarcity. Nor do they experience the same mix of coevolutionary ingredients (military and political organization, threat environment, war, political-economy strategies, and weaponry). As a consequence, there have been multiple and vastly different military-war trajectories in world history. The nature of coevolutionary movements in Mesoamerica, the Near East, or East Asia has been quite different. Mesoamerican changes were slow (Hassig 1992). When the Spanish appeared around 1500, they were opposed by groups not much better armed or organized than they had been hundreds of years before. The ancient Near East (see Gabriel 2002; Spalinger 2005; Hamblin 2006; Farrokh 2007) led in military developments and innovation but was eventually subordinated by first Macedonians and then Romans. East Asian armies (Peers 2006) were the first to exceed a million men in arms but became increasingly fixated on the threat from nomads on horseback after about 300 BCE.

Just how much variation in military-war trajectories has existed and what difference it has made remains to be seen. But we know enough to say that there has been substantial variation and that the variation should be expected to influence intersocietal selection. One very important characteristic of the western military-war trajectory (considered here to extend, to date, from Mesopotamia in the third millennium BCE to the United States in the early third millennium CE) is its marked upward escalation in political organization and warfare in an early phase centered on ancient agrarian empires and a later phase centered on a highly competitive European region after 1500.[26]

It is this post-1500 accelerated escalation that led not only to the western military trajectory subordinating all others in the system but also to the development of very strong political organizations within the states that survived the circa 1500–1945/1989 escalation in competitive competencies. It is not a coincidence that the states that survived this trajectory were also the states that were most likely to industrialize by the nineteenth century. Our argument is that the western military trajectory survivors became most likely to experience economic and political constraints on their war behavior that stemmed from the accelerated political, economic, and war developments.

The vast majority of states in the current system, however, did not experience this acceleration. As a consequence they have developed much weaker political organizations that are by definition much less capable of mobilizing the resources necessary for expanding interstate warfare. They can fight small wars briefly and on occasion but they are unlikely to fight the type of wars that are likely to lead to stronger states. These same political weaknesses—such as the inability to generate political loyalties or to monopolize armed forces within their territorial boundaries—encourage challenges to domestic authority structures and intrastate warfare.[27] Thus a situation mixing industrial states with relatively strong states and agrarian states with relatively weak states leads to distinctly differentiated war behavior.

The Very Long-Term Processes at Work

This differentiated war behavior of weak and strong states is one of the characteristics of the evolution of war that we need to explain, along with the origins and initial expansion of war. We can summarize the very long-term processes at work in the following way:

1. *Given weaponry, rudimentary military organization, and group identification, war emerged within contexts of scarcity, in response to threats from other groups and/or opportunities to subordinate or exploit other groups.*

Weaponry and rudimentary military organization in the form of coordinated hunting parties emerged initially for early food acquisition purposes (Ferrill 1997; Otterbein 2004). The hardware and software of hunting proved useful for killing other people as well (Cioffi-Revilla 2000).[28] Another necessary ingredient was the emergence of group identities that expanded beyond the nuclear family (Kelly 2000). This step was necessary to move conflict patterns beyond family feuding to intergroup warfare.[29] In the subsequent context of a number of political-economic changes—encompassing population increases, agriculture, political power concentration in chiefdoms and states, and environmental stress—the incentives for groups to make war on other groups increased (see, for instance, Carneiro 1970, 1990; Otterbein 2004; Haas 1990). So, too, did their political-economic, organizational, and weapons capability to do so. As a consequence warfare initially emerged and then escalated. There is no reason to assume that all parts of the world experienced exactly the same processes in the same ways. Warfare probably emerged in a variety of circumstances.

Aggressive and expanding chiefdoms may have been most critical in some places. Environmental stress was an important driver in other places.

2. *Once the practice of war emerged (and diffused), its escalation in terms of frequency, magnitude, and lethality expanded, depending primarily on the threat environment and increases in political-economic complexity, and secondarily on changes in weaponry and military organization. Macrochanges in the types of predominant production strategies (hunting-gathering, agrarian, and industrial) also hastened the coevolution of warfare and its related factors.*

Diffusion is an important factor in explaining the widespread resort to warfare throughout the planet. That is, once warfare emerged here and there, the practice was copied and refined by others who sought to apply the same approach to their own problems.[30] Still, the evolution of warfare experienced a number of different and distinctive evolutionary trajectories. For instance, Central American warfare tended to rely on elite warriors who fought on foot with shock weaponry that changed in form relatively slowly over centuries.[31] In Japan, the elite, sword-wielding samurai initially may have been Central Asian migrants who fought on horseback with bows in the classical Eurasian nomadic style. Over time they evolved into a warrior caste favoring swords and a distinctive code of appropriate behavior until overwhelmed by the advent of rapid firing guns. China, in contrast, moved very early and very quickly toward large infantry masses. Indian armies acquired an unusual reliance on the shock value of war elephants. Mediterranean and west European societies focused initially on various ways to concentrate the shock power of long spears, in conjunction with other weapons, before moving to an era of reliance on decentralized and heavily armored cavalry, and then later becoming specialists in the development of gunpowder, initially invented in China.[32]

Why these trajectories evolved differently can be explained in terms of our six master variables: war, political organization, military organization, political economy, weaponry, and threat environment. For instance, the contrast between Central American and European warriors, say around 1000 CE, can be explained in part by the fact that Europe is adjacent to Central Asia and Central America is not. The technology underlying European heavy cavalry was developed largely but not exclusively in response to light cavalry attacks from the east.[33] Central America had no horses in the pre-Columbian era and therefore no light cavalry threat with which to contend. Factors other than the differential threat environment were also involved, but in this case one does not need to complicate the analysis for present purposes.

Aspects of the threat environment can also help explain seemingly peculiar phenomena such as the virtual abandonment of a world lead in naval technology by the Ming dynasty in the early fifteenth century and the alleged suppression of gunpowder weaponry in Japan in the early seventeenth century.[34] The Ming dynasty perceived that the Mongol threat was its principal strategic concern and chose to concentrate on this problem to the exclusion of external involvements. Again, other factors were involved, and one could also say, with the advantage of hindsight, that the Mongol threat was exaggerated. But the Ming had overthrown a Mongol dynasty and not that many years had passed since the Mongols had subordinated a good proportion of Asian Eurasia.

In the Japan case, gunpowder weaponry helped to reunify Japan in the late sixteenth century (Ferejohn and Rosenbluth 2010). Once elites had centralized political power, they faced the question of whether to facilitate the possibility of subsequent domestic challenges by allowing advanced weaponry to be readily available, especially in a society in which elite warriors prided themselves on hand-to-hand combat skills. Finally, as long as an external invasion threat was minimal, superior weaponry was relatively dispensable. Contrast this outcome with the circumstances in highly competitive, early modern Europe. The European threat environment encouraged persistent attempts to improve and strengthen political and military organization and weaponry. The seventeenth-century Japanese threat environment did not.

Scholars have conducted relatively few comparative analyses of these multiple military-warfare trajectories, and this is an important task. In the interim, however, one strategy is to focus on a single trajectory that ultimately became the central one. The western Eurasian trajectory outlined in table 3.8 provides some clues to how these trajectories change over time. Some changes are very gradual but others come in fairly punctuated, episodic form and tend to be manifested by the "best practice" of a paradigmatic army (Lynn 1996). The success of these exemplars not only affects the political-military salience and first mover advantages of the principal innovators, it also leads to selective imitation of the innovations by competitors.

The western trajectory thus began in the intercity warfare of third millennium BCE Mesopotamia and evolved through various formats combining armored infantry with battle-wagons/chariots giving way to cavalry in the Assyrian iteration.[35] The Persian emphasis on cavalry was trumped by

TABLE 3.8 **The western Eurasian military-war trajectory**

Paradigmatic Leader in Military Innovations	Timing
Mesopotamia	Third millennium BCE
Egypt	Mid-second millennium BCE
Assyria	Early ninth century BCE
Persia	Late sixth century BCE
Macedonia	Late fourth century BCE
Rome	Early first century CE
Feudal (Carolingians)	Early ninth century CE
Medieval-stipendiary	Twelfth–thirteenth centuries CE
France	Late fifteenth century CE
Spain	Late sixteenth century CE
France	Late seventeenth century CE/late eighteenth century CE
Germany	Late nineteenth century/early twentieth century CE
United States	Late twentieth century/early twenty-first century CE

the Macedonian combination of cavalry with heavy infantry. The Romans began with essentially Greek phalanx formations but developed more flexible units with less dependence on the shock of long spears.

In the movement from third millennium BCE Mesopotamia to early first millennium CE Rome, armies and thus wars became larger in size and lethality. Two periods of acceleration focused around the beginning of the third millennium and the second half of the first millennium BCE increased the pace of change. States evolved from small cities to an empire encompassing much of western Europe, north Africa, and considerable parts of southwestern Asia. Yet this trend line of bigger but not necessarily better did not continue inexorably. The Roman Empire fragmented into many parts, leading to more decentralized political organization and corresponding political and military organization for nearly a millennium.

Numerous political actors attempted to overcome the decentralization but failed to recreate a pan-European-based empire.[36] Yet aspiring hegemons kept trying. The conflict between expansionary states and defensive coalitions (at least in Europe) did contribute a great deal to the escalating costs of warfare in the contemporary era.

In the process of coping with various French, Spanish, and German bids for regional hegemony (Kennedy 1987), competitive European armies returned to their infantry roots but this time combined it with increasingly effective firepower. Over the last five hundred years, during a third period of acceleration, warfare in Europe became frequent and then gradually declined in number but not in severity. Corresponding changes in political economy (for example, industrialization) and political concentration led to larger, faster-moving, and more expensive armed forces. Military organizations and warfare also became increasingly lethal. The combination of demands on state resource extractions to pay for war preparations, the expanding destructiveness of warfare itself, and the increased societal mobilization for war, in conjunction with other forces at work, all led to ever-higher costs of warfare that ultimately discouraged the perceived utility of the war option. Why contemplate warfare if the likely outcome offered so few positive payoffs (Kaysen 1990)?

3. *Warfare and political-economic complexity need not be monotonically related. At some point, highly developed actors are likely to find the practice of warfare too costly to achieve the traditional ends of this particular social practice, at least against each other. Thus we should expect warfare between highly developed actors to decline or become less probable at some point. This same expectation does not extend toward dyads combining less developed or agrarian actors. More asymmetrical situations—highly developed actors versus less developed actors—pose different cost calculations, in part because advanced industrial states tend not to use their full inventory of capabilities against weaker, nonindustrialized states. The result is different probabilities of warfare from those between the most developed actors in the system.*

The problem is that this process in which war has become excessively costly has been highly uneven. Affluent, industrialized states, located primarily in Europe and North America, are less likely to consider warfare an attractive option against other affluent, industrialized states. Decisionmakers in other types of dyads may arrive at different conclusions. Industrialized states continue to fight with nonindustrialized states. Nonindustrialized states also occasionally fight other nonindustrialized states. These same nonindustrialized states tend to be of recent origin and often are characterized by relatively weak political systems. As a consequence they have a higher propensity to engage in internal warfare than do older, stronger political systems. A central irony here is that the newer states are impeded in their development of strong political systems because they cannot emulate the state-making–war-making experiences of the states that survived the European centuries of conflict and bloodletting (Desch 1996; Hironaka 2005).

4. *The type of warfare that actors engage in also varies according to their political-military-economic capabilities.*[37] *Actors or political organizations with symmetrical capabilities are most likely to engage in symmetrical warfare (either between or within political organizations), whereas actors characterized by different levels of development are most likely to engage in some type of asymmetrical warfare (for example, guerrilla war, insurgency, or terrorism).*

The current, now world, military-warfare trajectory encompasses a highly heterogeneous set of actors with varying capabilities. Older states with substantial military capabilities still prepare for the possibility of major-power warfare—though based on a different model of war from those employed in earlier major-power wars—though they recognized that the likelihood of conventional major-power warfare is relatively remote until or unless the major-power threat environment changes radically.

Newer states often find they lack the capabilities to fight interstate wars either frequently or for very long times.[38] As a consequence they fight other states relatively rarely and for very brief periods of time. The twenty-one wars fought by less developed states between 1945 and 2007 that satisfied the Correlates of War project's minimal battle death threshold are enumerated in table 3.9. One lasted fewer than ten days. Six were completed in less than a month. As many as thirteen (roughly 62 percent) ended in fewer than six months. Only the Iran-Iraq war that persisted for some eight years really contradicts the generalization that wars between lesser-developed states tend to be short.[39]

For this reason alone the historical consequences of war-making in modern Europe seem unlikely to be realized in the Middle East, Latin America, or Africa. The great increase in new and weak states, however, is likely to expand the number of ongoing internal wars (Hironaka 2005). How these wars are fought depends very much on the relative capabilities and access to resources of the combatants (Kalyvas 2005). Combatants with equal access to powerful resources are likely to fight conventional civil wars with opposing uniformed forces. More probable, though, are situations involving unequal or limited access to resources. Rebels weaker than the states they challenge will most probably rely on insurgency and terrorist tactics that may vary over time (Van Creveld 1991; Rapoport 2004). When both rebels and states are very weak, some type of unconventional internal warfare is probable. Paramilitaries, militias, and even

TABLE 3.9 **Interstate warfare duration for less developed states, 1945–2007**

War	Duration	Lasted less than ten days	Lasted approximately a month or less	Lasted less than six months	Lasted more than six months
First Kashmir	10/26/1947–1/1/1949				X
Palestine	5/15/1948–1/7/1949				X
Off-Shore Islands War	9/3/1954–4/23/1955				X
Assam	10/20/1962–11/22/1962		X	X	
Second Kashmir	8/5/1965–9/23/1965			X	
Football	7/14/1969–7/18/1969	X	X	X	
Bangladesh	12/3/1971–12/17/1971		X	X	
Turko-Cypriot	7/20/1974–8/16/1974		X	X	
War over Angola	10/23/1975–2/12/76			X	
Second Ogaden War, Phase 2	7/23/1977–3/9/1978				X
Vietnamese-Cambodian	9/24/1977–1/8/1979			X	
Ugandan-Tanzanian	10/28/1978–4/11/1979			X	
Sino-Vietnamese	2/17/1979–3/16/1979		X	X	
Iran-Iraq	9/22/1980–8/20/1988				X
War over Aouzou Strip	11/15/1986–9/11/1987				X
Sino-Vietnamese	1/5/1987–2/6/1987		X	X	
Bosnian Independence	4/7/1992–6/5/1992			X	
Azeri-Armenian	2/6/1993–5/12/1994				X
Cenepa Valley	1/9/1995–2/27/1995			X	
Badme Border	5/6/1998–12/12/2000				X
Kargil	5/8/1999–7/17/1999			X	

Source: Based on information reported in Sarkees and Wayman (2010). All wars involving developed states as participants are excluded.

criminals are likely to constitute the principal fighting forces until or unless more professionalized military forces intervene from outside the combat zone (Kaldor 1999; Mueller 2004; Münkler 2005).[40]

Warfare has not and is unlikely to completely disappear in the near future. Its format has changed often in the past, and it will continue to change. Different types of warfare have been fought in different parts of the world. That propensity has not changed, but the differences have perhaps become starker. Part of the contemporary world is much less likely to experience external and internal warfare—aside from terrorism—than are other parts of the world. These differences in frequency, probability, and format are neither inexplicable nor random. They reflect differential evolution. Therefore their explanation requires a focus on differential changes over time or, in other words, the evolution of war as a social practice.

Transformations are not solely contemporary phenomena. An extended illustration is provided in the next two chapters, which focus on the three major accelerations in warfare and also on military and political organizations, threat environment, political economy, and weaponry. Indeed, these three earlier accelerations, which are outlined in table 3.10, set up the variation in the practices of warfare in the contemporary system.

In chapter 4 we start with two earlier accelerations—the early Bronze Age transition from chiefdoms to states and the early Iron Age escalation of competitive and warring states in the last half of the first millennium BCE. A focus on these asserted accelerations also allows us to describe and compare some early developments in multiple trajectories, thereby providing more opportunities to assess the utility of our theoretical framework.

In chapter 5 we concentrate on the third major acceleration in war's evolution. There are two reasons for singling out the last five hundred

TABLE 3.10 **Three accelerations in coevolution**

Acceleration	Location	Timing
First	Mesopotamia	Late fourth to mid-third millennia BCE
Second	Mediterranean and China	Circa 500–200 BCE
Third	Europe	Second half of second millennium CE

years of war/military evolution for special attention. First, European warfare and its coevolutionary covariates were clearly revolutionized and intensified after 1500. Revolutions and intensification, as we have seen, were not novelties after 1500, but the gap between what pre-1500 and post-1500 armies could be expected to do gradually increased immensely. Europe returned to standing armies that grew progressively larger. The standing armies, largely oriented toward infantry, became more professional and better trained. Their firepower became increasingly effective and lethal. The states that survived this intensification process became larger, more centralized, and more capable of mobilizing resources for increasingly expensive armies and navies. Improved capabilities in mobilizing the sinews of war, in turn, hinged on transitions away from agrarian economies toward economies more focused on commerce and industry.

The second reason for looking more closely at the past half-millennium of war coevolution is that during this time period the current European trajectory, which had descended from southwest Asian/Mediterranean roots, clearly surpassed other war-military trajectories (for example, China, India, Japan, Mesoamerican). This triumph did not happen overnight. Nor did it happen in 1500. In fact it took several hundred years for the European lead to become fully evident. Once it had emerged, with considerable assistance from a series of industrial revolutions beginning in the late eighteenth century, it proved very difficult to defeat. In the process the southwest Asia/Mediterranean/European trajectory ultimately fused with the modern North American trajectory and became the predominant war-military trajectory in the modern world system. As such it either extinguished or transformed radically the nature of other extant trajectories.

The established centrality of the western trajectory does not imply that the entire planet can now be located on the same evolutionary path in terms of warfare. Western Europe in the twenty-first century is debating whether to continue further along this trajectory and may well choose to exit rather than to develop more advanced military systems.[41] Other parts of the world are struggling to catch up with the technological ante demanded for competition within this trajectory. Much of the rest of the world will most likely simply be left behind. But such speculations run ahead of our evolutionary story. We need to turn our attention first to what happened in general in the first two accelerations—the topic focused on in chapter 4.

CHAPTER FOUR

The First Two Agrarian Warfare Accelerations

Scholars offer different classifications of major changes in warfare over the millennia. Richard Gabriel's (2002) thesis is that warfare has undergone three revolutions.[1] The first revolution took place between 4000 and 2000 BCE, the second encompassed the 1500 BCE–100 CE era, and the third followed the introduction of gunpowder sometime after 1650 CE.[2] We agree with the identification of three periods of extraordinary, accelerated change in warfare. Our sense of their timing is somewhat different, however, and we prefer to call them periods of accelerated evolution. To elaborate where we converge and disagree, we need to first outline Gabriel's arguments for the first two periods and note our points of agreement and disagreement. However, to show how accelerated evolution and coevolution interact, we will devote most of this chapter to an analysis of military change in ancient Egypt, Greece, Rome, China, and Mesoamerica.

Gabriel's First Two Revolutions

In Gabriel's first revolution, the emergence of complex urban societies in Mesopotamia and Egypt, predicated on the development of agriculture and animal domestication, led to three specific changes related to warfare. First, new weapons were developed, with stone giving way to copper and then to bronze. Second, governmental and societal structures were created that could command and support relatively large armies. Linking religious beliefs to ruler legitimacy further enhanced command and control.

Divine rulers helped convert family and clan allegiances into loyalty to the state. Governments and their bureaucratic infrastructures were further reinforced and stabilized. Third, population growth and density helped provide the men needed for army expansions. As a consequence, the scale of warfare—both in terms of geography and casualties—increased.

Gabriel emphasizes that prior to 4000 BCE there were no cities, no governmental institutions to speak of, no armies characterized by some degree of professionalization and organization, no specialized warriors, and that weaponry and agriculture had been developed in highly limited ways. Therefore, he argues, there could be no violence recognizable as warfare. By 2000 BCE, all of this had changed. Cities, food surpluses, population densities, governments, armies, and weaponry were all in place to create warfare on what Gabriel (2002, 3) views as "a modern scale":

> In this period warfare assumed truly modern proportions in terms of the size of the armies involved, the administrative mechanisms required to sustain them, the development of weapons, the frequency of occurrence, and the scope of destruction achievable by military force. The ancient world had given birth to a level of warfare that would have been instantly recognizable in all its elements by a soldier of the present.

We fully acknowledge the point that the emergence of agrarian-era warfare took place between 4000 and 2000 BCE. Before that time hunting-foraging-era warfare predominated, and was characterized by sporadic ambushes, raiding, and very limited participation. After 4000 BCE, the ingredients for a scalar increase began to come together. Yet the scope of these changes was restricted largely to southern Mesopotamia and to a lesser extent, Egypt. We know precious little about warfare in Sumerian Mesopotamia other than that intercity-state conflict increased after 3000 BCE, armored infantry troops are depicted in phalanx or concentrated spear formations, battle carts were employed, and that the first episode of imperial expansion with an army claimed to be five-thousand-man strong was underway in the 2300s BCE. These are impressive changes, especially in contrast to what had gone on before, as Gabriel emphasized, but we have only really vague impressions of what might have been taking place. These changes were quite revolutionary if one ignores the slow timing but still quite limited in geographical scope. Egypt, for a variety of reasons that will be discussed later in this chapter, did not follow the same path.

The common focus on military revolutions is probably misleading in some ways. Given our emphasis on evolution (and coevolution), the concept of revolution can be awkward if one insists that change be abrupt in form to qualify as revolutionary. Most people equate "evolutionary" change with slow-moving transformations. Thus we frequently encounter a revolutionary-evolutionary distinction that revolves around the amount of time required for change to be in place. There are, however, two problems with this common distinction. Evolutionary change can occur quite abruptly—as in a species extinction due to, say, meteorite impact. It is inaccurate, therefore, to restrict evolutionary change to the slow-moving variety when evolutionary change can be either fast or slow.

At the same time, political revolutions are often more slow moving than people recognize. A monarch may be overthrown abruptly, but ensuing changes to social structure, if they come, are apt to be much slower paced. If all palace coups were revolutionary the timing of sociopolitical changes would not matter. But we tend to restrict the term *revolution* to events that lead to widespread changes in how societies are structured.[3] Thus political revolutions can be abrupt affairs but are more likely to be drawn-out over years and perhaps even decades.

What, then, should we make of a claim that a two-thousand-year period was revolutionary for warfare in a corner of southwest Eurasia? As noted before, we acknowledge the scalar increase in behavior to which Gabriel has drawn attention, but we do not make too much of it. Perhaps if we knew more about what took place in Sumer, a better case could be made for focusing on it as a starting point. Sumer was not an isolated phenomenon, which is attested to by the probable linkages between battle carts and subsequent chariots and possible linkages between infantry-concentrated spear formations and subsequent Greek phalanxes. The light, spoked-wheel, horse-drawn chariots of the early second millennium BCE that emerged from the Black Sea area are likely to have been influenced by Mesopotamian heavy, solid-wheel battle carts of the fourth millennium BCE (Cotterell 2005, 42–47). Mesopotamian artwork also suggests the use of concentrated infantry armed with spears that clearly preceded the celebrated Greek formations some 2,500 years later. Whether the Greeks were influenced by older southwest Asian military practices, we will probably never be able to determine.

Coevolutionary changes were clearly in play with changes in political economy making political organization more necessary. Climate change encouraged greater reliance on irrigation techniques focused on the

Tigris-Euphrates, which, in turn, required political management. Cities grew because people had to live near the irrigation canals. Agricultural surpluses and expanded political organization facilitated the development of and support for specialized military forces. The initial nature of the threat environment is ambiguous, but there appears to have been increased conflict with tribal groups migrating first into the Fertile Crescent from the Caucuses in the last half of the fourth millennium and then into Mesopotamia from the Syrian Desert in the third millennium. Intercity conflict becomes more evident toward the end of the fourth millennium and is certainly manifested yet hard to pin down in the first half of the third millennium. The takeover of Sumer by Akkad in the second half of the third millennium led to imperial forays toward Lebanon, Anatolia, and the Gulf. Akkad, in turn, was overrun by nomadic tribes coming into the plains from the mountains, signaling an escalation in nomadic-sedentary conflict.

The transition to an agrarian political economy occurred first in southwest Eurasia, and it is hardly surprising that agrarian-style warfare first emerged there as well. We know that many firsts occurred there, but our general lack of information about what came first makes it difficult to advance causal linkages between the specific timing of various changes. We can say that substantial coevolution took place. We cannot trace precisely how changes in one sector led to changes in other sectors. Rather than defending the application of revolutionary terms to developments that occur over centuries, we choose to emphasize instead that changes tend to speed up from time to time. Mesopotamian changes thus represent the first evolutionary acceleration in warfare-linked coevolutions.

Gabriel's second period of military revolution (1500 BCE–100 CE) in warfare is better documented than the first. In this period, states and empires, based on military coercion, became standard and were characterized by near-constant warfare. The transition from bronze to iron in this period meant that states could make better weapons less expensively and therefore in greater supply. Combined with conscription and expanding standing armies, more reliable, cheaper, and more lethal weaponry led to increases in the frequency, scope, and scale of warfare that went unsurpassed until the advent of gunpowder weapons hundreds of years later.

In this period Gabriel emphasizes weapons and military organization. Table 4.1 summarizes some of the implications of switching from bronze to iron. Any given weapon is capable of doing x amount of damage, here measured in terms of energy produced. Bronze and iron armor can be

TABLE 4.1 **Energy (in footpounds) necessary to penetrate ancient armor**

Weapon	Energy Produced	Energy required	
		Bronze Armor	Iron Armor
Spear (underhand)	14	137	228
Sword (thrust)	21	182	302
Arrow	47	76	126
Javelin	67	99	165
Cutting axe	70	189	314
Spear (overhand)	71	137	228
Sword (hacking)	101	151	251

Source: Based on Gabriel (2002, 24).

TABLE 4.2 **Empire and army size**

Time Period	Empire Size	Army Size
Bronze Age:		
Sumer	250 by 125 miles	600/700–5400
Early Egypt	600 by 200 miles	60,000+
New Kingdom Egypt	1,250 by 200 miles	100,000
Iron Age:		
Assyria	1,250 by 300 miles	150–200,000
Persia	2,500 by 1,000 miles	200–400,000
Macedonia	2,600 by 1,000 miles	
Rome	3,800 by 1,500 miles	350,000

Source: Gabriel (2002, 9, 55, 61).

penetrated differentially, with iron providing at least 50 percent more protection than does bronze. Ancient weapons (spears, axes, arrows, and eventually swords) can be deflected by metal armor, but armies were rarely completely armored and only gradually increased the armor they possessed. Gabriel's point is that iron armor trumped bronze armor as part of an ancient escalation in weapon lethality and defensive precautions.

In conjunction with changes in weapons and armor, armies were also expanding in size just as foreign policy goals were expanding in geographical scope. Table 4.2 indicates the expansion in size and scope during the Bronze Age. Sumerian/Akkadian armies may have expanded from fewer than six to 5,400 soldiers. Old, Middle, and New Kingdom Egyptian armies eventually reached 100,000. Calculating the estimated areas in which they were expected to operate yields an increase from 31,250 square miles in the Sumerian case to 250,000 square miles in the New Kingdom Egyptian case.[4] The Iron Age cases in table 4.2 begin with Assyria and end with Rome. Army sizes increased from 150,000 to between 350,000 and 400,000. The areal mobility required expanded from 375,000 square miles to 5.7 million square miles. This area expansion represents a roughly fifteenfold expansion in contrast to the eightfold expansion in the Bronze Age.

The transition to iron had major implications for agrarian productivity as well as for weaponry and military organizations.[5] Iron plows were much more efficient than their predecessors. Population expansion and more food surplus were two of the consequences. These changes led to richer and larger states and states that were more capable of maintaining ever-larger armies and executing more ambitious imperial strategies. Threat environments became more intensive as expanding states and empires collided with one another, thereby generating ever-more intensive rounds of warfare.

Exactly where one starts the clock on this period is debatable, but we see a second evolutionary acceleration that is most evident in the last half of the first millennium BCE leading to the creation of the Roman and Han Empires.[6] Even so, the geographical scope of this acceleration is again uneven. It is most discernible in the Mediterranean and China, giving it the appearance of a pan-Eurasian scope. Yet there is no implication that all of the places in between the Mediterranean and China experienced the same evolutionary acceleration. Even the ways in which the Mediterranean and China experienced these evolutionary accelerations were not identical. Nor is there any evidence that similar accelerations were experienced outside of Eurasia. We hope to show how various trajectories worked by examining, comparing, and contrasting ancient evolutionary and coevolutionary developments in Egypt, the Greco-Roman Mediterranean, China, and Mesoamerica in the rest of this chapter. We view this as an opportunity to amplify the nature of the asserted second evolutionary acceleration and to test further the utility of our coevolutionary scheme.

The roles played by our four cases are not identical. The Egyptian case is exclusively Bronze Age in setting. We begin with Egypt in part because it possessed a distinctive threat environment for a time and in part to set the stage for the two predominately Iron Age cases: Greece-Rome and China. While these last two cases incorporate some material from the Bronze Age, they are intended to demonstrate what happened in the last half of the first millennium BCE at the two ends of Eurasia. The fourth case, Mesoamerica, which was characterized by the absence of a significant evolutionary acceleration of war and military organizations, is intended to represent what did not happen outside of Eurasia in the early Iron Age. One reason for the absence of an early Iron Age acceleration in the Americas was that metallurgy was not important for weapon manufacture there prior to the intrusion of the Spanish. However, iron was adopted in sub-Saharan Africa, albeit very slowly, without significantly influencing warfare and military organizations prior to the introduction of horses and gunpowder.

Case I: Ancient Egypt

Egypt became one of the twin pillars of concentration of military-political-economic strength in the ancient Near East, but its heyday was preceded by the rise and fall of the other pillar, Mesopotamia. Mesopotamia encountered serious salinity problems with its irrigation techniques, which led to a significant decline in agricultural productivity in the late third and early second millennium. Egypt avoided this problem for the most part because it relied less on extensive irrigation canals as in Mesopotamia and more on the fluctuations in the Nile River level to sustain agriculture in a narrow strip adjacent to the river. The annual fluctuations could not always be depended on—sometimes they were too high or too low—but the Mesopotamian problem of excess salinity was evaded.

What this meant was that ancient Egypt occupied a long ribbon of land adjacent to the Nile surrounded on both sides by desert. This provided Egypt with natural defenses against attack from peer competitors, but it also created some probability of fragmentation given the difficulties of overcoming distance and projection of force from a capital. The outcome was that ancient Egypt cycled in and out of periods of power concentration and deconcentration. The key to understanding the Egyptian threat environment is that when power was deconcentrated or fragmenting, it became more difficult to prevent the intrusions of desert nomads and other enemies. Regional conflict within Egypt thus encouraged non-Egyptian movements into Egyptian territory. When ancient Egypt was united, it was more likely to project force beyond its borders toward Palestine, Libya, or the south.

Table 4.3 summarizes Egyptian evolution and coevolutionary patterns between 4000 BCE and around 1000 BCE. Prior to the unification of Egypt toward the end of the fourth millennium by a southern Egyptian

TABLE 4.3 **Evolution and coevolution in ancient Egypt**

Period	Dating	Threat Environment	Political Organization	Military Organization	Weaponry
Naqada I to Pre-Dynastic	4000–2687 BCE	Trade/exploration protection and raiding tribes for manpower; increasing regional competition		Ad hoc militaries	Initially stone with bronze introduced after 2700; bows, javelins, mace, axe, spear
Old Kingdom	2687–2181 BCE	Trade and border protection with provincial governors becoming increasingly independent	Centralized imperial dynasties	Small contingents with Nubian auxiliaries; main armies controlled at provincial level; absence of specialized officer corps archer barrage followed by infantry melee	Copper weapons; royal fleet created to support amphibious troop movement
First Intermediate		Increased conflict within Egypt and on borders			
Middle Kingdom	2061–1786 BCE	Increased coercive expansion of Egyptian territory; temporary campaigns into Palestine	Centralized imperial dynasties	Egyptian levies called up for campaigns; Nubian mercenaries; armies still provincially based	Javelins/spears, bronze swords, bows, axe, animal skin shield; composite bows
Second Intermediate		Semitic immigration into Nile Delta and Hyksos control of northern Egypt			
New Kingdom		Confrontation with competitive states in Near East; Libyan/Sea Peoples invasions toward end	Centralized imperial dynasties	Chariot focus makes military more land-oriented with navy less critical for troop movements	Chariots-archers, new body armor, scimitar, javelins/spears, short sword, composite bow, shields

Sources: Based on information found in Gnirs (1999), McDermott (2004), Spalinger (2005), Hamblin (2006), and Darnell and Manasa (2007).

warlord, Egypt was divided into multiple chiefdoms that amalgamated into several competitive states. Bronze was introduced relatively late and weaponry tended to lag as a consequence, with stone and copper predominating longer than most other parts of the Near East. Military organization was rudimentary. Groups of armed men would be enlisted for specific campaigns against other local states or for raids into bordering areas for raw materials and slaves.

Unification in the late fourth millennium BCE was achieved through military coercion, and it ushered in a sequence of successive dynasties of pharaohs. The main sets of dynasties are referred to as Old, Middle, and New Kingdoms. The pattern consisted of one strong dynastic group seizing the throne at the outset of each Kingdom and then gradually giving way to the fragmentation of power as provincial governors became increasingly powerful while the central government became increasingly enfeebled.

One reason for this recurring pattern was that provincial governors retained principal control over Egyptian armies. The central government was initially served by a small contingent of mercenaries/bodyguards. This group would be supplemented for occasional campaigns by call-ups of soldiers supplied by the provincial governors from their respective populations. These campaigners lacked any specialized officer corps. Command would be retained by civilian bureaucrats appointed by the government for the duration of the campaign. As a consequence, Old Kingdom battles tended to begin with a barrage of arrows followed by soldiers fighting as individuals in a disorganized, melee fashion.

Each of the Kingdoms succumbed to periods of decentralization known as Intermediates. Similar to Dark Ages elsewhere, no central government either existed or lasted very long. Provincial (nomarch) conflict increased. Little could be done to prevent incursions from nomads in the east and west. Then political power would be reconsolidated by a new group of dynasts. One way of demonstrating central power was to conduct raids to the east and the south and return home with whatever loot could be acquired. Gradually these raids became more ambitious and enduring and the extent of Egyptian territory increasingly expanded with each subsequent Kingdom.

The Second Intermediate period following the demise of the Middle Kingdom was a period of external shock for ancient Egypt. Incursions from Palestine and the Levant were more persistent. Control over much of northern Egypt was lost to the migrants and, in particular, to a group the Egyptians called the Hyksos, who introduced chariots and compound bows to Egyptian weaponry inventories. Prior to the advent of the Hyksos, Egyptian forces had relied on Nile fleets to move troops up and down the river where they would be deployed in traditional fashion against usually fairly weak opponents. The Hyksos introduced weapons that were more common in other parts of the Near East and for which the Egyptians initially had little defense.

In part by adopting the new weaponry, the New Kingdom eventually was able to force the Hyksos out of northern Egypt. With the new advantage of greater land mobility offered by chariot forces, the New Kingdom foreign policies were the most ambitious of the three Kingdoms, leading to an Egyptian empire extending south into Nubia and beyond Palestine into Syria-Lebanon where it came into intensive conflict with other Near Eastern powers such as the Hittites based in Anatolia. The new weaponry and reconfigured military organization with more professionalization and training were able to support imperial expansion for a while. They were not able to forestall internal fragmentation propensities.

Gnirs (1999) argues that the prominence of the military in the New Kingdom facilitated a usurpation of the pharaoh-focused political system. New pharaohs could not rely solely on divine reinforcement but were expected to demonstrate their qualifications to rule. Military combat experience was helpful in this regard. Former military officers increasingly tended to dominate state administrative offices. Now that Egyptian strategic reach was greater than ever before, military garrisons were necessary to control newly gained territory in the south and east. In short, imperial expansion gave military officers a higher profile in Egyptian society than ever before (Spalinger 2005).

Invasions of Libyans and Sea Peoples (essentially migrations of people fleeing a sustained period of drought in the eastern Mediterranean) were resisted apparently with some success.[7] Yet Egyptian military power came to rely increasingly on Libyan mercenaries who eventually were able to assume a version of central power in a Third Intermediate period. In addition to an overreliance on non-Egyptian mercenaries, Egypt, buffeted by clashes with Hittites and then Sea Peoples, lost its control of its "Asian" territory and the revenues associated with them. The loss of important revenues, in turn, undermined the central power of the state, which encouraged political instability (Gnirs 1999). From this point on Egypt was controlled intermittently by a series of non-Egyptian conquerors (Assyrians, Macedonians, Romans, and so forth). Its natural defenses and local military forces were no longer sufficient to preclude successful invasions.

We can summarize the ancient Egyptian story in terms of our six-component model. The main feature is Egypt's unusually benign *threat environment* prior to the Hyksos and subsequent Egyptian insularity. Before and after the Hyksos shock, the external threat environment interacted reciprocally with the strength of *political organization*. In turn Egyptian *political economy*, tied to fluctuations in the supply of Nile water, created a cyclical foundation for ebbing and waning political centralization.[8] When the pharaohs were strong, the Egyptian state sought coercive expansion, mainly to the south and east, resulting in *war*. When the pharaohs were weak, Palestinians, Nubians, and Libyans penetrated into a fragmented Egypt. Pharaonic weaknesses were compounded by the tendency for *military organization* to focus on provincial (nomarch) lines. Even so, Egyptian expansion was limited until the Hyksos external shock or change in the external threat environment introduced chariots and compound bows. Adoption of this *weaponry* facilitated the expansion of Egypt toward the Fertile Crescent and a different and more competitive type of external threat environment, leading eventually to a showdown clash with Hittite forces. Throughout this several millennium story, the *interaction between external threat environment and political organization* seems most prominent. Yet political economy, military organization, weaponry, and war also played an important role.

Case II: Ancient Greece and Rome

Greece

The early and middle Bronze Ages in Greece are neither well known nor particularly interesting in terms of war and military organization questions. Tribal forces were armed and fought each other occasionally in disorganized melee fashion. Earlier, fighters in Greece had relied largely on hurling projectiles at their enemies. This practice had given way to closer combat. More specialized weaponry emerged as a consequence. So, too, did the scale of fortification throughout the Bronze Age. The Mycenaean early Bronze Age in the second half of the second millennium BCE was more interesting, if not all that better known, with increasing competition and armed forces utilizing chariots, accompanied by lightly armed infantry, and oared galleys. This period also ended in extensive conflict and destruction.

It is not clear how the chariots were employed in Mycenaean Greece. The majority opinion, based largely on a reading of the *Iliad*, suggests that they were used only to transport soldiers to the battlefield—as opposed to the Near Eastern (or Indian and Chinese) practice of using them as mobile weapons platforms. A dissenter is Robert Drews (1993; but see also Ferrill 1997, 95), who argues that since most others used chariots as mobile weapons platforms, the Mycenaean Greeks must have done so as well. Drews advances this inference as part of his contention that the Greek Bronze Age was brought down in destruction by better-armed, barbarian "infantry" that had learned how to overwhelm chariot-focused armies. The problem remains that there is simply little in the way of concrete evidence for or against such theories.

Foci on Greek military activities usually scrutinize what developed after the Dark Age interruption roughly between 1200 and 800 BCE in which population centers had fragmented and population levels had declined dramatically, presumably related to the same environmental deterioration problems that had generated the Sea Peoples fought by the Egyptians in the twelfth century. After several hundred years of decline, population levels and agrarian productivity began to improve after 800. Greece, naturally divided by mountains and valleys, was composed of a large number of polis or communities that were not populated all that densely initially. Alien incursions into another polis' territory, probably influenced by increasing population sizes, were met by ad hoc groups of farmers who came together to defend their turf and livelihoods.

Untrained, often without armor, these temporary and presumably volunteer soldiers relied primarily on spears that were thrown at the enemy and small round shields to protect against missiles thrown by the other side. Several things changed. Bronze armor began to be introduced or reintroduced in the eighth century BCE but remained expensive and therefore was distributed unevenly.[9] A full set of armor would cover the head, chest, forearms, and shins. A larger shield that was easier to carry was also introduced. Only the richest citizens could afford these full sets. Others would show up with a helmet, or a breastplate, or with weapons alone. In other words, amateurs brought their own equipment when needed.

The full details of how the hoplite formation developed may never be known, but gradually the better armored were placed in the first ranks. Throwing spears were phased out some time around 640 BCE (Wees 2004) and replaced by shielded soldiers using thrusting spears. With the shift from throwing to thrusting, the attackers and defenders assumed more concentrated formations that would attack one another, attempting to break through the first rank of their opponents. It is not known whether they maintained this phalanx formation throughout the fighting and pushed at each other (as some authors have described it—more on the order of a rugby scrum with few casualties) or, more likely, devolved into clashing shield wall combat with the front ranks attempting to thrust and slash their way through their opponents.

Ferrill (1997, 143–44) argues that the phalanx formation was less than maximally effective because it relied exclusively on shock tactics and ignored the advantages of composite forces that contained heavy and light infantry as well as projectile capabilities. He thinks this Greek commitment to what he calls an anomaly must be traceable to a break in the links between Greece and the more militarily advanced Near East between 1000 and 800 BCE. Otherwise, more sophisticated tactics might have been developed. Yet Ferrill (1997, 94), some fifty pages earlier, reproduces Minoan artwork depicting a line of spearmen with long shields and notes that the length of the spears shown may suggest an Egyptian influence. Even earlier Sumerian artwork also shows formations of armored spearmen with shields.

If we place the Minoans as preeminent in the Aegean in the first half of the second millennium BCE, the Mycenaeans as preeminent in the second half of that same millennium, and the emergence of the phalanx in the first half of the first millennium, it is not clear that we need to rely on severed Near Eastern links to account for the development of dense spearmen formations. What is really missing when the phalanx was emerging is the absence of an expansive Greek empire on the lines of Assyria. When such an empire did finally emerge in Macedonian form it did not rely exclusively on heavy infantry.

Part of the problem of reconstructing what took place is that the early phalanx combat is based on interpreting artwork on surviving vases and ambiguous written descriptions. For instance, as long as warriors are depicted carrying two spears, the inference is that at least one was thrown. When warriors are painted as carrying only one spear, the presumption is that a switch to thrusting has come about. Fortunately, the two-spear vases give way to one-spear vases, further reinforcing the idea of the evolution of weaponry and tactics.

In terms of phalanx tactics, the idea of deciding the combat issue by two opposing front lines pushing at each other does not seem very likely. There would have been less need for armor if the emphasis was on physically pushing the opposing line, and phalanxes, most likely, would have grown into deeper and denser formations, with victory going to whoever could recruit larger and stronger front ranks and more rear ranks pushing them in turn. Instead, armor became more uniform and complete over time, suggesting that the front line needed protection from spear and sword thrusts. Vases are not much help on this issue since they were not large enough to depict serial scenes from a battle between two phalanxes, assuming artists had witnessed them in the first place. Hans van Wees (2004, plate XIV between pages 210 and 211) makes a sly and easy-to-miss observation when he quotes from the *Iliad* about "dense ranks, dark and bristly with shields and spears") juxtaposed with a photograph of Papua New Guinean Dani warriors converging with spears before battle. Wees's apparent point is that the Dani subsequently broke ranks and fought in melee format—as demonstrated in other photos.

What is known is that the phalanx formations became denser, with the best-armored and best fighters in the front ranks and highly dependable troops toward the rear. Phalanx formations could have from eight to as many as fifty ranks. The idea was that the least useful troops in the middle would help propel the front rank forward, and the dependable troops in the rear would keep pressure on the middle ranks to prevent them from bolting in combat situations. At the outset the phalanx formations were relatively loose and went into combat accompanied by warriors on horseback, archers, and lightly armored soldiers. As political organizations grew stronger, they were able to impose more discipline on their phalanxes. The archers and equestrian and lightly armored fighters were excluded from the heavily armored, main formation and were assigned more peripheral roles to better maintain phalanx order and shock effects. Cavalry and light infantry could be used to protect one's own phalanx's flanks, harass the flanks of the opposing phalanx, and pursue soldiers when their phalanx formation broke down.

As political organizations became more capable of taxation and borrowing, the armor became more consistent. The hoplite heavy infantry became heavier (up to a point).[10] They also had to become better disciplined and trained, even if they were not yet standing armies. Regular taxation and state borrowing began only in the 500s (according to Wees [2004]), about the same time that the classical phalanx formation also finally took shape. Soldiers and sailors were not paid regularly before the 400s. Dividing the loot taken from a defeated foe had been their principal form of monetary reward prior to that time. No consistent, state-led training of hoplites, aside from the Spartan outlier, took place before the second half of the fourth century. The classical hoplite phalanx formation that is reasonably well known thus required nearly half a millennium to evolve and depended on coevolution in weaponry and political organizations.

The Greek case is often offered, going back to Aristotle, as a prime example of external threats of war, or, alternatively, new weapons systems leading to democratization. Elites were too few to man phalanxes by themselves. The need for military manpower implied some societal trade-offs in exchange for intermittent service. Therefore, anyone who could afford some armor was eligible for phalanx duty. More affluent farmers could qualify for hoplite duty and in turn expect and demand rights and privileges from the political system. Political systems more egalitarian than they might otherwise have emerged as a consequence.[11]

Some caution in causal interpretation seems wise in this case. The types of Greek political systems employing phalanx tactics varied in terms of their political equality, as suggested by a comparison of Sparta, a political economy based on helot slavery, with Athens, well known for its democratic tradition, if only for a relatively small proportion of its population. The greatest external threats—in the form of the Persian expeditions—came late to the Greek region. The phalanx system also took several hundred years to emerge in full form. To which phalanx formation—the mixed assemblies of the eighth century or the more professional variants of the fifth and fourth centuries—should we give credit for fostering egalitarianism? The leveling effects of the 1200–800 BCE Dark Age may be more responsible for any initial egalitarianism in Greek polis than was differential access to helmets and breastplates.

Raaflaub and Rosenstein (1999) argue that after the Dark Ages, farmers constituted a majority of the Greek population. Fertile soil required defense as population sizes began to expand once again. Farmers had excellent motivation to defend their own fields. Ad hoc farmer militias therefore formed to carry out this mission. Increases in the size of the massed militia presumably depended on increases in the size of the threatening groups. Thus the tendency to fight as clusters of spear-carrying soldiers preceded the development of the phalanx formation and probably also the later formalization of a linkage between property and military duty.

Once it evolved, the Greek phalanx (and, of course, the trireme about which we will say more) played a significant role in fending off Persian invasions carried out far from any home base with more lightly armored infantry. Not long after the Persian threat had been defeated, the Peloponnesian wars[12] became the focus of intra-Greek fighting, with one side (led by Athens) specializing in advanced warships, the trireme, and the other side (led by Sparta) specializing in the best-trained heavy hoplite infantry. Toward the end of the fifth century BCE, the Spartan alliance, heavily subsidized by Persian financing, was enabled to decisively defeat the Athenian alliance at sea and end the stalemate on the Greek peninsula. The long-lasting Peloponnesian wars aggravated the need for more specialized military forces, greatly expanded the mercenary pool, and imposed heavy fiscal burdens on the states that were most involved in the fighting. The states that could solve the financial sinews of war problem became the major powers of the Greek peninsula engaging in escalating and continuous warfare throughout the fifth and much of the fourth centuries BCE.

Kurt Raaflaub and Nathan Rosenstein (1999, 132) emphasize the contribution of naval warfare to the intensification of Greek warfare in this period. Building and maintaining fleets required extensive resources, docking and harbor infrastructures, and constant training. These activities required substantial financing by the states that could contemplate naval commitments. An obvious solution was to create an empire that could be taxed to sustain the fleets that were necessary to protect imperial linkages and trade routes. Causality flows in both directions, but the outcome leads to more complex state operations with an expanded fiscal base and a greater scale of operations. Greater resistance to expanding empire seems probable, and therefore the probability of warfare increased as well. Naval warfare was not only more expensive but also longer in duration than typical land campaigns and often more lethal in terms of the casualties inflicted within the fleets. The availability of naval fleets, moreover, made possible the movement of troops over relatively long distances and enabled the imposition of lengthy blockades on rival ports. All of these activities contributed to the intensification of Greek warfare in the 400s.

The changes to Greek navies of this era deserve special attention because roughly between the ninth and sixth centuries BCE, ships were designed and constructed that set the standard for first-line warships for the next millennia.[13] Lionel Casson (1991, 75–76) considers the design changes so revolutionary that he lists them as one of the top three naval innovations throughout history.[14] Shipbuilding goes back at least to early Mesopotamia and Egypt, and ships were employed for military purposes early on but primarily to convey troops to battle or to facilitate land battles on water by having enemy ships come alongside one another, which allowed oarsmen and marines to fight pitched battles at sea.

Mesopotamian shipping initially focused on using the Tigris and Euphrates Rivers to bring resources to southern Mesopotamia from the north. In the third millennium BCE, substantial trade via the Indian Ocean and Gulf route between Indus and Mesopotamia had been established. Egyptian ships initially focused on the Nile River and later specialized in eastern Mediterranean commerce between the Levant and Egypt.

In the first half of the first millennium BCE, Greek galley warships changed in two ways. Rams were added to the prow to enable ships to employ tactical maneuvers that would permit one ship to sink another. Ships also became more powerful by increasing the number of rowers through banked sets of oarsmen. Two banks of rowers had given way to three banks (the trireme) by sometime in the sixth century BCE and remained the standard in the eastern Mediterranean until the late seventh century CE (Casson 1991). Rams persisted to about the same time period as the main offensive focus until they were supplanted by the adoption of Greek fire—an early form of flame thrower—which continued to be used until at least the twelfth century CE (Rose 2002, 124).

The increasing size of ships and the number of oarsmen required to man them, along with the additional training necessary as naval tactics became more complex, necessitated more state expenditure to build and maintain galley fleets. The problem was compounded by the absence of regular taxation in the heyday of Greek prominence. The norm for Greek cities was to levy extraordinary taxes, sometimes obligatory and other times voluntary, when they seemed necessary (Chaniotis 2005, 120). The discovery and exploitation of nearby silver mines are thought to have been critical to the funding of Athenian maritime power.

Some argue that an increasing reliance on oared galleys and their rowers contributed to Athenian democratization because rowers had to be recruited from less privileged classes and yet be treated well because of their military significance in first opposing the Persians and later in the Peloponnesian wars. The problem with this argument is that if there was a contribution to democratization, it must have been highly localized and transitory, and perhaps limited only to the quite significant naval contribution to the defeat of Persian expansion. In addition, Athenian ship captains could only be recruited from the wealthiest elite while the crews remained poor, often non-Athenian in citizenship, and included a large number of slaves brought on by hired rowers to assist their owners (see Wees 2004, 209–14). Athenian fleets seem unlikely vehicles for domestic democratization purposes even in the restricted Athenian sense. The

Athenians soon ran into problems with rebellions within their extended maritime empire/alliance, and subsequent galley fleets (which continued to be used in the Mediterranean into the seventeenth century CE) are not usually given any credit for democratization influences.

Three or more generations of intra-Greek fighting over predominance in Greece was put to an end by Macedonian coercion and conquest. The Macedonians inhabited the northern frontier of Greece and unlike the rest of Greece were exposed to attacks from Celts and Scythian nomads. As a consequence of the distinctive nature of their own threat environment, they developed different military techniques than did more southern Greeks. One innovation, at least for Greek warfare, was the more prominent use of cavalry. Another was the adoption of an earlier, Athenian-abandoned experiment with longer spears. The twelve- to sixteen-feet-long Macedonian sarissas were considerably longer than the eight-feet-long Greek norm. This meant the spears of the Macedonian phalanxes would reach their opponents first, and in addition more spears from the nonfirst ranks would also be projected toward the enemy. Greater and more asymmetrical damage would usually ensue as a consequence, particularly given that the Macedonians were better trained to maintain and maneuver in tight formations than their adversaries in Greece and elsewhere. Other Macedonian innovations in siege craft, artillery, and logistics created a highly effective armed force that was capable of defeating much larger armies far from Greece.

Arther Ferrill (1997, 149–50) even considers the Macedonian episode a military revolution for Greece in that prior to the rise of Macedonia, Greeks could resist Persian attacks with phalanxes and triremes but they could not go on the offensive without expanding their tactical inventory.

> Before Greeks and Macedonians could penetrate the heart of Persia, they had to create an integrated army—heavy and light infantry, skirmishers, and heavy and light cavalry—and to learn the means of supporting such a force logistically. Furthermore, no invasion of Persia could succeed unless the attacking army had some chance of taking by storm the highly fortified strongholds on the Persian coast of the Mediterranean. . . . To take fortified sites by storm required an integrated army, but one that was supported by a corps of military engineers with far greater knowledge of the art of siege than the Greek world had produced by the end of the fifth century.

These innovations were not purely Greek or Macedonian inventions. The catapult was developed in Syracuse and Macedonia in the first sixty years of the fourth century BCE, but other forms of siege craft were Near Eastern in origin (Ferrill 1997, 170–74). Innovation often, perhaps always, involves a synthesis of already known factors—the genius is a matter of recombining what is known or suspected into a different and more effective package. Thus the Macedonians recombined their own techniques (greater utilization of cavalry, for one), some Greek practices (for instance, the phalanx with longer spears), and some Persian ones (such as integrating cavalry and infantry) to create an army that could and did conquer the known world.

Ferrill (1997, 150–66) gives much of the credit for this innovation to the manpower pool for mercenaries that was created by the Peloponnesian War. Greek mercenaries employed in the Near East were agents of diffusion, encouraging subsequent experiments with different tactics rather than relying on heavy infantry alone.

In the first half of this case, then, the Greek first millennium story, summarized in table 4.4, focuses on the interactions among *external threat environment*, *military organization* and *weaponry*, and *political organization*. As conditions improved early in the millennium, ad hoc farmer militias were organized to resist intruders. The militias gave way gradually, presumably in response to increased threats, to more heavily armored, hoplite infantry operating in phalanx formations. At sea, corresponding innovations improved naval weaponry, moving toward the trireme, and new tactics for ship-to-ship combat. Whether it was the nature of hoplite recruitment (which favored initially wealthier farmers who could afford the armor and later mercenaries) or the fact that most of the population consisted of farmers of variable wealth (the *political-economic* context), some political organizations featured more open mechanisms for circulation of political elites. More overtly, improvements to weaponry and military organization led to larger political organizations with greater expenses—some of which became increasingly ambitious in the scope of their military activities.

The ultimate product of this upward spiral in resource and military mobilization was the Alexandrian conquest of much of the then known world, predicated in part on the Macedonians facing a different type of external threat environment than the Greeks to the south. Macedonians were on the frontier facing Celts and Scythians and learned/developed techniques that were new to Greek/Mediterranean warfare. Subsequent amalgamations of other techniques, ranging from artillery to war elephants, facilitated the expansion of the Alexandrian empire, which fragmented quickly on Alexander's death because political organization (and succession

TABLE 4.4 **Evolution and coevolution in ancient Greece and Rome**

Period	Dating	Threat Environment	Political Organization	Military Organization	Weaponry
Early/middle Bronze Age	3100–1675/50 BCE			Hand-to-hand combat in melee	Swords, spears, javelins, daggers; metal weapons in MBA, leather/wood shields
Mycenaean/early Bronze Age	1650–1100/1050 BCE	Increasing competition in Aegean	Focused on networks of prominent men and followers	Chariot weapon platform with lightly armed support	Chariots, smaller leather/wicker shields for thrusting, more armor; oared galley introduced
Dark Age	1050–850 BCE	—	—	—	—
First half of Classical era	850–500			Initially groups of relatives, friends, neighbors coming together as temporary war bands, no regular or centralized training; hoplites provide own equipment	Spear (with throwing giving way to thrusting), short sword, round shield, bronze armor after 700s, bows

Era	Dates	Military Threats	State Development	Army Organization	Weaponry
Second half of Classical era	500–late 300s BCE	Persian expansion followed by Peloponnesian warfare	States becoming stronger, regular taxes, state borrowing	Separation of heavy/light infantry, horsemen, archers permits focus on phalanx	Throwing spear abandoned
Macedonian/Hellenistic era	359 to Macedonian wars with Rome in first half of second century BCE	Conquest of Greece, Persian Empire giving way to conflict among Hellenistic states and neighbors	Imperial fragmentation into separate states after Alexander's death (323)	Tight phalanx, cavalry, standing force with emphasis on training and drill	Long spear (12–16 feet), artillery and siege craft
Republican Rome	400 BCE–27 BCE	Initially intercity conflict, Celtic intrusions after fourth century, Punic Wars, central Italian expansion by Rome	Republic	Farmer militia, phalanx abandoned in favor of maniple and cohort	Sword and shield emphasis after phalanx abandoned
Imperial Rome	27 BCE–	Multiple threats to extended Roman frontier in Europe, Near East and North Africa	Empire	Professional army recruited from lower classes	Legion infantry increasingly augmented by sophisticated artillery and siege craft

Sources: For Greek warfare, Greenhalgh (1973), Ferrill (1997), Hanson (1991), Bowden (1993), Sage (1996), Monks (2000), Wees (2004), Chaniotis (2005), and Hall (2007). For Roman warfare, Keppie (1984), Harris (1985), Cornell (1995), Campbell (1999), Rosenstein (1999, 2009), Goldsworthy (2003, 2007), Southern (2006), Adams (2007), Alstone (2007), Gabrielsen (2007), Humphries (2007), Lee (2007a, 2007b), Rankow (2007), Rathbone (2007), Sekunda and de Souza (2007), and Serrati (2007).

processes) had not kept up with the expansion of other spheres. In this case, it could be argued that the main interaction is between *threat environment* and *military organization/weaponry*. But the causality patterns are not one way. Threats led to improvement in military organization and weaponry, which in turn led to a wider scope for war.

Rome

The Roman case is undoubtedly the best known of our five areas of focus, in part because it was so prominent in the Mediterranean for a considerable length of time. Yet not that much is known for sure about its early years. For both reasons briefly summarizing its story is a challenge. However, there are two main features of the Roman case that are worth highlighting for our immediate purposes. First, the Romans initially copied the Greek style, found it did not work in their threat environment all that well, modified it considerably, and then, later, conquered the Greeks. Second, the Roman political organization transited through monarchy to republic and then to empire. Its military organization changed in step with the political changes, but the easiest position to defend is that the changes in political and military organization were mutual causal influences on each other. Changes in warfare and military organization made political changes more likely and vice versa.

Early warfare in the Roman area initially took the form of raiding back and forth among more sedentary people residing in the plains and between them and less sedentary people inhabiting the hills. The sedentary warriors often consisted of small groups of armed men led by someone with social rank or wealth—much as in early Greece. At some point in time, the Roman area was subordinated to Etruscan rule, or at least Etruscan rulers. The Etruscans, competitive with Greek traders and colonists operating in Italy, had adopted the phalanx formation for their own armies. It is not known whether the Romans imitated the Etruscans or Greek colonists, but by the sixth century Roman armies had begun operating in a round-shielded, phalanx formation stratified by age and wealth and recruited from clans and tribes. Wealthier individuals served in the cavalry while relative levels of limited affluence determined the rank in the phalanx. The first rank was required to supply armor, sword, spear, and round shield. Other ranks needed to supply less military equipment. The last rank needed only a spear and a shield. The least affluent were relegated to a slinger group at the rear. This approach to organization presumably required some time to emerge, just as it did in Greece.[15] It also shaped Republican voting, with cavalry and first rank qualifiers given much greater weight than lesser propertied citizens.

The military problem was that the phalanx worked reasonably well against other similarly organized military formations. Celtic movement into Italy in the early fourth century, however, changed the nature of the external threat environment. Celts preferred less organized military formations and were able to overwhelm Roman phalanxes in pitched battles; they even managed to burn Rome once. Over roughly a half century following these defeats, Roman military organization was altered in several ways. The phalanx formation had proven too unwieldy in opposing a loosely organized foe. The solution was to reorganize around the maniple principle. This broke the larger formation into a number of smaller units, each of which could operate with more flexibility than one mass that had to maneuver as a group to succeed. Round shields were abandoned in favor of longer, more oval-shaped shields. Javelins were adopted for throwing at the enemy before the two groups came into full physical contact.

The size of the army was expanded, doubling in the first half of the fourth century and then doubling again in the second half. Later reforms introduced the cohort organization that amounted to expanding the size of the maniple by a factor of three, after people realized that maniples were too few in number to avoid being overwhelmed by large numbers of opponents (Rosenstein 1999, 198). In addition, dependence on supply trains was reduced—and mobility enhanced—by requiring soldiers to carry their own food. The property expectations for military service were gradually lowered, with the state assuming the responsibility for supplying military equipment. Swords were adopted as the principal weapon by at least the early second century, possibly copying Carthaginian mercenaries encountered in Spain.

The navy was created in the late fourth century and then greatly expanded in the mid-second century to deal with Carthage. Roman warfare at sea tended to export land combat techniques. Roman ships would ram and grapple or pin an enemy ship so that Roman soldiers could board the enemy vessel and turn a sea battle to their own military advantage. In this respect Roman naval tactics represented something of a regression, but they worked to eliminate all of the maritime competition.

These military reforms contributed to the development of a highly successful military machine. It was so successful in expanding lucrative

Roman territorial control that Roman citizens residing in Italy no longer were required to pay taxes after Macedonian mines were captured in the early to mid-second century BCE. In addition, a distinctive component of Roman power was its ability, through a system of diplomatic incentives, to integrate foreign peoples into Rome and to command their loyalty. This significantly expanded Rome's resource base for competition in the highly competitive Mediterranean system (Eckstein 2006, chap. 7).

The Roman Republic emerged in a constrained environment in which the initial focus of expansion was restricted to central Italy, motivated in part by a consistent demand for more farmland (Harris 1985). By the end of the sixth century, Rome had a population that was less than 40,000 and occupied a territory confined to about 820 square kilometers (Rosenstein 1999, 193). As they gained control of territory increasingly distant from Rome, military commands and commanders developed some autonomy. As campaigns dragged on, soldier-farmers returned home to neglected farms they no longer owned or could cultivate. The traditional recruitment pool began to shrink. Lower-class recruits became more common. The political system evolved along parallel lines with wealthy individuals who had worked their way out of the lower class being allowed to hold political office in the fourth century.

These outcomes had implications for the larger Roman political economy. Smaller farms were sold to people who operated large estates manned by slaves acquired in foreign conquests (Rosenstein 1999, 207). For one indicator of the significance of slave labor to the Roman economy, Harris (1985, 59) notes that sixty thousand people were enslaved in 297–293 BCE by a population that numbered two hundred thousand adult males. Shifting from local to more distant warfare also meant that Roman conquests would no longer expand the stock of public lands available to Roman citizens. The clamor for land redistribution in Roman politics generally centered on the redistribution of public lands to landless citizens. Domestic consequences included political unrest over demands for land reform and periodic slave revolts. Along similar lines, Hopkins (1977) contends that the key to the fall of the Roman Empire was its ultimate inability to continue expanding and thereby resupplying the slave labor force on which the agrarian empire increasingly relied.

Legions began showing more loyalty to their commanders than to the state, in part because commanders were expected to provide for the welfare of their troops during and after military service. Commanders and to a lesser extent soldiers also became richer by exploiting opportunities to gain loot in foreign conquests. Not surprisingly, campaigns against rich foes were favored over less lucrative garrison duty.

At the same time successful military commands became the primary route to political success in Republican institutions. Army operations were also one of the primary activities undertaken by the state. In short, the military organization's political salience in a state geared to widespread and highly profitable territorial expansion rose to the point that it could determine who ruled in the state should problems arise in the political succession process. Leading military commanders could utilize the legions they controlled and the resources of the provinces in which they were assigned to contest leadership. As a consequence the first century BCE was characterized by considerable domestic political instability and civil war.

The Roman Republic gave way to the Roman Empire. A state relying on a farmer militia gave way to a professional army recruited from the lower class. In the process the legions became more permanent, more cohesive, and better trained and disciplined. They developed more esprit de corps because members of a legion were likely to remain in one group throughout their military service. They could sustain more specialization in auxiliary combat skills such as artillery and siege craft. But they also became political weapons that could and were used repeatedly in domestic politics to determine who would become emperor. Soldiers had long since ceased being farmers who were part-time soldiers when no harvest was due. The gulf between civilians and the military became greater, and the support of the army became increasingly critical to political power. Even civilian politicians were eventually cut off from chances to command military forces when senators were denied the long-held right to command in the imperial period.

The Roman story (see table 4.4), therefore, can be reduced to a change in the *external threat environment* (the Celtic movement south into Italy) leading to a change in *military organization* and *weaponry*. The new military organization and weaponry worked quite well but their success undermined the agrarian *political economy* and the military organization's recruitment processes, leading to new military recruitment practices focused on obtaining soldiers from lower-class backgrounds. Relying initially on part-time soldiers who returned to their farms when not campaigning, longer-lasting campaigns farther away from Italy meant that soldiers were forced to stay away from their farms too long to hang on to them or to make them productive. Military organization worked better, given the demands of frequent and far-flung warfare, if soldiers stayed in the same units for long periods of time. A by-product, however, was that army commanders found that they could use soldier identifications with their legion as political weapons to influence decisions in the central *political organization*, or to simply take it over. In some respects it can also be argued that the overall system of empire could only be sustained by continuous expansion. Once the Roman Empire encountered limitation on its expansion in any and all directions, neither the military organization, its political economy, nor the central political organization could be sustained, any more than they were sustained in the shift from republic to empire.

Case III: Ancient China

Readers familiar with the Great Wall may have some sense of China's threat environment, but the obsession with holding off nomadic attacks from the northwest was something that took considerable time to develop (Di Cosmo 2002). Human settlements in the Yellow River valley go back thousands of years, but useful information about political-military developments only begin to surface after 2000 BCE. Even then the information is quite hazy. There may have been some form of political centralization focused on the Xia dynasty that engaged in occasional raids against peripheral tribes and vice versa. Bronze weapons first appear in this time period and may have been brought in via Central Asia. But not much more is known. Underhill (2006, 278–79) notes that the archaeological evidence speaks against the threat of warfare being a significant causal factor in the early development of Chinese states. As the Chinese state became more powerful, however, its warfare became more frequent and lethal. Nomads developed threatening offensive capabilities in eastern Asia in the second half of the first millennium BCE.

Table 4.5 looks at our key coevolutionary variables across various periods of Chinese political history. The cells start to become easier to fill with the Shang dynasty, the first undisputed episode of political centralization around relatively powerful clans that created a state with a reach of about one hundred miles away from the imperial center.[16] Li Liu and Xingcan Chen (2003, 141–48) contend that these earliest states in China cycled back and forth from more and less centralization because growth in urban cores exceeded the supply of available resources. One solution was the redistribution of population to more peripheral areas, which reduced pressures on the core and also expanded access to new raw materials (especially copper, tin, and lead). But some of the peripheral areas eventually became more densely populated, prosperous, and increasingly independent from the initial core area, which, in turn, experienced decline as its control of raw material flows from a less subordinate periphery declined.

The threat from tribes that were even more peripheral remained limited, but armies were created that were focused on elites operating in chariots used as moving platforms from which to fire arrows. Lightly armed infantry called up from peasants living near the ruling center supported the chariots. As a consequence, army operations had to be coordinated with agricultural demands. There seems to be no question that the chariots, although modified by the Chinese, had been introduced into China via Central Asia and, presumably, were important to the initial ascent of the Shang elites. Military expeditions of this era may have averaged three thousand to five thousand men in size (Peers 2006; Underhill 2006).

The Zhou had once been subordinate to the Shang dynasty, but with the help of western tribal allies they were able to overthrow Shang rule in the late eleventh century.[17] The Zhou created what was to become an increasingly decentralized political system of their own by bestowing the control over a number of walled towns to elites in the winning coalition. A number of the walled towns subsequently became increasingly independent.[18] The external threat from the "barbarian" tribes increased and by 770 BCE had forced the Zhou central power to move its operations farther east to a more secure site.[19]

Zhou armies were initially configured much like those of the Shang, but chariots gradually lost their central significance because they fared poorly in rocky or swampy terrain. They were supplanted by an increased emphasis on ever-larger infantries, which were less expensive and which were enhanced in effectiveness by iron weapons, improved armor, and crossbows (Lewis 1990). In the first half of the first millennium BCE, a large army might consist of thirty thousand infantry (Peers 2006, 18). Prior to the sixth century, however, ten-thousand-man armies were more typical, with their campaigns lasting only a few weeks and battles decided in a single day (Graff 2002a).

By the fifth century BCE chariots had declined in their military utility. Swords had lengthened and become the most predominant weapon. Iron had begun to appear in weapon/armor applications. The crossbow, with its improved range and penetrating power, also began to be used in this era. Armies swelled to several hundred thousands men; near-continuous warfare and battles that persisted for months were common (Graff 2002a).

TABLE 4.5 **Evolution and coevolution in ancient China**

Period	Dating	Threat Environment	Political Organization	Military Organization	Weaponry
Shang	2000–1500 BCE	Sporadic raiding			Bronze weapons
	1500–1000 BCE	Limited	Gradually increasing power over delimited territory	Elite chariot/archer-centered supported by peasantry infantry	Bows, spears, axes, leather shields
Zhou	1027–479 BCE	Increasing competition among states; increasing barbarian capability after 770 BCE	Increasingly decentralized as Zhou relative/allies become nobility in control of walled towns	Chariot-centered with peasant-based infantry becoming more important towards end; army sizes increasing substantially	Improved chariots and axes; sword appears
Warring states	479–	Hundreds of states reduced to small number in continuous warfare	Few states becoming stronger by absorbing smaller states and barbarian population	Chariot in decline; cavalry introduced; infantry larger and better trained	Sword predominates over bow; crossbow and iron weapons appear; mainly leather armor
Qin/Han	221 BCE–189 CE	Qin/Han empires established; interior demilitarized; main threat from Xiongnu nomads in steppes	Recentralized state with single autocratic ruler	Standing army emerges with infantry predominant but cavalry important in west	Crossbow significance increases; armor more common
Three Kingdoms/Ts'in	189–589 CE	Initial competition among three main states giving way to barbarian invasions after 316	Fragmentation devolving into multiple warlords	Increasing emphasis on heavy cavalry, along with infantry	Lances and bows; armored riders and horses; stirrups introduced

Sources: Based on information found in Lewis (1990, 2007), Yates (1999), Dreyer (2002), Graff (2002a, 2002b), Wright (2002), Li (2004), and Peers (2006).

Despite their declining utility, between the 600s and late 500s the size of chariot forces expanded by a factor of five. This was substantial, but the more significant point is that armies increased in size tenfold during the same period (Lewis 1990, 53).

Prior to the "warring states" era, which began in 479 BCE, China consisted of a large number of states of varying size contesting over their relative positions and the opportunity to recreate a centralized empire. Remaining competitive or even autonomous involved expanding the population size and wealth of the state. In some cases this could be accomplished by absorbing adjacent peripheral tribes. In others, peasants could be induced to move to a state by the lure of free land. Not coincidentally, the Chinese population more than tripled in the early Iron Age first millennium BCE. The demand for agricultural land expanded. Iron plows had increased the food supply and thus the size of the population that could be sustained. This meant larger armies as well (Graff 2002a).

Another strategy for remaining competitive was to defeat and absorb a neighboring state. Thus warfare became near continuous as literally hundreds of states were whittled down to initially eight major powers and then three large ones. One of the three, Qin, conquered the other two and briefly reestablished a centralized political organization in 221 BCE. By this time, cavalry had been introduced by copying the methods used by nomads. Very large infantries—armed with crossbows, increasingly armored, with longer periods of military training— became the competitive norm. Qin claimed armies ranging from one hundred thousand to six hundred thousand in size before it defeated its rivals (Peers 2006; Lewis 2007).

One of the by-products of this concentration process was the obsolescence of small city-states that could no longer compete successfully (Lewis 2007). Traditional aristocracies lost much of their power and autonomy to autocratizing states learning how to develop bureaucracies that could enlist peasants and collect taxes from them as well. Imperial administration was organized in terms of military districts. The new Chinese state was further militarized, at least initially, by creating social hierarchies based on military ranks and performance. The centralization of power was achieved by constructing an empire in the image of a military machine.

The Qin dynasty quickly disintegrated, but the Han took its place. One of the innovations of the Han was to demilitarize the interior of China and to place its military forces on the border to contend with what had become the main source of external threat, the Xiongnu nomads. The Xiongnu nomads, essentially a coalition of different ethnic groups, had only gradually become increasingly threatening on the northwestern frontier between the eighth century BCE and second century BCE. Acquiring horses and developing light cavalry prowess made a considerable difference. So did the coercive exertion of dominance over the nomadic tribes and forcing resistance to abandon their traditional territory (moving either east or west).

The demilitarization of the interior had the added advantage of making anti-Han rebellions less potent, but it also meant that if the border barriers were breached, there was little to stop external incursions into, and ultimately, conquests of China. Infantry, armored and armed with crossbows, remained the principal army arm, but cavalry, often recruited from nomads who were hostile to the Xiongnu, were indispensable on the steppe frontiers. Infantry recruitment was based initially on a mixture of conscription, volunteers, and prisoners.

Conscription was abandoned in 31 CE, however, as part of the interior demilitarization strategy. Why create a pool of peasants with weapon experience that might be used in a domestic revolt? Their place was taken by peripheral tribesmen who were able to deflect and defeat the Xiongnu threat but who became politically dangerous in their own right, as the Han lost control of the frontiers to their own cavalry and various warlords (Lewis 2007). As Mark Lewis (2007) notes, the Han empire could recruit nomadic enemies of the Xiongnu to serve as frontier cavalry, but they could not expect them to remain loyal to the Han once their enemies had been defeated (and after Han subsidies had diminished).

The Han dynasty persisted to 189 CE before a decentralized standoff among three large provinces (the Three Kingdoms) that had become effectively independent initiated a new round of warring states battling with one another for supremacy (and remilitarizing the Chinese interior to so some extent) and imperial reunification, which gave way eventually to successful northern invasions. Heavy cavalry armed with lances became increasingly significant in these contests, a switch facilitated by the invention of the stirrup.[20] Infantry were primarily used as bowmen, but that does not mean armies had become smaller. At least one army of four hundred thousand operated in this period (Peers 2006).

Ancient Chinese developments were thus focused on the interactions between *political organizations* (dynasties) and their cyclical attempts at ordering the *political economy*. *Weapon* innovations (bronze, chariots, iron, cavalry borrowed from nomads), at various points in time, appear to have contributed to the ascension of new elites and centralized political organization. The *external threat environment*, initially relatively benign, became more dangerous as nomads developed light cavalry skills. The *internal threat environment*, as central political organization decayed and fragmented, was probably more critical in leading to ever larger *military organization* and more bureaucratic states as epitomized by the Han empire. Once established, the Han empire had to turn its attention to defending its northern and northwestern boundaries from stronger opponents. The change in strategy, in response to a gradual change in the nature of the external threat environment, made the empire more dependent on its frontier cavalry since the interior had been demilitarized as a domestic political control scheme. The frontier cavalry, in turn, became more independent and less efficacious, eventually leading to the breakdown of the imperial center in the face of northern invasions.

Case IV: Mesoamerica

The Mesoamerican trajectory is the shortest one reviewed in this chapter, lasting only about 2,650 years. It is also the one characterized by the least evolution and coevolution in our key variables, as described in table 4.6. The trajectory involves a sequence of four powerful groups that barely overlapped at times and that operated, most of the time, in a limited threat environment prior to the arrival of the Spanish. Although there were some changes in weaponry, very few changes are discernible in political or military organizations.

Mesoamerica was initially characterized by the hunting-gathering mode of only occasional raiding due to the relative absence of anything to seize. Even territory was rarely worth fighting about because there was always other land to be had elsewhere. Agricultural development changed this state of affairs by making settlements larger and more permanent. The value of territory and territorial defense increased along with economic, social, and political stratification.

The foremost authority on Mesoamerican military development, Ross Hassig (1992), attributes the emergence of organized warfare to the rise of the Olmecs in the late second millennium BCE. While the Olmecs lacked threatening neighbors, they did engage in extensive trading activities that required defense. If the primary function of armed force is to provide security for trading groups, it should not be surprising to find that their

TABLE 4.6 **Evolution and coevolution in ancient Mesoamerica**

Period	Dating	Threat Environment	Political Organization	Military Organization	Weaponry
Olmecs	1150–550 BCE	Primarily raids on long distance trade		Very small	Spears, clubs, maces, slings; armor rare
Olmecs		Localized conflicts			Wood and leather shields appear
Teotihuacán	First century–750 CE	Relative absence of powerful and adjacent enemies; trade protection	City focused with theocratic rule	Relatively larger than predecessor	Thrusting spear predominant; atlatls, slings; helmets and shields; quilted cotton armor introduced
Toltecs	900–1200 CE	Initially trade protection; Chichimec invasion from north with bows toward end	City focused with theocratic rule giving way to warrior rule	Relatively larger than predecessor	Atlatls, slings, short sword supplants spear
Aztecs	1300s–early 1500s CE	Imperial expansion and subordination of resistance	Empire and indirect hegemony—warrior rule	Up to 8,000 for specific campaigns	Bows, broadswords, thrusting spears, clubs, shields, body armor

Source: Based on information found in Hassig (1988, 1992).

numbers were quite small—estimated to be between twenty-five and fifty specialized warriors. Initially oriented toward shock weapons (clubs and spears), the later development of slings provided some longer-range projectile capability. Combat would have been quite limited in duration and scope. As trade competition increased, the Olmecs apparently did not choose to defend their resource acquisition networks but instead simply withdrew from contested areas.

Teotihuacán was the next strong power to emerge. As in the case of the Olmecs, the Teotihuacáno lacked threatening neighbors but did engage in long-distance trading operations. Weaponry had improved. Wood and leather shields, helmets, thrusting spears, slings, and atlatls predominated.[21] Some quilted cotton armor came into use but only after the Teotihuacán activity had peaked. The size of the military forces increased but by precisely how much is not clear. Unlike the Olmecs, Teotihuacán was more prepared to defend its trading network as competition increased, but the costs of doing so may have made the trading operations too expensive to continue.

A few hundred years after the collapse of Teotihuacán, the Toltecs enjoyed a brief period of trading empire hegemony. Smaller in population size than their predecessor, Mesoamerican weapons development continued with short swords supplanting spears as the weapon of choice in hand-to-hand combat. The Toltec collapse was brought on by a conjuncture of drought, famine, rebellion, and nomadic incursions from the north. While on foot, the nomads, armed with bows, enjoyed an advantage in projectile capability over the bowless Toltecs. They did not conquer the Toltecs but contributed to the disintegration of their trading empire.

The fourth and last pre-1500 group to establish hegemony in central Mexico was the Aztecs. Originally Chichimec nomads who had moved south in the thirteenth century, the Aztecs imitated the more sedentary states they encountered in some respects. In particular they adopted local military organization and weapons, extending the lineage initiated by the Olmecs. One area in which they were less imitative was the empire they eventually established. The area in which they had settled was too lacking in agricultural potential to feed the newly settled tribe. One way to cope with that problem was to create a tribute system that could draw in food from surrounding areas.

Such a system required a fair amount of coercion. The Aztecs already possessed bows. They added a broadsword with greater reach than had been known previously. More elite warriors wore armor, helmets, carried shields, and wielded shock weapons. Nonelites specialized in bow and sling. Army size may have reached as high as eight thousand men under arms for specific campaigns. But since successful expansion could not lead to military occupation without exceeding a sustainable number of garrison troops, the type of hegemony that was established relied on indirect rule through local elites. Maintaining this system meant that the Aztecs had to convince their subordinated populations that they possessed military superiority in central Mexico. The more successful their reputation was, the less military force had to be applied. In return, the Aztecs would receive agricultural tribute and military assistance when requested.

As with other cases, the Aztec imperial dynamic was one that could not rest on its laurels. Army training in specialized weaponry, larger armies, and extensive logistical support structures had to be maintained. Population growth required more tribute. More tribute implied more population growth. The monarchy's elite political support, moreover, depended on sustaining elite prosperity. As long as Aztec success could be kept in motion, the system worked to the Aztec advantage and created an empire that did not resemble the weaker acquisition networks established by its predecessors in either intent or scale. But it also possessed an organizational weakness. If its reputation was seriously damaged, the Aztec imperial house of cards could unravel. This is precisely what Hernán Cortés managed to do with a relatively small number of Spanish troops, with the helpful assistance of indigenous allies eager to overthrow the Aztec hegemony, and with other important factors such as European diseases.[22]

In the Mesoamerican case, hunting-foraging *political economy* gave way to scattered agrarian settlements and an emphasis on trading in which Olmec, Teotihuacáno, and Toltec settlements initially led. *Military organization* and *weaponry* requirements were limited to protecting trading missions until the Chichimec intrusion from the north shifted the political-economic system to one of informal hegemony and empire. Throughout the Mesoamerican experience, military organizations and weaponry innovations remained restricted in part because the nature of *external threats* were limited and not subject to much change. Climate and little in the way of either wheels or metallurgy also helped limit the extent of change prior to the major shift in the nature of the external threat environment and the arrival of the Spanish. Climate, for instance, discouraged the development of armor beyond thickening the layers of cotton padding. So did the absence of bronze and iron for making protective plates to shield heads, chests, and shins.

Comparison of the Four Cases

Each of the four cases experienced evolution, coevolution, and acceleration. In the Egyptian case, the acceleration within the Egyptian trajectory occurred post-Hyksos during the New Kingdom, or shortly before the second half of the second millennium BCE. The Greek acceleration encompassed the Persian wars, the Peloponnesian wars, and the Macedonian conquests all in the second half of the first millennium BCE. Rome's accelerated trajectory began in the last few centuries of the first millennium BCE and continued into the first millennium CE. As in the Greek case, China's acceleration began in the warring states era and ended in the Qin-Han empires—all mainly in the second half of the first millennium BCE. Only the Mesoamerican case's acceleration, the most modest of the five, did not take place until near the middle of the second millennium CE.

Our starting point was the hypothesis that there were two eras of acceleration in agrarian warfare. The accelerations in the five cases encompass nearly three thousand years. How can we view a three-millennium interval as a period of acceleration without insisting on a conceptualization that is so elastic that nearly anything might fit? We see this problem as one of interpretation. Gabriel's (2002) first acceleration came in the Bronze Age and refers primarily to the states and armies that initially emerged in Mesopotamia and Egypt in the fourth millennium BCE. The Egyptian New Kingdom acceleration can be interpreted in several ways. One is to see it as a delayed culmination of the first acceleration—not unlike Sargon's Akkadian empire in Mesopotamia in the second half of the third millennium BCE. Another way is to view it as a premonition of what was to come in the Mediterranean a millennium later. Either way, it is something of a badly fitting oddity that might best be viewed as a bridge from one Bronze Age acceleration to the next one in the early Iron Age. What is clear is that the Egyptian trajectory faded away to a long series of foreign conquests after 1000 BCE. In this respect it can also be seen as an aborted trajectory.

The core of the second acceleration is best captured by the activities in Greece, Rome, and China. They share at least one background condition, the advent of iron metallurgy, which vastly improved agricultural productivity and consequently led to increases in population sizes. They also share the important common denominator of the intensification of warfare (and the threat environments) between competing states. The outcomes were similar as well in that one state (first Macedonia, then Rome in the west and Qin-Han in the east) defeated their competition and established geographically extended empires at the two ends of Eurasia that survived for a century or two into the first millennium CE. Eurasian military development was thus accelerated by a half-millennium of intensive warfare with various reverberations in related sectors of development. Weapons became much more lethal, military organizations became larger and more complex, and states became more powerful. It was not the last Eurasian acceleration. A third one occurred primarily in western Europe, but it was linked to gunpowder and industrialization, not agrarian productivity.

The Mesoamerican trajectory stands in contrast to the pace of development in Eurasia. For much of the time the Mesoamerican threat environment was much different from anything found in Eurasia. So were political-economic developments. Most noticeably, the advent of bronze and iron cannot be expected to have similar implications in areas in which metallurgy was much more marginally developed. Accordingly, the Mesoamerican trajectory evolved slowly. New weapons were added to the inventory. Military forces became larger in conjunction with larger populations. Panregional imperialism did not emerge, however, until Aztecs entered the picture. The Mesoamerican trajectory serves us here as a major contrast to what took place in Eurasia.

Thus the accelerations are characterized by marked unevenness. They did not occur everywhere and at the same time. The first agrarian/Bronze Age acceleration was limited initially to parts of the Near East or southwest Asia. The second agrarian/Iron Age acceleration was focused predominately in China and the Mediterranean.[23] It was certainly not a pan-Eurasian phenomenon. Smaller, lower-scaled accelerations can be found in sub-Saharan Africa and the Americas at other times, but none seem comparable to the two major agrarian accelerations focused on in this chapter.

Coevolutionary developments in the Eurasian accelerations and elsewhere are quite noticeable as well. Our six-sector ensemble seems to hold up well in another test of its applicability. Different threat environments tend to lead, among other things, to different types of political organizations, military organizations, and weapons, along with the interactions among these sectors. The initial ecological security of the Nile River environs led to a fragile political unification in which control over military force remained less than unified. Only when the security of the Egyptian niche was shattered did Egyptian military developments begin to catch up with the rest of the Mediterranean world.

First millennium BCE Greece, unlike the preceding Minoan/Mycenaean millennium, was initially divided into a large number of agrarian communities quarreling over farmlands that were defended by farmer militias. Over time, some of those communities became competitive states with increasingly professional armies. The Greek subsystem became increasingly integrated with the rest of the eastern Mediterranean as first Persians and then Greeks attempted to expand the scope of their geopolitical control. Rome went through a similar evolution and ended up as the largest empire ever experienced in western Eurasia.

China's threat environment began in a low-key version of sedentary settlements surrounded by nonsedentary tribes (initially on foot). The initial question was which dynastic families would rule the sedentary settlements. In the first millennium BCE, the threat environment had been transformed into a highly competitive, multistate system intensely caught up in continuous warfare. To survive this transformation (and at the same time to serve as agents of transformation), states and armies had to become larger and more militarily capable in terms of organization and weaponry. A third transformation of the threat environment refocused attention on horse-riding nomads and reinforced the coercive unification of China.

The Mesoamerican story is different from the Eurasian ones but still reflects coevolution. In Mesoamerica it is an interaction between an initially benign threat environment and the political economy of long distance trade that leads to limited military developments. When trade gave way to tribute, the Aztec state and military had little choice but to become more powerful and more complex than its predecessors in order to carry out its more demanding mission.

Yet it is not merely a matter of threat environments influencing the other five sectors. On occasion new weapons can lead to military reorganization. Chariots in Egypt and China are one example. Bows have had significant impacts as levelers of aristocratic stratification in China (crossbows) and later in western Europe. Although there are claims to the contrary, we think that weapons are not the most likely source of changes that stimulate sequences of coevolutionary change. Changes in threat environment, as noted above, may be one of the most important stimulator of coevolutionary change, but changes in political organization, political economy, and military organization also have had important repercussions.

In the Roman case it is very difficult to disentangle the chicken-and-egg nature of change in military and political organization within the context of a changing political economy. The legions were moving toward greater professionalism, autonomy from civilian society, and politicization at the same time as the Republic was transiting toward Empire. The changes in the political and military organizations mutually reinforced each other. Underlying and interacting with these changes were critical changes in the Roman political economy—small farms giving way to large estates, slave labor, and the expanding role of conquest plunder as the Roman imperial reach widened.

Equally striking is that each of the five trajectories is distinctly unique. None of the five exactly parallels any of the other four. Yet the six-factor framework appears to work equally well regardless of the time or location. In ancient Egypt, threat environment and political organization elements loom large. For the Greeks, a triangle connecting political organization, military organization, and weaponry is most prominent. The interaction between threat environment and political organization was most influential in initiating change in the Chinese trajectory. The Roman trajectory seems to have pivoted around political and military organization with a strong political-economic dimension. In the Mesoamerican outlier, political-economic changes in the form of creating successive trade acquisition networks took place in a relatively low threat environment. Military force supported the acquisition networks, and the military expanded in number over time but without much change in organization or weaponry.

Although it might be preferable to have a rigid theory specifying that a change in factor X always leads to a change in factor Y, the flexibility of the six-factor coevolutionary theory serves us well in explaining evolving relationships in ancient systems. The question is whether the same framework works equally well in more recent times. We think that will be demonstrated in chapter 6's treatment of the western trajectory as a long whole. Before we look at that long trajectory, however, we need to turn to the last five hundred years of the western trajectory and the third asserted evolutionary acceleration. This period is usually discussed in terms of arguments about various military revolutions. We think the six-factor coevolutionary package can do better and perhaps reduce some of the points of friction between contending interpretations. The third acceleration period also is important for our claims that this period ultimately generated new or more effective constraints on certain kinds of warfare. We seek to elaborate that claim in the next chapter as well.

CHAPTER FIVE

The Third Evolutionary Acceleration

After examining the origins of warfare—the first evolutionary acceleration centered in Mesopotamia and to a lesser extent Egypt, and the second evolutionary acceleration centered in the Greco-Roman Mediterranean and warring states/Qin/Han China—we now turn to the third evolutionary acceleration, which occurred during the last five centuries of the modern era. This acceleration was centered in Europe and was led by the European great powers, but its repercussions were experienced worldwide, and it played a central role in the evolution of the modern European and world systems.

In contrast with our case-oriented focus in chapter 4, in this chapter we focus on basic processes at work, in part because the circumstances are more familiar and allow us to say more. All of Europe did not participate equally in this acceleration and was not equally affected by the changes that occurred. On land, sequential Italian, Spanish, French, and German innovations led the way to new forms of army structure, weaponry, and logistics. At sea, the sequence of Genoa, Venice, Portugal, the Netherlands, and Britain as leading naval powers blazed new ways to engage in maritime combat. We will return to these innovators in chapter 6. In this chapter, however, our focus is placed on a more general explanation of why and how largely European great power warfare became more severe but also less frequent in the third period of acceleration. Not surprisingly, our explanation will revolve around coevolutionary changes in weaponry, military and political organizations, threat environments, political economy, and war.

There is little doubt that much of the increasing severity of war in the modern era is due to developments in military weaponry technology.[1] As Carl von Clausewitz ([1832] 1976) reminds us, however, war and the technology of war do not comprise a self-contained system, and an analysis of war cannot neglect its political core.² A complete understanding of war, and the increasing severity of war in particular, requires attention to the economic, social, and political factors that affect war's outbreak, conduct, and consequences. These other factors can affect war directly, but they also can affect the conduct of war through their interaction effects with military technology. In particular it is the weaponry, military and political organization, threat environment, and domestic political economy that combine to explain many of the changes in warfare over time. These are the core elements of our coevolutionary framework. They are also central, even if less explicitly stated, in historical analyses of the "military revolution" in early modern Europe.

Conceptions of Military Revolutions

Contemporary analysts and observers are probably familiar with the concept of the "revolution in military affairs" (RMA), which is commonly used to describe the fundamental transformation in the nature of warfare resulting from the application of new information-based technologies at the end of the twentieth century (Nye and Owens 1996; Arquilla and Ronfledt 1997; Owens with Offley 2000; O'Hanlon 2000; Gray 2002).³ The concept of a revolution in military affairs is quite familiar to historians who talk about the "military revolution" of early modern Europe (1500–1660), one that is often linked to the origins of the modern state (Roberts [1955] 1995; Parker 1988; Black 1991). Interest in the current revolution in military affairs, in conjunction with ongoing debates about the earlier military revolution, have led historians and some political scientists to speculate about additional military revolutions in the last six or seven centuries (Rogers 1995; Knox and Murray 2001). We build on that literature here, while acknowledging, as noted in earlier chapters, some potential analytic problems in both contemporary and historical applications of the concept (Gray 2002).

Scholars disagree on exactly how to define a revolution in military affairs, how we can recognize one when we see one, how many such revolutions have occurred, and whether the concept is in fact a useful one. Krepinevich (1994), for example, identifies ten military revolutions since the fourteenth century. Murray (1997) identifies four major revolutions and over twenty minor ones over the same period. Gray (2002) emphasizes three in the last two hundred years.

One thing many analysts agree on, however, is that there are different kinds of military revolutions, defined in part by their scope and impact. Some military revolutions are limited to changes in military technology, operational doctrine, and tactics. Others go beyond the tactical, operational, and strategic levels and encompass broader changes in the organization of military bureaucracies, civil-military relations, and the political and social organization of society. There is disagreement and confusion, however, as to how to label these different forms of revolutionary developments. Sullivan (1998) defines "military technical revolutions" (MTRs) narrowly to refer to changes that are limited to military technology, operational doctrine, and tactics, while defining the concept of "revolutions in military affairs" (RMAs) more broadly to refer to changes that go beyond MTRs to include broader organizational and political change. Murray (1997) does the opposite and defines "military revolutions" broadly to include organizational and political change and RMAs more narrowly in terms of technology and doctrine.

Another problem is that analysts are not always clear in differentiating the military revolution phenomenon from its causal antecedents or consequences, or in sorting out the precise causal linkages among these different variables. For example, lists of military revolutions in early modern Europe include a "gunpowder" and a "fortress" revolution (Krepinevich 1994), operational changes associated with each, and the development of the modern state (Murray 1997). Scholars are often not clear, however, whether the development of the modern state was constitutive of the military revolution, in the sense that it helps to define it, or whether the growth of the state was the consequence of such a revolution. It could also be both, of course, with reciprocal causal influences. What is important for our purposes is that military technology, strategy, and organization, along with the political organization of society and political economy, and their threat environment, all interact and coevolve together over time.

Table 5.1 charts the timing of a number of hypothesized military revolutions. Scholars clearly disagree about the timing of specific military revolutions. Our aim here, however, is not to work out these disagreements about which period of change is most significant. Rather, we interpret the list of changes identified in table 5.1 as a sequence of coevolutionary changes that define our third evolutionary acceleration period.

We have argued that evolution of warfare encompasses both continuity and change, and that some changes are revolutionary while others are gradual. One problem with standard conceptions of military revolutions is that they overemphasize the revolutionary components of change relative

TABLE 5.1 **The timing of hypothesized military revolutions**

Military Revolution and Focus	Timing	Source
Medieval organization of war	Twelfth–thirteenth centuries	Prestowich (1996)
Infantry	1330s–1340s	Rogers (1995)
Artillery	1420s–1440s	Rogers (1995)
Artillery fortress	1470–1530	Parker (1988), Black (1991), Rogers (1995)
Infantry	1560–1660	Roberts ([1955] 1995), Rothenberg (1986), Parker (1988), Rogers (1995)
Infantry	1680–1720	Black (1991, 1995)
Infantry	1792–1815	Paret (1983, 1986), Black (1991, 1995), Jones (1987), Parker (1988)
Infantry and artillery	1914–1918	Preston and Wise (1979), Brodie and Brodie (1973), Jones (1987)
Total war	1939–1945	Preston and Wise (1979), Brodie and Brodie (1973), Jones (1987)
Information age		Nye and Owens (1966), Cohen (1996)

Source: The military revolution information is based on a rearrangement of material found in Thompson and Rasler (1999, 9).

to more gradual elements (Gray 2002). Some argue that the evolution of warfare, and of military technology itself, is better described as a process involving incremental change (McNeill 1982). While some emphasize revolutionary change and others emphasize a series of incremental changes, a third perspective combines both revolutionary and gradual change components. This is the "punctuated equilibrium" model of warfare, which Clifford Rogers (1993) adapts from evolutionary biology (Eldredge and Gould 1972).

In the punctuated equilibrium model a sudden burst of innovation generates a new form of warfare and a period of stable equilibrium. The nature of warfare during such periods changes, but only incrementally, until a new burst of radical innovation—driven by incentives to gain an advantage, external shocks, and conceptual breakthroughs—transforms warfare once again. From this perspective warfare evolves through a sequence of discrete and relatively short revolutionary changes punctuated by long periods of gradual change within a stable equilibrium.[4] In this discussion we will give more attention to revolutionary developments, but we recognize that the relative impact of revolutionary and gradual factors, and the interaction between them, is an extraordinarily difficult theoretical and empirical question. Our more general solution to the conceptual problems inherent in discussing early modern and modern military revolutions is to refer to the last five hundred years as a third acceleration of warfare—not unlike the second one in duration, if not entirely in consequences.

One way to frame an analysis of the third acceleration in war's coevolutionary patterns is to seek an explanation for the declining frequency and increasing severity of great power war over the last five hundred years. Of course there are other questions we might ask, but this one should serve our immediate purposes well. We begin with the severity question because we think the trend toward greater severity is a major cause of its declining frequency. But the underlying causal relationships are more complex than a simple equation of greater severity leads to less frequency might suggest.

The Increasing Severity of Great Power War

Patterns in great power war during the last five hundred years are fairly clear, as we saw in figures 1.3 and 1.4 in chapter 1.[5] The frequency of great power war decreased continuously from the sixteenth to the nineteenth centuries, increased in the first half of the twentieth century, and sharply declined after that, culminating after World War II in the longest period of great power peace in the last five centuries. The severity of great power war, however, has been steadily increasing during the same period, while the duration of those wars has remained relatively constant. There is not much controversy about the nature of these trends. Our aim here is to explain them, and to do so within the coevolutionary framework developed in preceding chapters.

Military Weaponry and Technology

As we noted earlier, one unambiguous source of the increasing severity of great power war, and probably the first one that generally comes to mind, is the increasing destructiveness of military technology over time. The potency of weapons systems has increased steadily in range, accuracy, volume of fire, mobility, and penetrability. Along with improvements in the speed and efficiency of military transport and communications systems and the growth in the economic capacity to produce a larger quantity of weapons and support systems, this has contributed to the increasing destructiveness of war on the battlefield. Many of the advances in weapons systems derive from a series of relatively well-defined, radical innovations in military technology. It is important to note, however, that these radical innovations often overlay and reinforce one another rather than completely replace one another (Murray 1997).

One of the first major European innovations in military technology since the time of the Crusades was the development of the longbow in the fourteenth century. The longbow had an impact on European warfare despite the fact that it was used almost exclusively, and quite effectively, by the English, who developed the weapons and trained archers in its use.[6] By increasing the ability of archers to penetrate the armor of cavalrymen, the longbow, along with associated tactical innovations, contributed to a sharp increase in casualties on the battlefield. The need to give the knight greater protection led to the replacement of chain mail by plate armor, which significantly reduced the knight's mobility. One result was the short-lived dominance of heavy cavalry giving way to a return to the dominance of infantry, sometimes referred to as the "infantry revolution" (Rogers 1993). Along with a revival of military architecture stimulated by the Crusades, these developments contributed to the superiority of the defense in warfare (Levy 1984, 230–31).

The infantry revolution was followed a century later by the "artillery revolution" (Rogers 1993; Krepinevich 1994), which continued into the sixteenth century and which some call the "gunpowder revolution." The lengthening of gun barrels increased the range and destructiveness of artillery and the corning of gunpowder increased its destructive power, while breakthroughs in metallurgy (along with corning) reduced the cost of artillery and made it more widely available. These developments increased the severity of war on the battlefield. They also furthered the power of the offense, facilitated territorial conquest, and contributed to the expansion and consolidation of a small number of great powers (Wright 1965, 294). The new power of the offense was symbolized by the siege of Constantinople in 1453, where the Turks overran the greatest of all medieval fortresses in less than two months.

The increasing power of the offense was soon countered by the development of a new defensive fortification system, the *trace italienne*, which had thicker, ramped walls and protruding bastions (Parker 1988; Lynn

1995). The *trace* could better withstand bombardment than earlier fortresses, and its arrow-shaped bastions provided flanking fire (Parker 1988, 10–11; Lynn 1995, 172–73). The diffusion of the *trace* across Europe and the consequent increase in the importance of sieges led to changes in the composition of armies, which included an increase in the proportion of infantry, a decrease in the proportion of cavalry, and the emergence of specialized engineers who were trained in the science of fortification and siege craft (Parker 1988: 12–13, 156). It also contributed to a renewed power of the defense. Thus Ernest Dupuy and Trevor Dupuy (1977, 45) argue that "a 16th century fortress . . . was as impregnable as the 13th-century castle had been in its day." The hypothesized dominance of the defense in the sixteenth and early seventeenth century, however, is contested (Levy 1984, 231).

An important military revolution at sea also occurred in the early sixteenth century (Cipolla 1965; Guilmartin 1988; Palmer 1997; Parker 1988; Glete 2000; Sicking 2010), as sailing ships, which could carry large cannon, replaced light oar-powered galleys as frontline warships. Mediterranean galleys carried cannon, but only ones that could fire to the front or rear of the vessels. Once gun ports were built into the sides of sailing ships, it was possible to move well beyond the very few guns carried on galleys. Between 1500 and 1800 multiple banks of gun ports were created in a process that resembled the earlier Greek innovations in banks of oars. Gradually more and more guns were prerequisite to surviving frontline duty in naval fleets. It also took a century and a half for the changes in the number of cannon carried to change naval tactics. After the mid-seventeenth century, sea battle victories increasingly hinged on the ability to maneuver ships so that their cannon fire, concentrated on the sides of ships, could be maximized.[7]

This "revolution of sail and shot" (Krepinevich 1994, 32–33) was first conclusively demonstrated by the defeat of Turkish galleys at the Battle of Lepanto (1571), which ushered in a radically new era of naval warfare. The sailing ship contributed significantly to the ability of the European great powers to project their power and expand their commerce on a global scale. For much of the period prior to industrialization, indeed, it was only the European lead in sea power that enabled European traders to stay in the Eurasian commercial game despite substantial opposition (Thompson 1999b, 2000). The development of networks of bases built around *trace italienne* fortresses that could be relieved from the sea was another factor that kept Europeans in Eurasian commerce in the sixteenth though eighteenth centuries. Despite its profound impact on the nature of war at sea, this naval revolution, unlike most other revolutions in military technology, did not contribute all that much to the increasing severity of great power warfare.

On land the power of the defense was significantly reinforced in the mid-seventeenth century by the revival of military engineering and the development of a new science of fortifications by Vauban and others (Duffy 1985; Guerlac 1986). These developments are generally excluded from lists of military revolutions, but the new fortresses, invulnerable to artillery and to frontal assault, contributed to an era of geometric warfare defined by position and maneuver rather than pitched battle.

The eighteenth century witnessed some important tactical innovations under Frederick the Great and then Napoleon, but these innovations were independent of any significant developments in military technology. The most significant changes in warfare during this period were those associated with the *levée en masse*, a societal-level change linked to military organization, which we discuss later.[8]

The next major revolution in military technology did not occur until the mid-nineteenth century, when the combination of the industrial revolution, the development of the steam engine, and the introduction of railroads and telegraphs led to a "land warfare revolution" (Krepinevich 1994, 34).[9] This military revolution dramatically transformed the nature of war and enhanced the effectiveness of the mass army that emerged from the Napoleonic period.[10]

The development of the railroad greatly enhanced the rapid mobilization and strategic mobility of armies and facilitated the ability of states to fight two-front wars. It also contributed to the capacity to sustain larger armies in the field for extended periods of time. The invention of the telegraph further enhanced states' ability to mass forces quickly and to coordinate simultaneous military operations. The telegraph also had important implications for civil-military relations (Cohen 1996, 42), and hence for political and military organization. It gave political leaders timely information about developments on the battlefield and, hence, the temptation to dictate to generals and "micromanage" the war. At the same time, political leaders saw a reduction in their control over the distribution of war-related information to the public.

At the same time the technology of rifling improved the range and accuracy of small arms and artillery, and the introduction of repeating rifles and machine guns added to the volume of fire and reinforced the ability to defend entrenched positions against frontal assault (Fuller 1954–56; Fuller 1961, chap. 5; Brodie and Brodie 1973, chap. 6; McNeill 1982, chaps. 7–8). Eliot Cohen (1996, 44) refers to this as the "firepower revolution." Continued improvements in mass production made all of these weapons more widely available. Walter Millis (1956, chap. 4) refers to the aggregation of these changes as the "mechanization of war."

The result was a substantial increase in the destructiveness of war on the battlefield, accelerating the road to "total war" (Förster and Nagler 1997; Boemeke, Chickering, and Förster 1999; Chickering and Förster 2000). Despite the increased mobility of armies, there was a net shift in the offensive-defensive balance toward the defense (Levy 1984, 232–33).[11] Beginning with the American Civil War and extending to World War I, there was a trend, in Marion Boggs's (1941, 76–77) words, "toward enormous increase in masses of men under arms, and in the range, casualty-producing capacity, and rapidity of fire of infantry weapons, without any counteracting growth in the means of advancing this fire." There was a growing gap, however, between the "objective" balance in favor of the defense (as judged by a consensus of military historians) and the growing "cult of the offensive" (Van Evera 1984; Snyder 1984) shared by many military and political leaders. As J. M. K Vyvyan (1968, 165) argues, "Never has the dogma of the offensive been more prevalent; never, because of the lead of firepower over tactical mobility, has that dogma been less applicable."

This iteration of revolution in land warfare was accompanied by a revolution in naval warfare beginning in the middle of the nineteenth century. The sailing ship, which had dominated war at sea since the revolution of sail and shot in the sixteenth century, was replaced by the turbine-powered, metal-hulled ship and its long-range, rifled artillery. These changes contributed to a fundamental change in the nature of naval warfare (Brodie 1941; Krepinevich 1994, 35–36). The last decade before World War I marked the development of the all-big-gun battleship and battle fleet (Herwig 2001). This revolution in naval warfare extended under the seas with the introduction of the submarine and the torpedo, which could be used in strategic blockade and commerce raiding. The effects of these fundamental changes in military technology on warfare on both land and sea were evident in the conduct of World War I, though as before the direct impact of naval revolutions on the severity of war was limited.[12]

By the end of World War I another revolution in military technology was underway, one that is said to have defined the "birth of modern warfare" (Bailey 2001). It consisted of simultaneous revolutions in mechanization, aviation, and information. Significant changes on the battlefield were evident by the end of the war, but they were all accelerated by new technological developments after the war, including improvements in the internal combustion engine, aircraft design, and radio and radar. These technological changes facilitated the integration and coordination of larger-scale military movements with combined-arms tactics and operations. They led to new kinds of military formations, such as the panzer division, the carrier battle group, and the long-range bomber force (Krepinevich 1994, 36; Gray 2002, chap. 7). Land warfare was characterized by fluidity, speed, deep penetrations, and broad encirclements, and the stalemate of the trenches in World War I transformed into the blitzkrieg of World War II. These developments led to a significant increase in the destructiveness of war.[13]

The nuclear revolution in the mid-twentieth century, combined with the development of long-range strategic delivery systems, increased the potential human and economic destructiveness of war by several orders of magnitude, as evidenced by the bombing of Hiroshima and then by tests of the H-bomb a few years later. For the first time states could devastate enemy populations without first defeating their military forces (Schelling 1966, chap. 1). As a result, both sides in a crisis would almost certainly anticipate that the enormous costs of war would far exceed any potential benefits, leading to a situation of stable strategic deterrence between the leading nuclear powers (Jervis 1989).

The most recent revolution in military technology, and the one that triggered renewed interest in the concept of a revolution in military affairs, is the exploitation of new information-based technologies and the integration of complex information systems into a "system of systems" (Nye and Owens 1996). The result is a tremendous increase in the ability of military organizations to detect, identify, track, and engage a larger number of targets over a larger area in a shorter period of time and with greater precision and lethality (Krepinevich 1994, 41). This development was foreshadowed in the 1990–91 Persian Gulf War and was demonstrated beyond doubt by the performance of the American military operation in Iraq in spring 2003 (Murray and Scales 2003).[14] Unlike past military revolutions, however, the information-based revolution is likely to contribute to military effectiveness without increasing the severity of war.[15]

Yet there may be something even more fundamental than a sequence of military revolutions at work during the last five centuries. George Friedman and Meredith Friedman (1996) advance an interesting model that actually reflects a mix of emphases on military weaponry, political economy, and military organization. For the next five hundred years after Columbus initiated the European voyages of "discovery," Europeans increasingly perfected their employment of chemical explosions to military purposes. At first the emphasis was placed on exploding powder to propel projectiles from tubes. Cannon and musket-bearing infantry were the outcome from the fourteenth century on. A second major push came in the nineteenth century when hydrocarbon fuels (coal and petroleum) were first harnessed to move weapons platforms to places hitherto inaccessible and at speeds no longer dependent on muscle and wind. Each technological wave led to further successful expansion on the part of Europeans.

Yet the success of a technological juggernaut based on firearms was not without its liabilities. Firearms possessed two major problems. They were inaccurate and they took time to load and fire. Both problems were addressed and accuracy and firing rates improved over time. The solution to the technological problem required, however, that more men were mobilized for the firing line. Inaccuracy could be compensated for to some extent by expanding the volume of firing. More cannon and rifles firing were more likely to hit some desired targets than relying on fewer cannon and rifles. This meant the size of armies needed to expand to accommodate more shooters. More firearms firing meant also an incentive to expand the number of defenders so that the loss of soldiers hit could be managed more readily. The perverse logic (or liabilities) of relying on ballistic projectiles generated what Friedman and Friedman refer to as "ever larger armies, . . . larger war industries, . . . ever larger sums of money, and . . . ever larger casualties." The consequent escalation in technology and resource mobilization led ultimately to the exhaustion of Europe.

The battleship/aircraft carrier, tank, and bomber, as the principal weapons platforms of the twentieth century, were designed to transport projectiles close enough to the intended target, to find the target, and to attack the target while, ideally, ensuring the survival of the weapons platform to be used again. Inadvertently, the weapons platforms became increasingly complex and expensive—both to produce and to maintain. The development of countermeasures (for instance, aerial or subsurface attacks on battleships, antitank missiles, and early-warning radar defenses) meant that new ways had to be found to make the weapons platforms less vulnerable. Other weapons platforms had to be assigned to defend the principal combat platforms. The principal platforms themselves received more armor, guns with longer range, faster propulsion devices, and stealth capabilities. All of this meant more expense in terms of production, maintenance, and logistics.

At least another generation will be required to implement another major technological change in weaponry and military doctrine. By that time another round of military revolution will be launched, this time focused on nanotechnology or microscopically small computers. Entirely new types of weapons will be possible and most of these new weapons will entail much less human involvement. The initial expense of this new weaponry will favor the affluent states, and especially the United States, but eventually some nanotechnology weaponry could diffuse to less developed states.

Political, Economic, and Societal Coevolution

Although developments in military technology can account for much of the increasing severity of great power wars over the last five or six centuries, they cannot explain the full extent of those increases or their specific timing, and it is necessary to incorporate other variables. What begins as a change in military technology often affects military doctrine, strategy, and tactics, and sometimes these changes have a broader impact on the nature of military organizations, civil-military relations, the strength of the state relative to society, and political culture. These nonmilitary developments, once underway, have an independent and prolonged impact on the nature of warfare and can also create the conditions under which military innovation is more or less likely.

For example, the revolutions in artillery and gunpowder five or six centuries ago, and the tactical and doctrinal innovations that followed from them, had profound political consequences. The development of artillery and of the *trace italienne* created economies of scale that effectively priced nobles out of the market and contributed to the continuing shift in power from nobles to kings (Porter 1994, 31–32). These developments also ended the invulnerability of the castle and the security complex built around them and eroded the political influence and social status of the mounted knight by diminishing the battlefield relevance of the knightly virtues of individual strength, skill, and courage.

As kings accumulated more and more power and acquired effective control over more and more territory, their interests expanded, as did the imperatives to defend those interests. Thus there was a broadening of the interests for which wars were fought. The use of military force for the personal honor, vengeance, and enrichment of kings and nobles that characterized the Middle Ages gradually gave way to the use of force as an instrument of policy in pursuit of more expansive territorially based interests of kings and ultimately states. With the expansion of interests came an expansion of the means to secure those interests and an increasing severity of war on the battlefield. This expansion in the aims for which wars were fought continued in the late eighteenth century with the inclusion of the national ambitions of entire peoples at the time of the French Revolution.

Robert Osgood (1967) refers to this as the "rationalization" of military power under the state and dates its origins in the late fifteenth century, but this was clearly a process that evolved over time and intensified with the increasing centralization of power in the state in the modern system.[16] Military developments played an important role in this process of state consolidation (Tilly 1990). The advances in artillery and gunpowder in the sixteenth century led to important tactical and doctrinal innovations. The slow rate of fire of muskets led to the development of linear tactics, first by Maurice of Nassau and then by Gustavus Adolphus (Roberts [1955] 1995).[17] These tactical innovations produced continuous fire and resulted in a further increase in battlefield casualties by the end of the sixteenth century. With the replacement of the block by the line, one rank could fire while the other reloaded. This innovation was important since individual muskets were not very accurate. Their impact came in combination and in their effect in breaking up military formations, which left individual soldiers vulnerable to pike and bayonet and which placed greater emphasis on unit cohesion. These changes also led to more wide-ranging strategic movements, which required more extensive training and drill and which increased the inefficiencies of demobilization following the end of a campaign.

These factors combined to create incentives for the establishment of larger and permanent armies, which were enormously costly as were the new fortification systems. The administration of the expanded fiscal systems required an increase in taxation and larger state bureaucracies, and these in turn facilitated the further expansion of armies.[18] The increasing costs of creating and maintaining a military establishment led to fiscal crises in many states, to which monarchs responded in different ways and with varying degrees of success. These different responses in turn had a significant impact on state formation, prospects for democracy, wealth, and military power (North 1981; Rasler and Thompson 1989). The general result was a growing centralization of state power and an increasing ability of political leaders to extract resources from society and to use those resources for the expansion of the military. This interrelated complex of technological, economic, political, and social changes is generally known as the "military revolution" of early modern Europe, generally dated 1550–1650 (Roberts [1955] 1995; Tilly 1975; Parker 1988; Porter 1994).

The centralization of power in the state and the ability of the state to make war were further enhanced by the increasingly symbiotic relationship between the state and the commercial classes beginning in the early seventeenth century. This was driven in part by the growing access of private domestic interests to state institutions, which varied across states as a function of the degree of centralization of state power and the degree of concentration of parochial interests. The increasing assertiveness of the English Parliament under the Commonwealth in the mid-seventeenth century, for example, gave actors with concentrated interests in certain sectors greater influence on state policy in England (Wilson 1978) and in the Netherlands than in France (Martin 1997).

The reciprocal influences between state power and commercial interests was also driven by prevailing mercantilist ideology, along with the realities of power and wealth in the international system. Commerce generated the wealth necessary to sustain war, and war in turn became a means of expanding commerce (Viner 1948). In Clausewitzian terms, commerce was a continuation of war and war was a continuation of commerce (Howard 1976, 47). We might call this the "commercialization of war," but this was a more evolutionary than revolutionary development.

Azar Gat (2006, 480) takes this argument one step further in a very interesting way. He argues that the European trading system created after 1500 was the principal engine of European modernization, capitalism, and economic growth. Made possible by gunpowder, oceanic navigation, and the printing press, Europe leaped ahead of the rest of the world in power and wealth. Gat argues that these developments were more important than the military revolutions in European army size and firepower.

By the late eighteenth century the mercantilist system was beginning to be replaced by a more liberal, free-trading international economy. The greater ease of borrowing on international capital markets provided a new means for states to finance their military establishments and wars. This benefited some states more than others, however, and it was a significant factor contributing to Britain's rise as a leading world power (Thompson

1988). More generally, the efficiencies of a liberal, free-trading international economy generated additional wealth, more powerful armies, and the increasing destructiveness of war.

The major military revolution of this time, however, involved changes associated with the French Revolution. The rise of nationalism and popular ideology, the institution of universal conscription, the comprehensive economic mobilization of society, and the creation of the "nation in arms" combined to constitute a revolution in military affairs that led to a quantum increase in the size of armies in the field and consequently in the casualties of war (Murray 1997; Gray 2002).[19]

It is important to note that technology played a relatively small part of the military revolution associated with the French Revolution and the Napoleonic Wars. Barry Buzan (1987, 18) writes that Napoleon's victories were based "almost wholly on the innovative use of existing types of weapons, and scarcely at all on innovations in the weapons themselves." Richard Preston and Sydney Wise (1979, 189) argue that in some respects Napoleon was an "arch-reactionary toward new weapons and technological progress in the material of war." Napoleon integrated tactical and organizational innovations to create a highly mobile military force organized around the tactical offensive, a force that was significantly enlarged by mass conscription and by his own charisma (Ropp 1959, chap. 4; Gray 2002, chap. 6). Napoleon also exploited the revolutionary ideology and the enormous popular support underlying it to broaden state goals and war aims in unprecedented ways (Chandler 1966).

The consequences were enormous. People were much more willing to fight for the nation than for the crown (Posen 1993), and as a consequence the size of armies and the number of casualties that commanders and political leaders were willing to tolerate increased substantially. As Marshal Foch proclaimed with the end of the Prussian offensive at Valmy in 1792, "The wars of Kings were at an end; the wars of peoples were beginning" (in Osgood 1967, 52). European war began to reacquire, for the first time in centuries, a crusading spirit. As Winston Churchill predicted in 1901, at the beginning of the century of total war, "The wars of peoples will be more terrible than those of kings" (quoted in Gilbert 1967, 21–22).

Robert Osgood (1967, 51) refers to these developments as the "popularization" of war, while Walter Millis (1956, chap. 1) refers to them as the "democratization" of war. We prefer the former. Popularization carries less conceptual baggage and is less restrictive as to the types of regimes in which this phenomenon might occur. At the same time we need to be careful to not exaggerate the extent to which the populations of the Napoleonic War contestants were mobilized for war purposes. The point is not that the levels reached the heights encountered in the twentieth-century world wars, but that they were greater than had been experienced in the European wars prior to 1792.

Another important development, later in the nineteenth century, was what Osgood (1967) calls the "professionalization" of military power, or what Millis (1956, chap. 3) calls the "managerial revolution" (see also Huntington 1957, part 1). This refers to the development of a peacetime military establishment directed by a professional military elite that was independent of the aristocracy, headed by a general staff system, and supported by a system of military academies. We can identify some aspects of professional military establishments as early as the seventeenth century (Roberts [1955] 1995), and the system of military academies began early in the nineteenth century, but the new professional military systems did not become fully established until later in the century. The professionalization of military power increased the efficiency of the conduct of war and with it the severity of war. It had an enormous societal impact by enhancing the legitimacy of the military profession, which in some societies contributed to the growing militarism of society (Vagts 1959; Berghahn 1981; Ritter 1970).

The societal impact of war was even more pronounced in the period surrounding World War II.[20] The magnitude of the struggle resulted in the mobilization of entire societies for war, the preparation for war, or the deterrence of war. Far more than ever before, the entire scientific, technological, industrial, and educational capacities of the nation were mobilized directly for the war effort. This mobilization of the intellectual and educational as well as material and social resources of the nation for the purposes of enhancing military power continued, in peacetime as well as in wartime, at least for the leading states in the system. This "totalization of war" continued well into the Cold War. It was reflected in the United States in the emphasis on science education in high schools, in the pattern of research grants from the government and private funding agencies, in the resources directed to the space program, and to the more general impact of the Cold War on American culture.[21]

This "totalization of war" and its pervasive impacts may also have made both World War II and the Cold War much more probable than they might otherwise have been. Bruce Porter (1994, 153), for instance, emphasizes that the advent of industrialization in the nineteenth century led to the industrialization of war. Industrialized warfare had three dimensions. First, states improved their capability to produce weaponry. Factories could churn out mass-produced weapons, replacing what had been a crafts industry before the nineteenth century. Second, the weaponry they produced increased its rate of fire and in the process became much more lethal. A few machine guns, for instance, could pin down and decimate literally hundreds of soldiers. Third, the battlefield became increasingly mechanized in the form of weapons platforms that greatly expanded what individual soldiers were capable of accomplishing. In turn, states, particularly those that were most competitive with one another, had little choice but to increasingly mobilize more national capability to remain competitive in international politics and to be able to wage modern war. Wars became more total as more and more industrial production, the civilian working force, and finance were harnessed to the war effort—as they were most noticeably in World Wars I and II.

By saying that wars became more total, we do not mean to imply that all resources and individuals were mobilized for the war effort. Movement toward totalization is not the same thing as achieving totalization. Wars became considerably more total in Europe (and North America and Japan) than they had been previously in the last millennia or two. It is sometimes argued that warfare was more total in hunting-gathering times or in tribal situations in the sense that nearly all resources and individuals could be mobilized and the consequent proportion of casualties could be quite considerable as a proportion of the population (Black 2006, 5). Although this observation is accurate, it is not clear to us that this comparison between hunting-gathering or primitive agrarian circumstances and industrialized societies is all that useful. The complexity of military technology, state structures, and societies found in the industrialized world encompasses a different scale of "totalization" in resource mobilization than that which occurred much earlier.[22]

One outcome of this escalatory spiral in resource mobilization was greater political centralization. It could not be escaped in wartime. It also became more natural in the postwar eras so that states expanded their repertoires of activity to incorporate new functions such as social welfare and economic regulation. Socialist policies made major gains especially in Europe where the war impacts were so great and close to home.

World War I had other consequences as well. As Porter (1994) emphasizes, it created two basic categories among the major powers: winners and losers. The losers, a category that includes states that had been on the winning side at various times such as Russia and Italy but that either collapsed during the war (Russia) or felt that they had been poorly treated by their allies (Italy), were especially likely to see their traditional elites discredited by their war performance. In some cases intensive war also destroyed many traditional institutions that had served as the infrastructure of civil society.

This destruction of elite and societal structures created political space that could be exploited by various types of groups, fascists and communists in particular, in their struggle to gain power. This led to the rise of in the Bolshevik Soviet state, the fascist Italian state under Benito Mussolini, and the national socialist (Nazi) state of Adolf Hitler. Once in power these parties of the radical left and right took the momentum toward state centralization to its maximal degree by expanding the power of the party/state and largely eliminating individual autonomy from the dictates of the party/state. They also militarized their societies for intense international conflict.

For Porter (1994), then, the social welfare and totalitarian states primarily in Europe of the twentieth century both stemmed to a considerable extent from pressures to prepare for, and to engage in, industrialized warfare. Centralizing states needed mass participation in war mobilization processes and needed to be prepared to expand the services they exchanged for loyalty and increased taxation. Mobilized populations, moreover, felt more responsible for the welfare of fellow citizens. Some groups in countries that failed to do well in World War I, in addition, felt strong incentives to develop radical strategies to ensure the military viability of their states. Although expanded welfare functions probably mitigated pressures to go to war, the consequent ideological conflicts of the twentieth century encouraged the second iteration of total war and a Cold War in which the Soviet Union mobilized resources as if it were engaged in a third total war.[23]

Porter (1994) does not pursue the irony that the escalatory spiral in war intensification contributed ultimately to the exhaustion of states in both western and eastern Europe. That exhaustion may have greatly and permanently reduced the probability of further warfare among the most economically advanced countries in Europe. Many of the states in Europe seem also to have broken free of the escalatory spiral in coevolving political and military organization. For the most part their armies are small once again and are neither well armed nor well funded. That could change sometime in the future but it seems more likely that substantial parts of Europe have simply dropped out of the coevolutionary orbit of many of war's organizational and political-economic implications. In what may prove to be a fundamental evolutionary shift, albeit one that is concentrated in geographical space, they have kept the political organizations shaped by centuries of warfare but are unlikely to use them for the traditional purpose of interstate warfare.

We cannot emphasize too strongly, however, that the trend toward more intensive warfare has been predominately a characteristic of European interstate relations, or more precisely, a characteristic of European interstate relations since the early modern period beginning in the sixteenth century through the bloodletting that culminated in 1945. Other regions did not experience the same coevolutionary spirals, but for reasons that are consistent with our coevolutionary model. Contemporary regions outside of Europe and North America have not confronted external threat environments similar to the one faced by early modern European states. As a consequence, different environments have contributed significantly to different coevolutionary histories.

The Declining Frequency of Great Power War

The frequency of great power war declined continuously in each of the last five centuries, the only exception being the increase in the first half of the twentieth century. The most basic explanation for this trend is that over time the increasing costs of war relative to its perceived benefits have gradually reduced the utility of war as a rational instrument of state policy. Casualties and human suffering have increased enormously, as have economic costs associated with the destruction of infrastructure, lost productivity, and the maintenance of a competitive military establishment. The nuclear revolution has increased these costs dramatically, though some argue that conventional warfare had become so destructive that war between major powers was becoming obsolete even in the absence of nuclear weapons (Mueller 1995).

The declining legitimacy of war, at least among the advanced industrial and democratic states of the west (Knorr 1966; Mueller, 1995, chap. 9), has further increased the diplomatic and domestic political costs of war, and the spread of democracy and nationalism have increased the costs of territorial conquest and occupation. The growth of economic interdependence among the great powers has increased the economic opportunity costs of war.[24] In addition, the shift in the foundations of military power and potential away from land and population to industrial might and, more recently, information-based technologies, contributed to the declining value of territorial conquest, at least for the great powers (Knorr 1966; Van Evera 1990/91).[25] This, together with the increasing congruence between state territorial boundaries and national identity groups for the leading states (Miller 2007), and the associated settlement of major territorial disputes between advanced democratic states (Gibler forthcoming), has reduced the potential benefits from and hence incentives for great power war, at least among the most economically advanced states.[26]

Some observers would go even further and argue that it is not merely that the potential benefits of great power war have been reduced. Rather, they have been extinguished completely. John Mueller's (1989) *Retreat from Doomsday* contends that great power warfare has become "subrationally unthinkable." What this means is that decision makers and populations no longer even consider warfare as a conceivable option in settling disputes between major powers.[27] This is not simply a matter of distaste, revulsion, or disdain for a primitive problem-solving approach. The option simply no longer comes to mind as even a remote possibility.

Mueller's (1989) argument is fundamentally ideational rather than material. He contends that the increasing obsolescence of war basically reflects a twentieth-century shift in attitudes. Before 1914 most people continued to approve of war as an acceptable policy option. War was not only a means of resolving interstate disputes, it could also enhance the prestige and glory of the nation, values that were reinforced by the Social Darwinist ideology of the day (Joll 1984, chap. 8). Moreover, war was perceived as inevitable, a fact of life that could not be avoided. The costs and horrors of World War I fundamentally changed these attitudes, at least in the west. A majority of opinion no longer thought of war as a reasonable way to resolve disagreements. Neither the winners nor the losers could expect to gain enough to make the sacrifices associated with world war tolerable, given the increasing destructiveness of warfare.

Even so, not everyone learned the same lessons from World War I.[28] Political leaderships in Italy, Germany, and Japan, for example, clung to earlier conceptions of the utility of force and of virtues of war, and they were quite willing to resort to—and some argue that they even preferred—military force to negotiation and compromise for dealing with conflicts of interests. This raises potential problems for Mueller's argument about a fundamental shift in underlying attitudes toward war and its violence-inhibiting consequences. Mueller (2004, 54–65) defends his position by arguing that World War II occurred because of the beliefs and actions of one man, and that the war would not have happened without Hitler.[29]

World War II did occur, however, and it further reinforced the views of peoples and leaders in most advanced industrial countries that major power warfare had ceased to be a desirable policy option. Although many scholars have argued that the advent of nuclear weapons contributed significantly to these changing attitudes toward war (Schelling 1966; Jervis 1989), Mueller (1989, 1994) insists that the growing destructiveness of conventional warfare would have induced an attitudinal shift against the utility of war even in the absence of nuclear weapons. The Cold War, in his view, reflected a situation in which the winners were satisfied with the prevailing status quo and the losers came to accept that same status quo without being forced to accept it due to military inferiority or fear of nuclear attack.

Carl Kaysen's (1990) critique of Mueller's (1989) interpretation is most helpful in underscoring some of the coevolutionary implications of the recent pacification of older, more affluent states. His central criticism is that Mueller fails to explain how the world shifted to the belief (which Kaysen accepts as accurate) that war between advanced states had ceased to be a viable instrument of national policy, that Mueller focuses on the outcome without providing a full explanation for how it came about: "The retreat [from doomsday] appears to take place in a vacuum, or at best in a highly rarefied atmosphere in which the forces of technological change, economic change, and change in the internal structures and workings of the polities that fight or avoid war are barely detectable" (Kaysen 1990).

Attitudes are unlikely to change unless the environment in which they are formed undergoes substantial change. Kaysen (1990) suggests that major power warfare has become unthinkable because potential war makers no longer consider it profitable. Mueller says much the same thing, but Kaysen's take on the evolution toward war's unprofitablity is much longer in historical scope. The costly world wars of the twentieth century are not insignificant, but much more is involved.

Kaysen begins by stipulating that a necessary and sufficient condition for war disappearing as a policy option is the emergence of a world in which all potential war makers believe that the likely costs of going to war exceed the likely benefits of doing so.[30] The questions then become whether we have reached that state and, if so, how did we get there?

One of the keys for Kaysen is the observation that territorial control has long been the focal point for acquiring and maintaining economic and political power. As long as agricultural production constituted the principal economic activity, the ability to expand territorial control meant more farmland, more agricultural output and surplus, more farmers, and a greater ability to transform the production into material resources and symbolic displays of power. The war calculus, in this context, remained relatively simple. What was the likelihood of territorial expansion, and at what estimated cost in lives and treasure? As long as weaponry and army size remained fairly limited, the consequent scale of warfare was also likely to remain restricted. Therefore, the costs of warfare in terms of damage to farmlands and loss of population were apt to be both temporary and small. Restricted costs of warfare made perceived net gains from warfare more conceivable.

This state of affairs persisted for millennia but hardly forever. A variety of important changes crept into the war calculus. Initially, political elites and military warriors were indistinguishable. Most of the population was not involved in combat, and those who were tended also to be the primary beneficiaries of war gains. Yet increased governmental complexity led to greater specialization in roles, thereby separating political and military elites. Cities and trade became increasingly important to economic productivity. Standing armies and gunpowder expanded the scale of warfare. While these changes altered the war cost calculus, especially in the European region between the fifteenth and eighteenth centuries, the costs did not escalate so greatly so as to preclude the possibility of perceived net gains from warfare.

Changes that took place in the nineteenth century, however, led to fundamental changes in the war calculus. Kaysen identifies five basic types of change. First, industrialization led to the development of new forms of locomotion. Animal power was replaced by mechanical and electrical power. Manufactured goods became more important than natural materials. Forms of communication accelerated the speed of information transfer. Changes in the civilian world were paralleled by the industrialization of warfare, a second major change. Weaponry became more lethal. The size of armies expanded. Combined with economic industrialization, the scale of warfare intensified dramatically. A third change involved the expansion of urbanization. By the middle of the nineteenth century, half of Europe lived in cities. A fourth consideration is that the gap between elites and masses had been diminished as well thanks to expanded literacy, expansion in the ranks of the middle class, and changes in prevailing formulas for political legitimacy (for example, democratization). Fifth, political systems, as a consequence, became more inclusive and better integrated. Integration was furthered by the breaking down of various particularistic loyalties. Education, expanded transportation infrastructures, and military service all contributed to national identification and the homogenization of the state.

The consequences of these changes were also fivefold, in Kaysen's (1990) view. First, the value of land and therefore the perceived value of territorial expansion diminished. Second, industrialization had multiplied the scale, cost, and lethality of warfare. Third, the probability of war-related losses of life expanded significantly and so too did the likelihood of lost economic growth due to war participation. Fourth, conquests of nationalistic populations implied that the probable costs of political repression could exceed the economic gains of expanded territorial control. Fifth, governments had become dedicated to servicing the welfare demands of its citizenry. Popular consent and attaining and maintaining political office had become increasingly focused on guaranteeing economic security and social harmony. Major power warfare meant major mobilizations, losses of life, and sacrifices of economic welfare. Taken together, these changes—which combined how individuals related to their societies, how leaders viewed their roles, and how wars were executed—made major power warfare increasingly unattractive. To the extent that it had become unprofitable, it also became unthinkable.

Many of these changes had occurred in significant magnitude by 1914 or 1918. Why did it take longer for major power warfare to become less attractive? Mueller's (2004, chap. 4) explanation focused on Mussolini, Hitler, and Tojo. Kaysen's explanation of the pace of changes focuses primarily on the generalization that ideas change more slowly than the environments in which they are formed. Moreover, changes in the environment are uneven and require amplification. Thus the transformations involving leaders more attuned to public welfare considerations did not take place simultaneously everywhere. World War I, especially, resulted in the removal of old-fashioned hereditary elites in a number of places. The

Depression of the 1930s and World War II constituted strong influences on the elevation of economic security to the peak of the political demand schedule. Ballistic missiles armed with nuclear warheads further escalated the lethality and potential costs of warfare. The diminished probability of major power warfare, in Kaysen's view, required hundreds of years of change and changes that continued to take place throughout the twentieth century.

These evolving calculations about warfare do not apply to all types of war. Short and limited wars can still be regarded as potentially profitable (in the sense that gains could be greater than the costs). States still prepare for the threat of major power war while recognizing that such wars make little sense for rational actors. As long as national security dictates a premium on defense, war between major powers is something less than totally unthinkable. In addition, the changes that Kaysen emphasizes are not universal in application. They apply primarily to western Europe, North America, and Japan. As long as the rest of the world remains unindustrialized, the theoretical consequences experienced in the north are much less likely to apply to a less developed south, in which internal and external conflict should be expected to persist.

Kaysen's (1990) argument emphasizes the various impacts of industrialization. Reduced to its essence, the argument is that political-economic changes have intensified weaponry and expanded military organizations thereby making war less rational. Industrialization-driven political-economy changes have also transformed political organizations into entities more oriented toward welfare than warfare consideration. Thus industrialized states, at least, are less likely to engage in increasingly costly warfare than did the leading states in past historical eras.

The prediction that industrialized states are less prone to intramural warfare than in the past seems quite plausible. The irony of the most technologically advanced coevolution is that development processes have removed many of the most affluent states from the ranks of likely war participants, at least in wars against each other.[31] They have too much to lose to make war against other leading states very attractive. But only a rather small proportion of the world's states are industrialized. Nor are all possible contenders for elite status in world politics economically developed. While wealthy states are significantly less likely than in the past to fight one another, warfare between the rich and poorer actors (states and nonstate groups) cannot be ruled out, especially if current resource scarcities (especially oil and water) become more acute in the future. To the extent that have–have not conflict increases, one can expect that a leading actor on the have side is likely to be the state with the most advanced economic and military technology. To summarize: future wars between developed states are quite unlikely, but little in Kaysen's argument excludes conflict between developed states and nonindustrial states.

Turning back to long-term changes over the last half millennium, we might have expected that the increasing severity of war could have created incentives for shorter wars, and that this tendency would have been reinforced by improvements in communications and logistics that increased the speed of military operations on the battlefield. It is pretty clear, however, that the duration of great power war has not significantly diminished during the last five centuries, though there is an observable downward trend in the duration of major-minor wars (Levy 1983, 124–28).

Several factors have worked against the earlier termination of wars. The gradual industrialization of agricultural societies has increased states' economic capacities to sustain a war and bear these costs. The increasing number of great powers participating in each war (Levy 1983, 120–28), reflecting a gradual shift from dyadic wars to more complex wars (Vasquez 2009, chap. 2) creates military coalitions of greater staying power. Allies provide military support, and they also provide the economic support that allows states to continue fighting (Kennedy 1987). In addition, one might argue, along with Clausewitz ([1832] 1976), that over the long term the defense always manages to keep up with the offense, so that it takes equally long to obtain a decisive advantage on the battlefield.

Internally, the growth of larger and more powerful national security bureaucracies has increased the extractive capacity of states and their ability to finance a war effort through direct taxation, borrowing, or deficit financing (Roberts [1955] 1995; Ardant 1975; Rasler and Thompson 1983). The growth of liberal democracy has increased governments' access to capital by increasing their accountability and consequently the expectation that their debts will be repaid (Schultz and Weingast 2003). The growth of government bureaucracies has also created a set of vested interests and organizational routines that reinforce existing policy and make it more difficult to reverse course and bring an end to fighting (Iklé 1971; Levy and Thompson 2010b, chap. 6). The growth of democracies, the rise of nationalism, and the occasional tendencies for democracies to adopt a crusading spirit in war (Doyle 1983) also contribute to the difficulties in ending inconclusive and costly wars. Finally, uncertainty about military outcomes, along with uncertainty about adversaries' future power and future intentions (Fearon 1995; Powell 1999; Wagner 2007, chap. 4; Reiter 2009) is a major factor contributing to the persistence of wars, and there is little reason to believe that such uncertainty has diminished over time.

Conclusions

This discussion of the various factors contributing to the increasing severity and declining frequency of major power warfare over time and to the evolution of war more generally suggests that innovation in military technology, while important, has not been the only factor driving the contemporary process, and not always the most important. Williamson Murray (1997, 70) may exaggerate when he claims that, with respect to military revolutions, "The historical record suggests that technological change represents a relatively small part of the equation." The two most recent military revolutions, involving nuclear weapons and then information-based technologies, were each technologically driven (though each had important consequences for military organization and society). Murray provides a useful corrective, however, to the technological determinism argument.

Organizational, political, social, and economic variables also play significant roles, and where weapons technology has a major impact it is often through its interaction effects with these other variables. The incorporation of new technologies into existing military systems and strategic doctrines is generally not sufficient for success. The advantage often comes to those who create new operational units that integrate new technologies with other systems in innovative ways. Thus some of the key innovations are conceptual (Krepinevich 1994, 30). The basic elements for a military revolution in the period between the two world wars of the twentieth century, for example, were available to many of the major European states, but it was German leaders who learned the correct lessons from World War I, developed a vision, and made it work (Murray 2001). The panzer division and the blitzkrieg were organizational and conceptual innovations, not technological ones.

More generally, though, the last of our three accelerations appears to reinforce the utility of our coevolutionary theory. It's a bit like unraveling a ball of string, but it appears that this acceleration was initially stimulated by radical changes in *weaponry*, longbows and gunpowder in particular. *Military organizations*, competing in an intense *threat environment*, refocused their efforts on infantry and artillery and adopted more mobile tactics, which required larger number of soldiers. *Political organizations* had to find ways to pay for expanding armies, expensive artillery, artillery fortresses, and sailing fleets that once could be assembled intermittently but quickly became more permanent fixtures.

New weaponry contributed to the growing vulnerability of the castle, which undermined the sustainability of feudalism and facilitated the continuing shift to the state as the foci of political organization. The increasing centralization of the state facilitated the mobilization of revenues through taxes, which paid for growing military expenses and profoundly affected the *political economy* of Europe. Some states utilized the innovations in sailing ships to create global networks of resource acquisition, which also accelerated the commercialization of the European political economy.

Subsequent changes in political economy, most spectacularly industrialization, then transformed weaponry by making it much more lethal and giving European states much larger military organizations and longer military reach. The sharpened competition among the main European contenders in the first half of the twentieth century accentuated the trend toward total war, with all of their implications for strong states and mass identifications with the state. The lethality of military technology increased significantly, until the extinction of all human life had become a possibility. The fiscal and human costs of total warfare also expanded greatly. All of these ballooning costs altered the nature of perceived benefits associated with warfare between major, industrialized powers, and a number of competitors have simply dropped out or been priced out of the military competition game.

It is extraordinarily difficult to anticipate these complex and coevolutionary kinds of innovations, whether technological or conceptual, and therefore difficult to extrapolate past trends and predict the future of warfare. That is one of the liabilities of an evolutionary analysis. The complex interaction of constantly changing military and political organization, political economy, threat environment, and weaponry, all within the crucible of war and contingency, render long-range forecasting very difficult. Although in one sense military revolutions are the products of "objective" technological and social forces, they also emerge from the conscious efforts by military and political agents to initiate or accelerate fundamental change. As Jeremy Shapiro (1999, 137–38) argues in distinguishing between the perspectives of strategists and historians on revolutions in military affairs: "The strategist's revolution is made; the historian's happens." Shapiro goes on to say that "the utility of the historian's viewpoint to inform the current debate is very limited... their ability to predict military revolutions is virtually non-existent. These revolutions only seem clear in retrospect." Shapiro undoubtedly underestimates the extent to which the strategists' military revolutions are endogenous to underlying political, economic, and technological developments, but he is certainty correct about the difficulty of predicting the military revolutions of the future.

Still, we have theoretical reasons for anticipating less, rather than more, interstate war between the affluent survivors of the third evolutionary acceleration of warfare. Industrialization made military weaponry and warfare more deadly, thereby accentuating processes already underway in early modern Europe since the vulnerability of aristocratic cavalry and the attractions of gunpowder were established. World Wars I and II brought that point home, especially in some of the areas that suffered the most destruction. As a consequence industrialization expanded the scale, scope, and lethality of warfare but not without creating built-in constraints on that expansion. It is too soon to declare warfare between major powers a thing of the past, but its probability certainly seems to have declined markedly—and for good reason. If there are likely to be many losers and few, if any, winners, the incentives for engaging in major power war have been greatly reduced.

Whereas chapter 2 looked at the distant origins of war and chapter 4 followed up with an examination of early accelerations in the evolution of warfare, this chapter has looked more specifically at the last five hundred years of warfare escalation in the western trajectory. The next chapter takes an even longer look at the western trajectory—from Mesopotamia to the United States—and focuses on tendencies for paradigmatic armies to lead coevolutionary processes in sequential patterns of power concentration and deconcentration. We think these tendencies are generic to most if not all trajectories. We have already seen some of this behavior in chapter 4's discussion of ancient coevolutionary changes in various parts of the world. The next chapter, however, will focus exclusively on the western trajectory—in part because it ultimately subordinated other trajectories and in part because many of its features are already familiar but perhaps not as a single trajectory.

We also wish to highlight an element of the third acceleration that may not be generic to all trajectories. It is not just paradigmatic armies (and navies) that lead the way. It is also aspirations for regional hegemony that leads to the construction of paradigmatic armies. If there is sufficient resistance, periods of "warring states" and upward spirals in military lethality result. We saw these phenomena at work in the second acceleration, both in China and the Mediterranean. It may also have been characteristic of the intercity warfare of Mesopotamia in the early third millennium BCE, but we do not know enough about this time period to state that it was with any certainty. That it was an important factor in the third acceleration seems incontestable.

CHAPTER SIX

The Coevolution of the Western Military Trajectory

The complex interaction of threat environment, political and military organization, weaponry, political economy, and war leads to variable developmental trajectories across time and space. The distinctive Japanese trajectory has little in common with the equally distinctive Mesoamerican trajectory, which, in turn, is radically different from the trajectory that emerged in the ancient Near East. As a consequence we have a number of different trajectories that have developed throughout the world. Granted that there are many differences, is it possible to impose even more common denominator structure on these trajectories? We think we can. By combining John Lynn's (1996) paradigmatic shift model with Joyce Marcus's (1998) dynamic of consolidation and dissolution model, we can create a common structure for trajectories that move from successive iterations of military-political predominance based on demonstrated superiority in organization and weaponry.[1] We propose to focus on the long western trajectory to demonstrate these processes.

One distinguishing characteristic of the western military trajectory is that it moved into phases of warring states as many as three times: the intercity struggles of southern Mesopotamia in the early third millennium BCE (about which we know little), the Persian-Greek-Roman-Carthaginian conflicts of the second half of the first millennium BCE, and the last five hundred years of European international relations. Those three periods are also our three periods of evolutionary acceleration. We argue that intense periods of warring states are responsible for upward spirals in coevolutionary change or accelerations.

In chapter 4 we examined several cases of states involved in the first two accelerations. We switched gears in chapter 5 to focus on the multiple changes related to the third acceleration. That serves our purpose of being able to note numerous changes but gives the impression that the changes simply happened without specific agency. We want to correct that impression in this chapter by reexamining the western trajectory again. This time we focus on the trajectory in its entirety from its Mesopotamian roots to its current leader, the United States.

Military trajectories are propelled by various influences, but particularly prominent are what Lynn (1996) has referred to as paradigmatic armies (and navies) that develop the innovations that fuel what we call coevolutionary change. Moreover, as pioneers and leaders in developing military organizations and technology, paradigmatic armies tend to experience some notable degree of success linked to their states' aspirations for regional hegemony, and paradigmatic navies tend to be successful in their states' aspirations for global political-economic leadership. One of our key hypotheses is that periods of acceleration are most likely to occur during periods in which multiple actors engage in intense competition and in which no state actually acquires a position of hegemony or dominance in the system. Once a state achieves regional hegemony, we hypothesize that the absence of intense competition should lead ultimately to the deacceleration of coevolutionary change.[2]

Lynn (1996) emphasizes a sequence of paradigmatic armies and the associated changes in military organization that accompany each paradigmatic shift. Lynn refers to each iteration in the sequence as a "military style" and describes the movement from one style to the next as an evolutionary process. He begins in the eighth century CE and summarizes the evolution of contemporary western military style to the current period in a seven-iteration model, with accompanying observations on the impact of change not only on military organizations but also states, warfare, and political economy.

Marcus's (1998) dynamic model, which she develops for ancient states, emphasizes a historical sequence of consolidation, coercive expansion, and dissolution. This cycle is initiated by a chiefdom that defeats its rivals and creates a unitary state based on its superior political-military organization. Expansion against weaker groups proceeds until some maximal territorial size is attained. After an expansionary peak is reached, the unitary state begins to dissolve. New and/or stronger rivals may emerge. Peripheral provinces break away. A period of decentralization ensues until another period of consolidation is attempted.

Marcus makes no claim that this cycle is universal. Yet it is fairly common in ancient history. Her examples include Mayan, central Mexican,

Andean, Mesopotamian, Egyptian, and Aegean cases. There is no exact periodicity in the cycle. Periods of centralization and decentralization vary greatly and presumably can be explained in terms of a combination of general and idiosyncratic factors—although that is not something Marcus takes on.

The models constructed by Lynn and Marcus are quite illuminating, and we want to adapt them, with some modifications, to the study of evolutionary trajectories. There are many trajectories in which powers succeeded one another as the predominant military-political power in a region over several millennia. Good examples include the Mesoamerican trajectory (Olmec, Teotihuacán, Toltec, Aztec), the Andean trajectory (Moche, Wari, Chimu, Inca), the Egyptian trajectory (Old, Middle, New Kingdoms), or the Chinese trajectory (Xia, Shang, Zhou, Han, and onward).[3]

How do these trajectories work and what difference do they make? Although we could examine any of these trajectories, we use the western trajectory—stretching from Mesopotamia to the United States—as our test case in this chapter. Its length is useful. Its subordination of other trajectories also gives it additional distinction. Lynn has looked at the modern end of this trajectory. We exploit the opportunity to connect his modern end to its earlier track.

Military Styles: Lynn's Model

Lynn's spatiotemporal focus is on Europe and the United States, or what we call the western trajectory. Perhaps not surprisingly in his capacity as a historian, Lynn evades the question of generalized motors that propel his seven evolutionary iterations over more than a millennium. He also uses the term evolution merely as a synonym for change. Lynn makes an important contribution, but he passes up an opportunity to develop an explicit and comprehensive evolutionary model that could account more generally for the movement from iteration to iteration. We think our coevolutionary model can help in this respect.

In Lynn's (1996) framework of the evolution of military styles, paradigmatic armies play a central role, and other armies either converge or diverge away from these models of "best practice." Yet paradigmatic armies have tended to be more than simply models for imitation. Given their military capability advantages, political organizations with paradigmatic armies tend to be aspirants—successful or otherwise—for regional hegemony, as captured well in the Marcus model.[4] A focus on military institutional centrality need not blur the simultaneity of political-military centrality and its implications for changes in world or regional politics. A more explicit evolutionary model should help to clarify this issue.

We also think that Lynn's starting point in the eighth century CE, while it does allow him to examine twelve centuries of evolution of modern military styles, is unnecessarily limiting. So, too, is Marcus's emphasis on the evolution of what are essentially chiefdoms. Lynn's model can be extended backward in time, and Marcus's model can be extended forward in time. We will demonstrate this assertion by tracing the full western Eurasian military trajectory as parsimoniously as Lynn traces the last millennium.

Consider, for instance, Lynn's eighth century CE starting point. Arguments about military revolutions in early modern Europe stress the movements away from the predominance of heavy cavalry and political decentralization toward the predominance of infantry and political centralization (Roberts [1955] 1995). A longer perspective suggests that both reliance on heavy cavalry and political decentralization were departures from the normal western military trajectory in which increasingly centralized states privileged infantry in conjunction with various types of artillery forces over cavalry. Early modern European political-military developments represented a return to the trajectory's trend line rather than a departure from it.

Another concern of ours refers more to other peoples' work on the western military trajectory than it does to the analyses of Lynn or Marcus. Some writers are especially impressed by the distinctiveness of the western trajectory and its cultural superiority to other military styles. Yet while the western military trajectory is certainly distinctive, perhaps one of its most distinctive attributes has been its openness to outside influences and its propensity to absorb nonwestern military technology, ranging from the stirrup to gunpowder. This adaptive propensity has reinforced the long-term pattern of the trajectory and, at times, encouraged deviation from the norm. It suggests that we need to be careful about exaggerating the uniqueness of a western trajectory that has been highly dependent on nonwestern inputs and influences for its success.[5]

Our aims in this chapter are to address these four concerns: the need for an explicit and general model that explains movements in political-military change from iteration to iteration, the need to develop further the centrality of the lead army (and its state) for specific eras, the need to sketch parsimoniously the full western military trajectory from its conception to contemporary developments, and the need to demonstrate the strong role of exogenous stimulants for endogenous military changes.

There are many other questions that we could raise—such as how does the western military trajectory differ from others (for example, Chinese, Japanese, Indian, Mesoamerican); why the western trajectory has prevailed over others; and what difference does the nature of the trajectory make to contemporary questions of war, peace, and world politics? Although these questions should be addressed as well, they require separate attention in other chapters and elsewhere.[6] Our aim here is to continue to develop a long-term perspective that might facilitate the analysis of various related questions. We turn next to particular components of the Lynn and Marcus models. Of the two, the Lynn model is far more complex and will demand most of the attention.

Lynn (1996) sets out to define and categorize successive army styles in the west beginning with the eighth-century CE European feudalism. He is well aware that other analysts have promoted the significance of weaponry and tactical developments as prime movers of change, but his main assumption is that institutional changes are more important than changes in technology and tactics. Lynn assumes that the infrastructural contexts supplied especially by states, but also societal structures, economies, and cultures, will have reciprocal influences on military institutions. He does not dismiss the possibility that technological change can change military institutions, but he views military institutions as filtering weaponry innovations—selecting some while rejecting others according to perceived institutional interests. Warfare also looms large for its demonstration effects. Success in warfare invites and even compels imitation at the risk of continued failure for those who decline to adopt new innovations. All in all, this is a very evolutionary perspective.

For Lynn, war is a principal vehicle for accelerating convergence in military structures and practices. The principal agent in this convergence process is the paradigm army, which for a period of time sets the standard as the model for other armies to imitate and converge upon until a new core leader supplants it. In the European context Lynn notes that the paradigmatic cores tended to be located on either side of the Rhine. Geographical centrality is thus important to this process, because that is where the incentives for innovations to ensure survival are apt to be greatest.

Given the relative success of the paradigm army and its set of military institutional characteristics, it has little incentive to reform. Fundamental changes are usually introduced by more peripheral and, initially, less successful armies. Nor is there any expectation that all armies will converge on the paradigmatic model. Financial problems, geographical barriers, different threat environments, and population limitations—to name some of the factors at play—are likely to intervene and restrict the extent of convergence. Accordingly, a core-periphery military structure is likely to develop in which convergence is greatest within the core and least likely as one moves away from the core and toward the regional fringe.

Lynn proceeds to employ this framework in constructing a twenty-six-factor matrix of core army style in Europe from the eighth century to the end of the twentieth century. Table 6.1 summarizes a select few of these factors in an attempt to capture the essence of the argument. A taxonomy of seven institutional styles is associated with changes in political and military organizations, political-economic context, and weaponry and tactics.[7] The seven iterations include: the feudal (eighth to tenth centuries), the medieval-stipendiary (twelfth to thirteenth centuries), the aggregate-contract (late fifteenth to early sixteenth centuries), the state-commission (late sixteenth to early seventeenth centuries), the popular-conscript (1789–1810), the mass reserve (1866–1905), and the volunteer-technical (1970–95).

Starting with European feudalism, the decentralization and temporary call-ups of feudal vassals is seen as a product of political decentralization, a nonmonetized economy, and the availability of and appreciation for heavy cavalry technology.[8] Although Lynn does not elaborate on the interdependence of these factors, the implications are reasonably clear. The expense of maintaining heavy cavalry led to a decentralized strategy for paying for security. Rulers exchanged land and rank for the privilege of summoning feudal levies in emergency situations. Once summoned, it was not always clear that feudal levies would appear at all, do so in a timely fashion, or stay long enough to accomplish their mission.

Heavy cavalry also became increasingly vulnerable to common soldiers armed with crossbows and longbows that were capable of penetrating aristocratic armor. The medieval-stipendiary era thus encompassed the emergence of hired infantry used in conjunction with feudal levies. As states grew stronger, economies came to be monetized, and as warfare became more complex with gunpowder, cannon, and *trace italienne* artillery fortresses, mercenary specialists in warfare emerged who could be hired as full-fledged infantry units, regardless of nationality—leading to the aggregate-contract style of the late fifteenth and early sixteenth centuries.[9]

Foreign mercenaries had to be fed and paid. When their demands were not met, they were often a greater threat than the armies of a state's external opponents. Strong states, increasingly absolutist, could develop their

TABLE 6.1 **Lynn's abbreviated matrix of core military style**

Core Military Style	Change Period	Incoming Rationale	Outgoing Rationale	Paradigmatic Army	Technical/ Tactical Changes
Feudal	Eighth–tenth centuries	Political disintegration; lack of money economy	Feudal levy unreliability	None	Heavy cavalry dominance
Medieval-stipendiary	Twelfth–thirteenth centuries	Need for more reliable troops; increased use of infantry	Superiority of new infantry skills	No strong candidate (France, England, Switzerland)	Fortifications; increased use of infantry, bows, and artillery
Aggregate-contract	Late fifteenth–early sixteenth centuries	Political centralization; money economy; mercenary emergence	Unreliability of mercenaries; growing national expertise	France (late 1400s/early 1500s) and then Spain	Gunpowder revolution; artillery fortresses; tactics/discipline; revolution
State-commission	Late sixteenth–early seventeenth centuries	Absolutist state; need for controllable military	Lack of army dedication, initiative, and effectiveness	France to 1740s/1757, then Prussia	Gunpowder weapons refinement; cavalry resurgence; continued tactics change
Popular-conscript	1789–1810	Political revolution requiring dedicated national army	Limitations and expense of long-service professional armies	France to 1860s, then Germany	Infantry tactics; mobile artillery; initial industrial revolution advances
Mass-reserve	1866–1905	Population increase; industrial technology; representative political institutions	Lack of need for and great expense of large armies; political costs of conscription	Germany to 1918, France to 1939, then US and USSR from 1945	Full impact of industrial revolution (machine guns, tanks, planes, atomic weapons)
Volunteer-technical	1970–1995	Technology not dependent on army size	—	United States	Electronic revolution; continued improvements in weapons platforms

Note: Lynn (1996) offers twenty-six factors that we have very selectively reduced to four for this table.

own national armies and have some expectation of paying for their maintenance. The true nationalization of the army, however, had to await the advent of nationalistic recruits in the French Revolutionary/Napoleonic Wars—most prominently demonstrated in France (Lynn 1997). More or less simultaneously, the fruits of the British Industrial Revolution began to appear on battlefields, thereby expanding the firepower, lethality, mobility, and complexity of army operations.

At the same time, though, the financial and political implications of popular conscription encouraged states to proceed cautiously with armies that were usually smaller than those generated to fight between 1792 and 1815. Professional, long-service troops were needed to respond quickly to security threats, but maintaining too many of these troops on hand was costly. Too great a reliance on patriotic enthusiasm might also lead to threats against the postwar societal status quo, which was invariably more conservative than that of France in 1792. As a consequence, popular conscription gave way to mass-reserve armies in which trained reserves and popular conscripts could be called up in times of emergency to bolster the professional standing army.

The attractiveness of the mass-reserve concept was diminished by a constellation of late twentieth-century changes. The number and intensity of external enemies diminished as the Cold War waned and ended. Army missions became increasingly less reliant on bulk size and more dependent on the deployment of high-tech weapons platforms. The idea of conscription became increasingly unpopular just as ways to cut military costs became more popular. As a result, the mass-reserve paradigm gave way or, more accurately, is giving way, to the volunteer-technical style that involves a downsized armed force utilizing vastly improved technology to carry out its missions.[10]

Note that throughout the seven iterations, the main movers, from Lynn's perspective, are the unreliability of current military organizational arrangements (and the consequent impulse to develop a better arrangement), material/political costs, and political-economic changes that allow larger armies to be maintained. If levies cannot be trusted to show up in time, a ruler needs to move toward a standing force. If foreign mercenaries cannot be trusted to go unpaid or to always follow orders, a ruler needs to move toward a standing national force, which may or may not be facilitated by patriotic sentiments.

All of these changes presume the increased availability of the financial sinews of war, which are predicated, in turn, on economic development to pay for the changes and stronger political organizations to manage them. Costs rise as armies grow very large, creating incentives to find strategies for limiting army size (reserves and professional volunteer cadres). As political systems become more sensitive to voter preferences, conscription becomes increasingly costly to maintain. It is clear that although Lynn focuses primarily on military institutions, his explanatory factors emphasize political-economic changes and the desire to maintain military competitiveness, with an occasional dash of technological change thrown in.

Lynn's framework offers an attractive way to summarize more than a millennium of change in military "style," though we would make two specific amendments to Lynn's model. Charlemagne's imperial project is a strong paradigmatic feudal candidate for the eighth century. One could also add something between the state-commission and popular-conscript periods and dated around late seventeenth to early eighteenth centuries, based on Black's (1991, 20–35) argument that European armies changed more between 1660 and 1710 than in the previous century on which much of the early modern European military revolution debate is centered. Black's argument is admittedly based more on weaponry (bayonets) and tactical changes than on changes in military organization and therefore does not suggest the need for an eighth iteration.

A more significant omission in Lynn's (1996) framework is a model capable of explaining in general terms how one moves from one style to the next. Lynn provides many specific hints about how things have evolved historically, in that he offers explanations for the particular factors that influence the comings and goings of a particular style (see table 6.1). Yet these are descriptive explanations. In one century Lynn states that military unreliability, increased political centralization, and increased economic monetization are important influences. In another it is technological improvements and political costs that matter most. Lynn's answers are certainly plausible and useful but they are anchored to the specific time period for which they are put forward. We think we can generalize the argument even further, in part because the seeds of greater generalization are strongly evident in Lynn's matrix if we relax the privileging of military institutions as the central focus and give equal emphasis to the other elements of our coevolutionary framework.

We also need to integrate Marcus's insight on the successive preeminence of leading political-military states. Her process is not limited to chiefdoms becoming unitary states only to dissolve into smaller units. The basic driver is exploiting political, military, and economic advantages to subordinate competitors. That process began early and still operates, although the forms taken have evolved over time. Yet coercive territorial consolidation persists as an ongoing process, and the most recent breakdown of a prominent unitary state dates only to the early 1990s.

Coevolution, Regional Hegemony, and Constraints on Escalation

The coevolution of the six variables introduced in chapter 3—war, political and military organization, political economy, threat environment, and weaponry—is the first theoretical principle. That is, these six variables tend to coevolve with a significant change in one or more of the six probably leading to significant changes in the other variables/processes. The second theoretical statement is about changes or innovations in the six variables. Change or innovation in warfare, threat environment, military technology, political and military organizations, and political-economic milieu is both episodic and gradual, but the most radical innovations and changes tend to be made episodically. Third, these radical innovations will tend to be highly concentrated spatially and then diffuse gradually depending on the ability and willingness of others to emulate the innovations. Fourth, the advantages accruing to first movers in warfare, military technology, and political/military organizational capability are tremendous. They lead to the probability that one group will tend to predominate to the extent that they can seize the war-making initiative and, for a while, maintain their military capability lead. The magnitude of this advantage can vary, however, as a function of the scope of the institutional or technological change and the rate of diffusion of these innovations.

If this bellicosity advantage is highly concentrated for a finite period of time, it follows that the modal propensity is for some movement toward regional hegemony on the part of the group enjoying the war-making lead.[11] Adjacent opponents will be defeated and either absorbed or subordinated. Regional empires will emerge with sizes varying as a function of a variety of constraints—technological, organizational, logistical, financial, demographic, geographical, and climatological.[12] Political-military expansion on land has always encountered some limit beyond which it proved difficult to move successfully. The histories of Assyrian, Persian, Alexandrian, Roman, Islamic, and Mongol expansion, among others, provide ample illustration. As a consequence, regional hegemony has been the ultimate prize for aspiring conquerors. The development of maritime and later aerospace capabilities allows for the projection of military force at greater distance, but no one yet has attempted global hegemony based on direct territorial conquest. More indirect strategies of power and influence are another matter (Robinson and Gallagher 1950), but that is an analytically distinct form of global hegemony.[13]

Still, the propensity is only for movement toward regional hegemony, not always for its successful implementation. More competitive situations can characterize the period leading to the imposition of hegemony and the period following its probable disintegration. Most patterns of hegemonic decline (on land, at least) involve some sort of resource overextension. Aspiring regional hegemons attempt to expand too far, take on too many enemies, and/or deplete the resource base necessary for maintaining a hegemonic position (Gilpin 1981; Kennedy 1987; Snyder 1991; Kupchan 1994). Thus warfare should be expected normally to be characterized by a three-phased sequence of prehegemonic competition, hegemony and resistance, and posthegemonic competition.

The imposition of regional hegemony is not guaranteed by the mere possession of superior military capabilities (and, presumably, the will to exploit those capabilities). Without suggesting a tautology, the success of expansion depends in part on the nature of resistance to expansion, which, in turn, may depend on the threat environment. The greater is the resistance, the less probable is successful expansion. Resistance, in turn, can be generated in a variety of ways. Expanding groups can encounter climate and terrain changes that tend to neutralize their initial capability advantages. The Mongols, for example, found it difficult to penetrate India successfully, due in part to climate changes (Grousset 1970, 242; Wink 2004, 119). Expanding groups can collide eventually with another group that also possesses military capability advantages that equal or exceed their own. Or the chances of successful resistance can be augmented by the coalescing of other units against the threat of coercive expansion (as in balance of power processes).[14] In situations in which resistance is great, therefore, it is conceivable that a region would never move out of the prehegemonic competition phase. Since there is no assurance that coevolutionary processes will move forward rapidly, it is also conceivable that a region could experience extended periods of posthegemonic competition as well. An example here is post-Roman Europe. Depending on how one interprets the Carolingian imperial expansion, there is little in the way of attempts to establish regional hegemony for more than a millennium after the fall of western Rome (Santosusso 2004,

64–65). Other regions have also experienced long interludes of continued fragmentation.

Nor is political-economic milieu the only possible source of constraints on the direction of coevolutionary patterns. The historical record is not one of universal movement toward an escalation in the scale of warfare, the number of soldiers, the size of the state, or the lethality of the weaponry. At least two other countervailing processes are discernible within the six-variable complex. One is that increasing minimal expectations for competitive warfare capability, in addition to real-life demonstrations of these rising minimal thresholds on the battlefield, force some states to drop out of competition. This tendency is reinforced by changing expectations and demands of populations for greater attention to welfare, as opposed to warfare—a factor that can be traced to the evolution of the political-economic milieu, at least in some parts of the world.[15]

A second countervailing process is that the increasing lethality of weaponry, which is related to its expense over the long term, appears to have constrained the application of some but hardly all of the most lethal military technology. Poison gas was used in World War I but not very much in World War II. Atomic weapons were employed at the end of World War II but not, so far, since then. The advent of nuclear weapons did lead to an escalation in the development of nuclear weapons but, in retrospect, need not have done so. Students of deterrence argue that a minimal second-strike capability may suffice to deter a nuclear attack.[16] Alternatively, innovations in artillery/bombing coordination and accuracy have encouraged a perceived need for smaller, more technologically sophisticated military organizations as opposed to ever-expanding armies, as suggested by the contemporary literature on the information-based revolution in military affairs.

The combination of these countervailing processes leads to strong constraints on the ultimate coevolution of warfare, military technology, political/military organization, threat environment, and political-economic milieu. Rather than an ever-ramping-upward spiral of expense, organizational capability, and lethality, some go up to a point and then spiral downward. Many of the most powerful military powers of the past are no more. In some cases they have been defeated or exhausted by combat, and may even have ceased to exist. In other cases the increasing costs of military competition have forced former competitors to the sidelines. They are simply no longer able to compete effectively on the political-military playing field. By default, and of course holding other sources of threat constant, the world has become a safer place by reducing major power competition. Whether this condition persists will depend on the maintenance of the high costs for entry into competition at the highest level and the reduced incentives to tolerate these high costs. After a brief post–Cold War interval in which there were no major power rivalries, evidence for the reemergence of major power rivalries, albeit of less-than-Cold-War intensity, is reappearing (Thompson and Dreyer 2011).

There is another dimension to these cost constraints on competition and conflict. The vast majority of contemporary state organizations have never experienced the upward coevolutionary spiral of warfare, technology, and organizations associated with what we are calling the third acceleration. It is quite likely that many will never do so. There is an ironic outcome of this basic divide in historical experience. The greater the extent that states have experienced and survived political-military competition and its domestic implications in creating loyal and patriotic citizens and governments capable of monopolizing coercive power at home and mobilizing resources to meet external threats, the more likely they are to be strong political organizations. States lacking this experience are more likely to be weak states beset by debt crises and internal warfare and increasingly unlikely to transform themselves into strong states in the traditional fashion.[17]

Weak states will still engage in external warfare, but most likely it will be short in duration, close to home, and inconclusive. Most weak states lack the capability to engage in extended combat at any distance or to resolve their grievances on the battlefield without external help. External intervention in such conflicts is just as likely to prevent any possibility of breaking out of the "weak state trap" or the "state-strength dilemma" (Holsti 1996, 116–17), which refers to the limited likelihood that decision-makers seeking to transform their weak states will overcome their domestic and external constraints. External financial and military assistance makes it less likely that local decision-makers will need to develop domestic strategies to pay for military organizations and technology. The occasional appearance of weak state military expansion (against even weaker foes) is also likely to encourage external efforts to prevent it on behalf of maintaining local and wider status quos, a process that has been reinforced since World War II by the emergence of strong international norms against territorial conquest (Zacher 2001; Hironaka 2005).[18]

The combination of weak states, many of which lack much military capability, and strong states, many of which no longer develop their military capability, leads to a world that is selectively more pacific in its interstate relations than would be the case if there were more strong states with ambitious foreign policies or if there was a better chance of breaking out of the weak state trap.[19]

There is more that could be said about strong and weak states and the implications of coevolutionary spirals for such processes as taxation, liberalization, and regime type formation (Ardant 1975; Hintze in Gilbert 1975; Rasler and Thompson 1989). The theory advanced so far is sufficiently complex, however, to warrant stopping at this point and considering whether or to what extent the historical evidence supports these theoretical generalizations. There are also a number of distinctive emphases in the theory as currently developed that work against testing all dimensions simultaneously. Some choices have to be made among the implications of coevolutionary spirals for regional hegemony in contrast to the implications for strong and weak states. Both subtheoretical emphases deserve testing. Yet doing so would take us in much different directions. In this chapter we choose to focus primarily on the link between coercive advantages and thrusts toward regional hegemony formation that might permit us to extend the western military trajectory back in time. In chapter 7 we return to the strong-weak state distinction.

More Testing of the Coevolutionary Theory of War

Testing our theory of the evolution of war requires considerable work. We are talking about multiple dimensions of behavior encompassing thousands of years and formidable variety in different parts of the world. No single test, however comprehensive, is likely to touch upon all of its various dimensions. Each test should be looked upon as just another trial that can produce a supportive, nonsupportive, or simply an inconclusive outcome. Still, tests can be characterized as either central or peripheral to the thrust of the theoretical argument. Central tests examine core axioms while peripheral ones focus on more tangential elements. Not surprisingly, the former type of test is more important than the latter type to assessing the utility of the theory.

One of the central assertions of this evolutionary war interpretation is that technology, organizations, threat environments, war, and political-economic context have coevolved and led to intermittent bouts of regional hegemony, or attempts to achieve regional hegemony, by the group most favored by the coevolutionary spiral at a given point in time. How might we test this proposition? The traditional and time-honored way would involve reliance on anecdotal references to behavior that seems to resemble the predicted tendencies. Yet such an approach falls short of tackling the serial implications of the coevolutionary spiral. Scattered examples will not suffice to demonstrate, successfully or otherwise, that one round on the coevolutionary spiral led to another round, which led to another round, and so on up the spiral. We need, then, to trace the full history of warfare from its outset to its contemporary manifestations in at least one military trajectory. Fortunately, inasmuch as there are a number of different trajectories, we need not attempt to take them all on at one time. Instead, tests of this idea should concentrate on establishing the nature of one evolutionary warfare trajectory at a time before attempting more comparative statements.

If we can accept Lynn's seven-step iteration, we already have a good handle on the modern end of the western military trajectory. Accepting the iterations implies adopting his periodization and interpretation of prevailing army organization type, critical military technology, political-economic context, and types of war and war styles. To encompass the full span of the western trajectory, the question is whether we can augment Lynn's data back to the origins of western warfare. As it turns out, this augmentation involves adding another 10,000 or 11,000 years to Lynn's 1,300 years.

This test of the coevolutionary dimension of the warfare theory comes down to questions about serial continuity in tendencies for organizational, technological, political-economic, and warfare processes to proceed in rough unison over time and about tendencies for the primary beneficiaries of the changes to seek the temporary domination of their region. In earlier chapters we have sought confirmation for the first part of the proposition. We have yet to examine the second part on regional hegemony.

Table 6.2 summarizes the effort to extend Lynn's interpretation of more recent developments further back in time for the western trajectory.[20] Table 6.2 begins around 12,000 BCE. As we saw in chapter 2, one of the perennial debates in the warfare literature revolves around the question of whether the human species is inherently violent or whether warfare is an acquired trait.[21] It is unlikely that this debate will be resolved any time soon, but the available evidence strongly supports the idea that warfare is a behavior that emerged over thousands of years before it came to be manifested in ways that we might now recognize as warfare.

TABLE 6.2 The coevolution of organizations, technology, warfare, and political-economic context

Time	Army Organization Type (Lead Land Power)	Military Technology	Types of War and War Styles	Political-Economic Context
Pre-12,000 BCE	None	Primitive clubs/spears	Sporadic violence but not war	Hunter-foragers/low population density
12,000–8,000 BCE	Sporadic groups—informal column and line tactics may have been used in combat	Bow, sling, dagger, mace	Intermittent clashes; raiding; ambushes	Neolithic hunting-foraging groups
8,000–4,000 BCE	Noninstitutionalized	Fortification of cities begins to appear?	Intermittent clashes and sieges	Beginning of agriculture and population settlements of slowly increasing density
4000–2000 BCE	Presumably imperial conscript/mercenaries—standing army in second half of third millennia (Akkad)	Heavy infantry phalanx?; bronze piercing axe, later composite bows in Akkadian era, and solid-wheeled battle carts; siege craft	Chronic intercity combat but more siege than battles	Decentralized urban network giving way to Akkadian empire
1500–1000 BCE	Imperial conscript/mercenaries (Egypt)	Integrated heavy and light infantry; chariots, compound bows	Punitive expeditions against weaker opponents giving way to full scale warfare between major powers	Increasing competition among major powers in region leading to Egyptian-Hittite showdown
900–600 BCE	Feudal levies give way to imperial conscript/mercenaries (Assyria)	Iron weapons; integrated force of heavy/light infantry, chariots (emphasized), and cavalry introduced; siege warfare	Multidirectional imperial campaigns to extend/protect borders and suppress rebellions	Assyrian imperial expansion, organization, and hegemony
550–350 BCE	Imperial conscript/mercenaries (Persia)	Integrated light infantry and emphasis on cavalry, with weaponry subject to ethnic specializations	Imperial campaigns to extend/protect borders and suppress rebellions	Persian imperial expansion and hegemony

490–338 BCE	Property owners available for short campaigning seasons	Hoplite heavy infantry phalanx	Initially short, ritualized wars for limited gains, escalating to longer wars for major stakes in Greek wars with Persia and subsequent intra-Greek wars	Greek city states as regional subsystem in larger eastern Mediterranean
350–200 BCE	Imperial conscript/mercenaries (Macedonia)	Integrated heavy and light infantry, sarissa phalanx, and cavalry; siege warfare/catapults, logistical reforms	Frequent warfare to unify Greece and to conquer the Persian Empire	Initially, Macedonian expansion followed by decentralization of Alexandrian empire
200 BCE–300 CE	Evolution from citizen militia to standing force of imperial conscript/mercenaries (Rome)	Heavy infantry in maniples/cohorts using short swords and spears permitting great maneuverability; siege craft	Frequent warfare against usually less organized opponents in extension and protection of imperial boundaries; frequent civil war	Extension and maintenance of Roman imperial hegemony
700–1000 CE	Feudal (Carolingians?)	Iron age arms/armor, stirrup reliance	Mainly local contests with other power centers and raiders	Political decentralization with aspirations to greater centralization; limited monetary economy and agrarian economy with landed elite
1100–1300 CE	Medieval-stipendiary	Increasing use of infantry; crossbow, longbow; stone fortifications; early gunpowder impact	Expeditions at increasing distance relying on mercenaries while feudal forces provide home defense	Initial formation of national monarchies; expansion of money economy; military service commuted into money payment

TABLE 6.2 (cont.)

Time	Army Organization Type (Lead Land Power)	Military Technology	Types of War and War Styles	Political-Economic Context
Late 1400s–early 1500s	Aggregate contract (France)	Real impact of gunpowder revolution; artillery fortresses; initial tactical innovations	Great reliance on mercenaries in offensive and defensive operations	Increasing political centralization—absolutist state; money economy established; commercial expansion; expansion of credit essential to hiring large numbers of troops
Late 1500s–early 1600s	State-commission (Spain, Sweden, the Netherlands)	Gunpowder weapon refinements; continued revolution in tactics/administration	Wars with relatively limited goals	Continued commercial expansion; initial expansion of middle-class wealth
Late 1700s–early 1800s	Popular conscript (France)	Continued tactical changes; initial impact of industrial revolution	National contests at greater distance from home	Industrial and political revolutions; expanding middle class wealth; diminishing status of agrarian aristocracies
Late 1800s–mid-1900s	Mass-reserve (Germany)	Full impact of industrial revolution; machine guns, rapid fire/heavy artillery, trucks, planes, tanks, atomic weapons	Total war	Industrial societies/industrial working class; less authoritarian and more authoritarian political systems
Late 1900s and continuing	Volunteer-technical (United States and, to lesser extent, Soviet Union)	Sophisticated technological improvements in vehicles, planes, and weapons systems; electronic revolution	Altered threat structure placing greater emphasis on skill and mobility in conflicts of limited duration against opponents with less capability	Wider distribution of wealth; apparent Cold War triumph of democratic systems in the west

Sources: Anglin et al. (2002), Archer et al. (2002), Ferrill (1997), Gabriel and Metz (1991), Jones (1987), Lynn (1996), and Nicolle (1995, 1996).

As implied in chapter 2, the basic limitation on the emergence of warfare was population density. Small hunter-forager bands made up of people of all ages and both genders could inflict only so much damage on other bands of similar size.[22] At worst, they might seek to eliminate them altogether. Yet the archaeological evidence for massacres on this scale is limited in time. No evidence of combat involving groups of people as attackers, defenders, or casualties has been found before some 13,000 years ago.

Table 6.2 suggests that changes in military technology preceded political and military organizational changes without leading to major changes in the types of warfare that were exhibited. It was only after concentrations of population began to appear and also after people began to develop technology to protect themselves against raiders that intermittent clashes began to escalate into combat engaged in by groups beginning to resemble armies. The span 4000–3000 BCE appears to mark an initial watershed in this respect, with the emergence of multiple cities in southern Mesopotamia, along with infantry formations, improvements in military technology, and intercity warfare. This era also gave way to the first clear episode of imperial expansion centered on Sargon's Akkadian takeover of northern and southern Mesopotamia (after 2350 BCE) and attempted movements into adjacent areas in the Fertile Crescent and Gulf. Sargon may also have possessed the first standing army of impressive size, perhaps 5,400 men (Gabriel 2002, 55).

As the first episode of imperial expansion, some might opt for either the fourth millennium BCE Urukian expansion of Lower Mesopotamia's resource acquisition network to encompass the area between Anatolia, Iran, and Egypt, or the coerced unification of northern and southern Egypt toward the end of the fourth millennium (Algaze 1993). However, while the Urukian expansion appears to have involved the movement of a substantial number of Sumerians into non-Sumerian territory, it does not appear to have had an explicitly coercive nature. Sumerians created trading enclaves in areas already populated and colonies in areas that were underpopulated, not unlike the Greek expansion of the first millennium BCE. It is also possible that the Urukian expansion imitated an even earlier, fifth millennium Ubaid resource acquisition network, but no evidence exists to suggest military coercion in that instance either (Stein 1999). The expansion to the north of Upper Egypt has a better claim to the earliest imperialism. We do not know much about the circumstances, however, and it was initially restricted to the Egyptian area, with some extension into adjacent Palestine and to the Nubian south of Egypt. Sargon also united the north and south of his core region but then proceeded to move beyond the Mesopotamian borders in several directions.

The next significant iteration in table 6.2 highlights the Egyptian New Kingdom expansion into the Fertile Crescent area (as well as south into Nubia) of the last half of the second millennium BCE. Army size had escalated by a factor of more than two to eight over the probable maximum sizes found in the preceding millennium. The Egyptian army's integration of light and heavy infantry, in addition to its shock chariot component and bowmen, illustrate the expanding sophistication and complexity of military organization. Political organization had also become increasingly complex as occasional razzias, or raids into adjacent territory, gave way to expanded territorial control and rivalries with other major powers in the region.

The iterative pace of the western trajectory accelerated in the first millennium BCE. Whereas the Akkadian and Egyptian empires represented third and second millennium enterprises, the first millennium experienced an Assyrian-Persian-Macedonian-Roman sequence before slowing down in the first millennium CE.[23] It is in this same sequence that the west Asian–west European gap was also bridged. How this happened is due in part to the Greek city-state interval inserted in table 6.2 between the Persians and the Macedonians. This insertion is not meant to give equal status to the Persians, Greeks, and Macedonians, as Greece never developed a lead land army. If the Greek city-states had been located in the west Asian threat environment, they would probably not have developed the hoplite heavy infantry innovation. It is dubious, for that matter, if they would have emerged as city-states in the first place if they had been surrounded by more hostile adversaries, as they would have been if they had been located on the other side of the Mediterranean.

One way to simplify the changes in military technology and organization of the first millennium BCE is to note that the Assyrians developed their primacy in part on the basis of a combination of infantry, chariot, and siege warfare emphases. Their successors, the Persians, placed greater emphasis on cavalry that had been introduced initially by the Assyrians (courtesy of Cimmerian and Scythian nomads). Alexander the Great merged the eastern emphasis on cavalry with the western emphasis on heavy infantry to become the first European to conquer a goodly proportion of west Asia and northeast Africa.[24] The Romans then took the Macedonian phalanx one step further by breaking heavy infantry units into more flexible, smaller numbers of men, who were less dependent on long spears. We should note, however, that these changes in military technology and military organization evolved in warfare and were accompanied by various changes in the threat environments and the nature of the political economies supporting these expanding empires.

Alexander, for example, increasingly relied on eastern military units only after fighting in the east had reduced his Macedonian core troops. The Romans initially fought in phalanx formation and moved toward the maniple cohort formation only gradually. The political-economic evolution is seen most clearly in the Greek and Roman experiences. Initial reliance on property owners (Greek hoplites) or citizen militias, as in Rome, gave way to more specialized military organizations composed of soldiers with more longer term commitments than had originally been the case.

The disintegration of the Roman Empire in the west gave way to an extended period of decentralization, although that generalization may not give sufficient credit to the relatively short-lived and spatially limited Carolingian effort. As Reuter (1999, 14) argued, the Carolingian expansion probably proceeded as far as was possible for its era and ran out of enemies worth conquering. This extended period of political decentralization, moreover, was paralleled and encouraged by a strong reliance on cavalry to deal with nomadic and Muslim light cavalry raiders and to use as heavy shock instruments against infantry.

Even so, many of these heavy cavalry were more likely initially to use their horses as transportation to the battlefield and to then fight on foot (Bachrach 1993a, 1993b). Another myth of the western trajectory is that infantry was displaced by cavalry as early as the Battle of Adrianople in 378 CE. The source of the myth appears to be Oman ([1898] 1991) but as Burns (1973) demonstrates, this Roman-Goth battle was primarily fought by infantry, and Roman cavalry actually outnumbered the Goth cavalry. There is no question that the arrival of the Goth cavalry, possibly on a less than premeditated basis, proved to be a significant contribution to the Goth victory over the Romans, but the ascent of heavy cavalry in western Europe was a long way off into the future. The Battle of Adrianople probably says more about Roman imperial and army dissolution than it does about the relative predominance of infantry versus cavalry.

Contrary to the usual image associated with the birth of European feudalism that was long thought to be associated with the emergence of the stirrup (White 1962), heavy cavalry appears to have been a legacy of the earlier Roman period, in which Roman armies had utilized Alan heavy cavalry to also fight nomadic light cavalry units in the east and had then distributed Alan units throughout the empire. The Germanic tribal successors to the Roman Empire subsequently imitated and expanded on the Alan example. This eventually led to the emergence and dominance of the European feudal knight for a few centuries.[25]

Table 6.2, which integrates Lynn's seven iterations with the older cases, indicates that roughly the last millennium of the western trajectory was characterized by a return to accelerated change in military technology, military organization, and political-economic context. Gunpowder, *trace italiennes* (artillery fortresses), and a renewed emphasis on disciplined infantry tactics brought fundamental changes in military technology that were only revolutionized in subsequent iterations by the changes wrought by industrialization changes after the late eighteenth century. Military organizations expanded greatly in size and professional training. Political organizations and national societies also underwent a great deal of change, in part due to attempts to keep up with the mobilization requirements associated with the changes in military technology and organization. It is precisely this activity on which the lion's share of debate about early modern European military revolution is focused. Moreover, the debate is not centered so much on whether there were military revolutions between approximately the medieval era and today, but when, where, and to what effect.[26]

We agree with Lynn's (1996) argument that these changes can best be viewed as successive transformations in military technology, military and political organizations, and warfare, all aided and abetted by corresponding changes in the European political economy and threat environment. We go beyond Lynn, however, in arguing that each round after the late 1400s tended to be initiated or led ultimately by one aspirant to regional hegemony. The French inaugurated the acceleration when they marched into Italy in 1494. The Habsburgs countered with tactical innovations leading to the Spanish *tercios*—a line of development that was followed by subsequent tactical innovations introduced by northern Protestant states (the Netherlands and Sweden), leading ultimately to the French development of a nation in arms.[27] Expansion in the size and discipline of armies eventually was accompanied by a full array of transformed military technology made possible by a series of industrial revolutions after the late eighteenth century. In support of these transformations, European states became more complex and powerful. Their populations underwent a transformation as well from nominal subjects to patriotic citizens. Warfare moved toward the total involvement of populations experienced in World Wars I and II.

These developments were not coincidental. They were instead the product of an intense coevolutionary spiral in technology, organization, and warfare that transformed Europe in ways that have not been experienced to the same extent in much of the rest of the world. They were changes brought about by paradigmatic armies (and navies) within the dual context of aspirations to regional hegemony that were repeatedly thwarted by the intensely competitive nature of European international relations of this period. We think this combination of paradigmatic innovation, thwarted hegemony, and intense competition led to the third acceleration.

Deciphering the "Western" Military Trajectory

How should we summarize this western military trajectory? Table 6.3 provides one possible interpretation. Over a roughly five-thousand-year span, the predominant emphasis has been placed on infantry (heavy and light), in integrated combination with chariots, cavalry, and tanks, and with various ways to fire projectiles over an increasing distance. Although not fully illustrated in table 6.3, the size and lethality of western armed forces has intensified steadily but nonlinearly. Army size escalated from Sumer to Persia, declined with Macedonia, expanded again with Rome before declining again in the feudal era. After the feudal era, size steadily escalated again until the latest volunteer-technical phase. Western political organizations and their financial strategies for paying for these changes have always had to scramble to keep pace with the escalating military costs. To the extent that some political organizations succeeded, the complexity, strength, and size of the political organizations reflected this form of arms race.

The main exceptions to the infantry intensification norm are the chariot era (roughly 1700–800 BCE) and the feudal era (roughly 500–1300 CE), in which heavy cavalry gradually came to predominate due to changes in the threat environment, the political-economic landscape, and the availability of weapons technology.[28] Although Egyptian and Assyrian armies had strong appreciations for chariots, they used them in conjunction with a strong emphasis on infantry, and not as a substitute for them. Egyptian chariots were used as mobile platforms for archers and to chase fleeing

TABLE 6.3 **The western military trajectory**

Leading Army	Infantry	Chariot/Cavalry/Armored Cavalry
Sumer/Akkad	Central component	"Battle-wagons" (used primarily for elite transportation)
Egypt (New Kingdom)	Central component	Strong focus on chariots
Assyria	Central component	Chariots still significant but becoming obsolete/Cavalry introduced
Persia	Central component	Cavalry role expanded
Macedonia	Central component	Cavalry also significant
Rome	Central component	Cavalry significance decreased until the last few centuries of the western empire
Feudal (Carolingian)	Present but largely secondary	Heavy cavalry emphasis
Medieval-stipendiary	Significance begins to be restored	Cavalry significance persists
Aggregate-contract (France)	Central component	Cavalry of declining significance
State-commission (Spain)	Central component	Some cavalry significance restored
Popular-conscript (France)	Central component	Cavalry retain significance
Mass-reserve (Germany)	Central component	Armored cavalry
Volunteer-technical (US/USSR, then only US)	Central component	Armored cavalry (significance declining?)

infantry (Gabriel and Metz 1991, 331–32). Charioteers might also dismount and fight as infantry. Assyrian chariots were used as shock forces and to carry infantry into battle so that Assyrian charioteers tended to end up fighting as infantry as well.

From this perspective, the late medieval and early modern European military revolutions (again roughly between 1300 and 1800) appear less as a discontinuous break in the long-term pattern and more as the reassertion of western path dependencies. The intensification of infantry tactics (and firepower)—some of the hallmarks of the early modern European changes—has been more central to the western military trajectory than the respective "flirtations" with chariots and heavy cavalry.[29]

Chase (2003) makes a strong argument for the predominance of cavalry in areas characterized by nomadic threat and for the development of gunpowder firearms elsewhere in the Old World (western Europe and Japan) in the period between 1300 and 1750, but he overlooks the infantry/artillery path dependency of the western (but not the Japanese) military trajectory. Otherwise, we do not find Chase's theory and its emphasis on the initial inadequacies of gunpowder firearms incompatible with the one advanced here. Archer et al. (2002, 222–23) argue that technological advances in firearms were most probable in the frontier areas separating antagonistic cultures/religions and characterized by chronic warfare. The idea is that the nature of the threat environment literally forced actors to try new technology and tactics in order to survive. They point to the Hundred Years' War, which does not seem to fit their argument because of the absence of a religious-cultural frontier, and the Christian-Islamic frontier in southern Europe, the Mediterranean, and North Africa, which does.

One last question remains to be explored. How western has the western trajectory been? John Keegan (1993, 289–91) lauds the "Western way of warfare" for triumphing over the rest of the world. For Keegan, the western military culture combines three ingredients: (1) an emphasis on face-to-face combat on foot and to the death (as opposed to more ritualized behavior), (2) an ideological justification for war as sanctioned by Christianity, and (3) an openness to new technology leading to the gunpowder revolution and its increasingly lethal weaponry descendants. The first element Keegan attributes to the Greeks, the second to the Crusades, and the third as culminating in the eighteenth century CE.

Victor Hanson (2001, 21–22) also focuses on the "western way of war," but he reads a lot more into western military culture. He describes it as amoral because it elevates military necessity over religious scruples and individualistic due to citizen-focused societies from which the military are recruited. He also emphasizes the heavy infantry characteristic, which he attributes to the high premium placed on property ownership and the relatively large numbers of people who have been able to own property in the west. Free inquiry, rationalism, and the marketplace of ideas explain the superiority of western military technology and the adaptability of its armies. For Hanson, though, all of these traits can be traced back to the Greeks in which he specializes. The curious irony here, however, is that Greek phalanx formations were designed to suppress the exhibition of

TABLE 6.4 **Nonwestern influences on the western military trajectory**

Army Leader	Nonwestern Imports/Influences
Sumer/Akkad	Composite bow?
Egypt	Composite bow, chariots
Assyria	Chariots, cavalry
Persia	Cavalry
Macedonia	Persian cavalry, Indian "very heavy" cavalry (elephants)
Rome	Legion-maniple formation adopted and phalanx abandoned after defeats fighting northern tribes; heavy cavalry needed to fight Parthians, Huns, and others
Feudal	Heavy cavalry, stirrup
Medieval-stipendiary	Gunpowder, cannon (naval—masts, compass, rudder)

individualism in combat. Phalanxes either moved well as a group or they were prone to disintegration under stress.[30]

One problem with emphasizing the distinctiveness of the western military experience is that it plays down the long history and extent to which the western trajectory has been strongly influenced by nonwestern stimuli and contacts. Table 6.4 summarizes some of the most important military imports. The origin of the composite bow in the Akkadian era is unclear in part because the only evidence that such bows were used is a picture on a memorial to a victory over highland tribes to the east of southern Mesopotamia. Did urbanized Mesopotamians develop this weapon or was it developed far from the cities in the mountains or steppes and then captured by Akkadian forces? Or, as William H. McNeill (1963, 46) suggests, did Akkadians innovate the composite bow because they represented a group that was transitional between northern "barbarians" and southern "civilization"? In fact, McNeill argues that Sargon was only the first of many "marcher lords" to exploit barbarian military techniques for imperial expansion purposes.

The situation is much clearer in the Egyptian iteration thanks to the introduction of both chariots and composite bows by Hyksos invaders from the east. Although the Hyksos came from the Syrian/Palestinian area, chariots with spoked wheels and pulled by horses had been developed in the area around the Black Sea before diffusing throughout the Old World. The Egyptians had to imitate the Hyksos arsenal to win back control of

Egypt prior to the beginning of the New Kingdom. The Egyptians, with their own preexisting military technology, could not have ousted the Hyksos, but that imitation was only a necessary condition, not a sufficient one, for the defeat of the Hyksos.

Both Assyria, which was already strongly committed to the use of chariots, and Persia imitated to varying extents their horseback-riding nomadic opponents from the central Eurasian steppes.[31] Macedonia later integrated Persian cavalry with the Greek hoplite heavy infantry strategy. Rome first abandoned the Greek phalanx for the more flexible legion-maniple system after disasters experienced in combat encounters with Celtic and Samnite tribal groups. Rome later hired Alan heavy cavalrymen migrating west for deployment against light cavalry attacks on its eastern and northern frontiers.

The heavy cavalry emphasis of the feudal era appears to stem in part from the deployment of these Asian-Roman heavy cavalry throughout the empire, where the cavalrymen either remained and/or were imitated by indigenous warriors. That the heavy cavalry could become heavier over time was due in part to the import of the stirrup—possibly a Chinese invention, but definitely an eastern innovation—toward the middle of the first millennium CE. The stirrup enabled more heavily armed men to remain in the saddle, though this was facilitated by larger horses, which were not eastern imports. Other Chinese inventions—gunpowder and cannon—began to filter into Europe in the thirteenth century CE and contributed to the dethroning of the medieval heavy cavalry emphasis in Europe. It is also worth noting that crossbows were first invented and utilized in China roughly a millennium before they were used to defeat armored cavalry in Europe. Whether European crossbows were based on Chinese models, however, is not clear. European naval capabilities, however, owe a great deal to borrowed Chinese innovations, including rudders, compasses, and multiple masts.

The western military trajectory, therefore, owes a great debt—chariots, cavalry, and gunpowder—to eastern imports and "out-of-area" influences. The debt is more than simply a matter of the occasional introduction of novel weapons. These weapons permeated the trajectory and also contributed to the near-continuous intensification of military lethality, even if they sometimes diverted the direction of the trajectory.

Thus the western military trajectory was far from autonomous. More significantly, the west was adjacent to areas with different path dependencies, terrain, political organization, and military trajectories. In the absence of these repeated alien military inputs and openness to their utility, the trajectory might have developed much differently—perhaps more like the relatively insulated Mesoamerican military trajectory, which evolved very slowly from Neolithic weaponry onward until confronted with the alien military inputs of Spanish conquistadores. Thus the intermittent but pervasive intervention of new strategies and technology stimulated by contact with outsiders is also part of the western military trajectory—particularly since the specific impacts of these borrowed strategies and technologies were not always similar to the impacts manifested in other military trajectories in which they originated.

Keegan (1993) is right to emphasize the fighting face-to-face, on-foot, to-the-death element. As he notes, this is very much an infantry characteristic, which we have argued is one of the major hallmarks of the western Eurasian military trajectory. Charioteers and cavalrymen, on the whole, have been more likely to develop aristocratic rituals and norms of chivalry. Infantry soldiers moving in tight formation are trained to kill collectively as quickly and as efficiently as possible. The question is whether this western cultural trait is of Greek origin or perhaps even older if infantry formations began to appear several thousand years before the Greeks developed their hoplite version of heavy infantry.

It is worth noting that infantry operating in looser formations (for instance, Celts in western Europe or Aztecs in Mexico) have developed more ritualized battle behavior focusing on individual face-to-face combat. The phalanx formation did not encourage one-on-one combat because massed spearmen depended on overlapping shields for their protection. As it happens, though, the Celts employed both shield walls and individual combat challenges. Ellis (1998, 102–10) suggests that the Romans learned about shield walls from their Celtic opponents even though Celtic battles could sometimes be determined by a fight between two champions representing the opposing armies. Roman champions were prepared to engage in this form of contest as well, but their participation was banned after it was realized that Celtic champions tended to be much larger (and therefore more likely to win) than the typical Roman volunteer.

As for the other two traits, it is difficult to imagine that westerners (including Mesopotamians, Egyptians, Assyrians, Persians, Greeks/Macedonians, and Romans) had to wait until the early second millennium CE to begin invoking gods as ideological justification for warfare. Nor is the technological openness a latter-day development. It appears to have been present almost from the outset—aided by the presence of porous frontiers with and intermittent shocks and examples from the rest of Eurasia.

Keegan (1993, 390–91) argues that "Asian" culture encouraged elites to be conservative and to retain a monopoly on traditional weapons, no matter how obsolete, as a type of arms control. There have been several different military trajectories in Asia, however, and so a single cultural prescription cannot explain less openness to military technology at the other end of Eurasia. Nor is it clear that "Asians" in general were less open to new military technology (see, most recently, Sawyer 2004). Chariots, cavalry, crossbows, and gunpowder were hardly strangers to eastern Eurasia. The Chinese reluctance to focus more resources on gunpowder in the face of a nomadic threat is explained well by Kenneth Chase (2003) in terms of the early ineffectiveness of gunpowder weapons against light cavalry. In the long term, this ineffectiveness was overcome. In the short term, light cavalry threats had to be defended against by cavalry maintained in the sedentary target areas. This is a problem due not so much to culture per se as it is to the differences in eastern and western Eurasian threat environments.

Where does this leave our evolutionary war interpretation? The western trajectory is but one of several distinctive historical vectors to experience the interaction of technology, organization, and warfare. No two trajectories are likely to have experienced exactly the same mix of ingredients. Nor are they likely to achieve exactly the same outcomes. That is not what our theories predict. What they predict is that the coevolving, interactive mix of technology, organization, political economy, threat environment, and warfare will lead to the probability of one state getting ahead of its competitors in developing a coercive edge. This advantage is not infinite in time, and it does not always lead to success on the battlefield. It is likely to lead to attempts at regional expansion and conquest. That is precisely what we find most of the time in the history of a western trajectory encompassing change from the early Sumerian armies to the current US Army.

There also appears to be some relationship between periods of intensely warring states and accelerations in coevolutionary dynamics. The western trajectory is the only one to have experienced all three accelerations. Not looking at other trajectories in this chapter limits our ability to fully test this question, but there at least appears to be some correlation. What is most needed to test this idea adequately is a comparison of several trajectories with an eye toward the correlations of warring state phases and acceleration. Although we do not argue that coevolutionary development occurs only in periods of acceleration, the question of whether more significant coevolutionary development occurs in acceleration periods than in nonacceleration periods remains open.

Conclusion

Our arguments about coevolutionary dynamics—based on interactive and reciprocal changes in military and political organizations, technologies, political economy, threat environments, and wars—suggest that we should not focus too much on which single factor is most important because a change in one of the factors tends to bring about changes in the other factors. The theory also speaks to regional hegemonic tendencies, balance of power processes, strong and weak states, and transformations toward less bellicose environments.

Advancing theories is one thing. Testing them is quite another. In this chapter our assessment proceeded by first constructing and then examining the western military trajectory over thousands of years. The questions guiding our inquiry concerned whether there is a pattern of one state creating a coercive advantage based on relative endowment, threat environment, and the organizational-technological-political-economic-war coevolutionary spiral over its rivals sufficient to encourage attempts at regional hegemony. Once the prerequisites had been satisfied, there appears to be a clear pattern of succession encompassing Sumerian/Akkadian, Egyptian, Assyrian, Persian, Macedonian, Roman, Carolingian, Habsburg-Spanish, French, German, US Army superiority.

With the partial exception of the last army in the series, each state used, or appeared to use, its coercive advantage to seek regional hegemony.[32] The first seven realized variable success in this endeavor, although not without ultimately encountering successful resistance to further expansion. The post-1494 western cases have been less successful. As long as the differentiated outcome can be attributed to even more successful resistance than was encountered in the earlier segment of the trajectory, the outcome conforms to our theoretical expectations. Admittedly, however, there is no exploration in this chapter of the causal processes associated with the ultimate failures of modern hegemonic aspirants and the resistance they inspired and encountered.[33]

The patterns summarized in table 6.2, therefore, constitute reasonably strong support for the coevolutionary model. One hastens to add that evolutionary theories cannot be tested quickly. There are too many warfare trajectories to examine. While we have looked at one, there are a number of others that need investigation. Even if all trajectories prove to operate on roughly similar coevolutionary principles, there remain a number of other issues to explore. Is the western trajectory unique in eventually developing constraints on the propensity toward regional hegemony? Is it also unique in moving from a long series of regional hegemons to the most recent case in which the leading global sea power has become the leading global land power?[34] Is this latest wrinkle in the trajectory a temporary phenomenon, or is it the harbinger of a new era in world politics? Have other trajectories experienced evolutionary shifts that transform warlike environments into more pacific settings? Do states that have experienced coevolutionary spirals become different types of organizations as compared to those that never experience anything similar? How do different regions mix strong and weak states? Do regions composed exclusively of weak states operate on different principles from regions with some strong states? Or, more generally, what other processes can be linked theoretically to the organization-technology-war coevolutionary spirals?

Our evolutionary interpretation is rich. The questions are numerous. Not surprisingly, then, the empirical challenges are great. None of that is a bad thing, but much remains to be done before we will have a good sense of just how useful this coevolutionary theory is. We cannot take on all of the relevant questions at one sitting, and consequently we have needed to be selective. In our next chapter we shift the analytic focus away from the Eurocentric past and present and look instead at the trajectory of warfare outside of the west, and in particular at the rise of internal as opposed to external war in less affluent parts of the world.

CHAPTER SEVEN

Nonwestern Military Trajectories

We have argued that the third acceleration of coevolutionary developments led, through two different causal paths, to two important transformations of warfare. For industrialized states, the escalating costs of war have reduced the likelihood that they will fight each other. For nonindustrialized states, their relative weakness and inefficiency in mobilizing resources have left them less able to engage in interstate warfare and much more vulnerable to internal warfare. Having focused in earlier chapters on the transformation for industrialized states, we now turn to nonindustrialized states.

One of the keys to understanding why there are two different worlds of warfare—one for the more developed, affluent part of the world and another for the less developed, less affluent part of the world—lies in the differences in the nature of the two worlds' historical threat environments and the ways in which those environments affected the political organization of states.[1] Ann Hironaka (2005: 6–7) captures the evolutionary shift in threat environments:

> In the seventeenth and eighteenth centuries, interstate warfare was frequent and intense . . . in those days any sufficiently strong entity could become a state, and conversely, any state that was too weak was likely to cease being a state. In that international climate, states that were unable to hold out against their militarily more powerful neighbors were in danger of losing large pieces of territory, or even their existence. . . .
>
> After 1945, however, the rules and behavior changed. If one considers the international system as promoting a particular ecology of states, the population of states before 1945 was composed mostly of strong, battle-scarred states that had proven their capability to withstand both interstate and civil war. Since

1945, most colonies have achieved independence and sovereign statehood not through victory in war, but through the encouragement and support of the international system. Furthermore, international norms and laws increasingly discouraged territorial reshuffling through wars of annexation or secession.... In a sense, the international system has locked the problems of states into specific territorial arrangements and perversely created conditions that encourage lengthy civil wars in recently independent states.

Hironaka (2005) attributes the shift to what we would call an ecological change in the nature of the international system. States born after 1945, generally as the product of decolonization after World War II, are generally weaker than those that survived the competitive international system of the past. In addition, international norms that have emerged and developed after World War II have worked against the kind of territorial conquest that might make some states stronger while at the same time weed out weaker states. In contrast to earlier centuries, where unresolved conflicts of interests were often settled on the battlefield, such conflicts are now much less likely to be resolved in that manner. This shift has two major consequences.

One, which Hironaka (2005) emphasizes, concerns internal warfare. Divergent groups compete for power and influence within states. In many states that competition involves violence, especially where ethnic groups are concerned about their security and seek either partial control over the state apparatus or political independence from states in which they are a minority. Many states are too weak to suppress or control internal violence, which only increases incentives for coercive strategies by groups dissatisfied with the status quo. As a result, in the contemporary world there is an interaction between the nature of the threat environment and the weakness of political organization, which creates conditions for internal warfare.

The second facet of the ecological change is that states, new as well as old, are less likely than they once were to go to war with other states. Internal warfare is on the rise but interstate war is not, as we documented in chapter 1. Old states face decreasing benefits and increasing costs from war and consequently a reduction in the incentives to resort to military force to advance or maintain state interests. New states often lack the resources to fight frequently, for very long, or at a distance from their immediate boundaries. They also have fewer incentives to fight if they are likely to be denied territory captured in battle by external powers that enforce norms against territorial conquest (Zacher 2001; Hironaka 2005). As a consequence a few new states may acquire some battle scars, but their wars will not lead to the strong state outcome realized by the survivors of the early modern/modern European/North American warfare escalation. The wars of weak states are unlikely to transform political organizations because they are too infrequent, too short, involve too few participants, mobilize too few resources, and, often as not, are too often lost or indecisive.

How this state of affairs came about needs more discussion, though the principal processes involved are not dissimilar to the developments discussed in the previous chapter. Once we have elaborated the circumstances that have led to this bifurcated ecological setting, we can turn to some illustrative models that have been developed to account for the heightened salience of internal conflict in the present and, presumably, into the near future. These models have some utility, but they lack a sufficiently long-term evolutionary perspective.

Threat Environments

Table 7.1 summarizes a number of facets of the external environment found in early modern Europe and contemporary sub-Saharan Africa, the Middle East, and Latin America.[2] The first point is not that these last three regions share identical external environments. They have not experienced identical histories, they do not confront the exact same types of external problems today, and they are not equally weak. In comparison to early modern Europe, however, they are sufficiently similar to cluster as a single group, recognizing some variation within them across a number of dimensions.

The second point is that the external environment in early modern Europe was a highly competitive one in which defeat in war sometimes meant the loss of independence, while success in war generally led to territorial expansion.[3] The victor sometimes absorbed the loser in a lethal game in which control of more territory and people meant more relative power in the European region as long as each surviving state could keep up with the gains of its nearby competitors. Boundaries remained flexible and subject to force, negotiation, and inheritance.

Early modern Europe also enjoyed an unusual sense of autonomy in the sense that European states intervened in other regions but non-European states did not have the power to intervene in Europe until

TABLE 7.1 **A comparison of external environments then and now**

External Environment	Early Modern Europe	Africa, Middle East, Latin America
Intensive geopolitical competition at regional level	Present	Variable — least in Africa and Latin America
Continuous interstate warfare	Present	Relatively absent outside of Middle East
Potential for long wars	High	Low
Mass/total war	Increasingly	Limited
Preoccupation with domestic threats to order	Moderate	High
Extraregional intervention	Low at outset	Strong
State boundaries established at independence	No	Yes
Possibility of expanding control of territory and keeping territorial gains	Strong	Weak

Source: Based on observations advanced in Heydemann (2000), Centeno (2002), and Herbst (2003).

much later in the modern era.[4] In these circumstances, warfare was nearly continuous somewhere in the European region and increasingly outside of it as well, as European states sought extraregional resources for their intraregional competitions. Given plenty of ambition, rough capability symmetries, and intermittent financing, wars persisted for many years. Increasingly they affected a greater proportion of the populations at war, and eventually the mobilization of human and material resources for war became more total.

The nature of early modern Europe's external threat environment — and particularly its structure of multiple independent actors that had not been coercively unified into a single overarching empire — allowed the co-evolution of war, political and military organizations, political economy, and weapons to proceed without much in the way of constraints, and in fact contributed to the acceleration of that coevolution. The survivors of these processes, by and large, were states that were successful at making war. Their military organizations became increasingly professional and efficient. Their weaponry became increasingly lethal. Their bureaucracies expanded and became more efficient, extracting resources from society using those resources to build military power. Their populations were increasingly drawn into war preparations and war making, and they were transformed into national citizens with an intense sense of identification with their nations.

In contrast, most of the new states in the modern, largely post–World War II era (outside of Latin America) have been exposed to much different external environments (while sharing some aspects of the system structure in terms of multiple independent state actors). Geopolitical competition has certainly existed in regions outside of Europe. Latin American states fought occasional wars throughout the nineteenth and twentieth centuries that reflected external expansion ambitions. Yet no state in South America ever sought to conquer the entire region.[5] Territorial conflict was usually over adjacent territories with or without some valued resources (oil, nitrates) or with access to the sea or the Amazon. Boundary lines were inherited from the days of Iberian empire, but they were often fuzzy due in part to limited penetration and population of the interiors. As South American states developed and pushed inward on their allocated territory, they tended to collide with other states doing the same thing. Brief wars sometimes clarified who controlled what territory. Sometimes the warring states withdrew from their encounter without fully resolving the boundary demarcations.

The territorial boundaries of African states were often demarcated in nonsensical ways, generally reflecting European imperial convenience more than ethnic/economic realities. At the same time African decision-makers, so far, have been reluctant to contest state boundaries for fear of opening up a Pandora's box of uncertainties and escalating conflict. The regional norm of avoiding clashing over boundary claims may be in the process of disintegrating, but so far most of the fighting in sub-Saharan Africa has been within states rather than between them. A significant exception was the Congo War, also known as Africa's World War (1996–2003), which involved eight African states and numerous armed factions within states (Clark 2002; Prunier 2009). Yet most of the very large number of casualties in this conflict died as a result of civilian non-combatants experiencing famine and disease in an environment characterized by extreme turmoil.

The Middle East is a much different story with the ongoing Arab-Israeli conflict—with its occasional interstate wars and ongoing border conflicts and insurgencies—and with Arab-Persian and intra-Arab conflicts as well. Yet as in Latin America and sub-Saharan Africa, war losers

TABLE 7.2 **Implications of differences in external environments**

Linkage Between:	Early Modern Europe	Africa, Middle East, and Latin America
War and state formation	Strong	Weak
Defeat in war and state elimination	Strong	Weak
War preparations, war making, and development of state extractive capability	Strong	Weak
War making, industrialization, and capacity for technological innovation	Strong	Weak
War, national identity, and nationalism	Strong	Weak

Source: Based on observations advanced in Heydemann (2000), Centeno (2002), and Herbst (2003). See also Barnett (1992).

continue to exist as sovereign states.[6] Moreover, with the exception of the Iran-Iraq war in the 1980s, Middle Eastern wars tend to be very short and subject to less than total mobilization outside of Israel. Material losses have been made up by major power patrons external to the region and by Arab oil states. Most radical efforts to reorganize the region, similarly, have been curtailed by external major powers seeking to maintain a balance of power in the region. This process goes back at least to early nineteenth-century attempts to prop up the Ottoman Empire from external and internal attacks. The 1956 Suez/Sinai War, with American coercive pressure against Britain and France to end the conflict, demonstrates that major powers have not always agreed on how best to accomplish this role.

We lack the space to go into much detail about the similarities and differences that characterize the Middle East, sub-Saharan Africa, and Latin America, or for that matter early modern Europe. Our main point is that vastly different external environments in the contemporary era have led to various restrictions on war and consequently on the coevolution of war, political and military organizations, political economy, and weaponry. Table 7.2 summarizes some of these distinctions. The principal message is that political organizations and economies in Africa, the Middle East, and Latin America (and elsewhere) are weaker, in part, because they did not experience the same type of high threat/continuous and escalating warfare, and external environment that characterized early modern–modern

Europe and that helped strengthen strong states and weed out weaker ones (Desch 1996; Hironaka 2005).

Whether or not one laments this missed "opportunity" of experiencing intense warfare, the ways in which coevolutionary processes have worked in the nonwestern trajectory have differed from those in early modern Europe. Political organizations are weaker in terms of extractive capability and popular identification with the state. Political-economic development has been more stagnant. Military organizations, too, while often stronger than the political organizations of which they are a part, remain less than competitive outside their immediate home territories and sometimes not even within their home territories.

The different outcomes of these coevolutionary processes have three general implications worth noting: the "regional displacement" of warfare away from Europe (Singer 1991), a significant shift in the ratio between internal and external warfare (Holsti 1996), and increasing concerns with the threat of terrorism. Some observers might add a fourth—the crystallization of American primacy after the disintegration of the Soviet Union. Our position, however, is that the three processes with which we are most concerned here are more fundamental and in addition preceded the advent of US unipolarity.[7] Let us discuss each in turn.

The "regional displacement" idea is simple. Looking at the last two centuries, a rather large number of wars took place in Europe. Between 1816 and 1945, twenty-two of fifty-two interstate wars (42 percent) were fought in Europe. Yet between 1946 and 2007 only four of thirty-eight (10 percent) wars occurred in Europe.[8] Something has clearly changed. We think we have explained the major changes in our earlier discussion of the European escalatory spiral, intensification of warfare, and the consequent exhaustion of much of the region's potential for further interstate combat.[9]

Still, the switch in interstate war away from Europe to other regions carries a number of auxiliary implications. Interstate wars fought by weaker states generally will be shorter and less decisive. States that have not been through the European war-making vortex are more likely to lack the military capabilities, popular enthusiasm, and financial wherewithal to subsidize longer wars. They also frequently lack the logistical infrastructure and maritime/aerospatial capabilities to project coercive force at much distance. The "bright" side of this development is that fewer people should be killed in interstate wars that are fought with less intensity than in the total wars of the twentieth century. The dark side is that the wars of the future could be more on the order of intermittent but frequent border clashes that resolve little in the way of outstanding grievances and issues. It may also be that our understandings of how warfare was fought over the past two centuries will not serve us very well in deciphering the next century's warfare pattern.

The changes in the ratio of internal to external warfare can be seen in the following figures. Between 1816 and 1945, there were 166 internal or civil wars and as we have seen, fifty-two interstate wars. These numbers yield a ratio of about three civil wars for every interstate war before 1945. After 1945 the number of states in the international system practically tripled. Other things being equal, this increase in the number of states, and hence in the number of potential war makers, should have led to an increased number of all types of warfare, but not necessarily a different internal/external ratio. Between 1946 and 2007, however, 168 civil wars were initiated—only two more wars than took place during the entire 1816–1945 era, which was more than twice as long. The post-1945 period also witnessed the outbreak of thirty-eight interstate wars. True, this is not much short of the fifty-two interstate wars in the 1816–1945 period, but it is relatively modest given the substantial increase in the number of states during that period. Thus the frequency of interstate warfare is less than we might have expected based on past patterns, while the number of civil wars approximates what might have been expected.

More importantly for our immediate purposes, though, is the ratio of internal to external wars. In the 1946–2007 period there were about 4.4 civil wars for every interstate war, in comparison to the 3.2 civil wars per interstate war for the century and a half prior to the end of World War II. A comparison of the total number of deaths attributed to warfare further reinforces our point. James Fearon and David Laitin (2001) attribute 12.1 million deaths to civil wars in the second half of the twentieth century in comparison to 4.6 million for interstate wars.

There is no guarantee, of course, that the higher ratio of internal to external wars will persist throughout the twenty-first century. Some increased proneness to civil war can be associated with new states in general and especially with new states created in the aftermath of imperial disintegration, as illustrated by the case of the collapse of the Soviet Union and the communist bloc that characterized the 1990s. Fearon and Laitin (2001) calculate that the probability of a civil war breaking out in new states was 0.022, nearly twice the probability (0.012) of a civil war erupting in states established before World War II. They also find that civil wars are roughly five times as likely to start in a country's first year of independence as they are in other years.

This might imply that as the Cold War recedes, so will the blip in civil wars and hence the ratio of internal to external wars. The changes in the internal/external war ratio, however, cannot be attributed solely to the end of the Cold War.[10] The mean number of interstate wars ongoing after World War II demonstrates no secular trend, and fluctuates around the 0.01 level.[11] The mean number of ongoing civil wars, however, clearly began to trend upward from the mid-1950s and only began to decline at about the end of the Cold War in the late 1980s. A future reduction in the onset of civil wars conceivably could reduce the ratio of internal to external warfare. Yet even so the point remains that internal warfare is a relatively more prominent activity in the current era than is conventional interstate warfare.[12]

This outcome is entirely compatible with a heterogeneous world system composed of a mixture of old (and in some cases exhausted) war-making state organizations and a very large number of weak states that are unlikely to replicate the histories of the older, surviving and mainly European states. Some states will work very hard to avoid warfare while others will stumble into lower-intensity clashes. Still others will fall apart internally because relatively new states are highly vulnerable to fragmentation.

These patterns raise the question of whether these contemporary developments are entirely novel. Has there been some type of evolutionary shift in the nature of warfare in the global south? A number of scholars have engaged this question. Here we examine two models that focus on contemporary behavior in the less developed world and argue that this behavior is historically unprecedented, though the scholars' respective assessments of how contemporary wars differ from past wars are quite different.

One assessment is Mary Kaldor's (1999) interpretation of the new types of war produced by the interactions among globalization, identity politics, and disintegrating states. The other is John Mueller's (2004) emphasis on thuggery as the residual of disappearing warfare. We first sketch each model briefly so that readers have a sense of their arguments. We then consider the extent to which each model can be reconfigured in the coevolutionary terms used in earlier chapters. We identify the limitations of each of these models and argue that neither provides an interpretation that is fully compelling in comparison to our perspective.

New Wars and Old Thugs

Kaldor's Model

Kaldor (1999) argues that warfare has changed in significant ways. She contrasts "new wars" with "old wars" and emphasizes the role of globalization in shaping the new war phenomena, but she also suggests that the new wars are a somewhat more localized phenomenon in time and space. She also stresses that in many ways the new wars reverse the processes that led to the development of the old wars.[13]

Table 7.3 summarizes Kaldor's characterization of old wars, a characterization that will be familiar to many readers. The type of warfare that became most prevalent in the past three to four centuries was closely tied to the relatively recent emergence of the nation-state organizational format. The primary goals of interstate warfare moved from a focus on territorial delineations and aristocratic inheritance squabbles to national and ideological disputes.[14]

The late twentieth century encompassed one imperial collapse (the Soviet Union), the disintegration of a number of formerly communist states,

TABLE 7.3 **Kaldor's evolution of old wars**

Kaldor's variables	Seventeenth–eighteenth century	Nineteenth century	Early twentieth century	Late twentieth century
Predominant state type	Absolutist state	Nation-state	State coalitions; multinational states/empires	Ideological blocs
War foci	Reasons of state; dynastic claims; border consolidation	National conflict	National and ideological conflict	Ideological conflict
Army type	Mercenary/professional	Professional/conscript	Mass	Scientific-military elite/professional
Military technology	Firearms; defensive maneuvers; sieges	Railways; telegraph; rapid mobilization	Massive firepower; tanks; aircraft	Nuclear weapons
War economy	Taxation/borrowing regularization	Bureaucratic expansion	Mobilization economy	Military-industrial complex

Source: Based on Kaldor (1999, 14).

the end of the Cold War, and the failure of a large number of regimes established in the wake of the withdrawal of European empires. Further accelerating fragmentation are globalization processes that create winners (people able to participate in the new age of transnational, information technology) and losers (people excluded from participating and forced to cope on marginal local resources). All of these changes interact. The end of the Cold War and globalization were reciprocal influences on each other, with the demise of the Cold War (itself influenced by information technology) knocking down the last areas attempting to remain aloof from the world economy. The collapse of the Soviet Union created a number of new states with discredited formerly Marxist regimes, and the end of the Cold War diminished superpower incentives to bolster client regimes throughout the world.

In a context of economic deterioration, expanding unemployment, and growing inequalities, a number of new and some older states were beset with increasing political illegitimacy and disintegration. The new wars, focused on capturing political control largely within the disintegrating states, are increasingly privatized as state control breaks down. As a result of an interaction between these breakdowns and globalization, the consequent political violence over claims to political control involves a confusing number of actors, including traditional armies, private and paramilitary armies, warlords, self-defense militias, mercenaries, guerrillas, criminal gangs, armed children, journalists, foreign military advisers, international organization workers, and peacekeeping forces—all usually operating somewhat independently. In terms of our coevolutionary framework, Kaldor gives primary emphasis to the interaction of threat environment, political organization, and war.[15]

Actors' goals and tactics in the new wars have also changed substantially. Group leaders play upon particularistic sentiments (ethnic, racial, and/or religious) to generate rallying foci for movements stressing substate group identities, and sometimes invent those identity-based sentiments if that will serve their interests. They capitalize on peoples' sense of insecurity, stoke fear and hatred of some other group, and often see violence as desirable because it focuses identity differentiations more clearly.[16] They often emphasize the removal of the targeted group as the principal short-term goal and the creation of more homogenous groups as the long-term goal.

The new population displacement campaigns take place in a context of increasing economic deterioration, crime, corruption, and violence. Fight-

TABLE 7.4 **Kaldor's main distinctions between old and new wars**

Kaldor's variables	Old Wars	New Wars
Goals	Geopolitical/ideological	Particularistic identity politics
Nature of warfare	Capture of territory by decisive battles	Guerrilla avoidance of battle combined with population expulsion and intimidation
Military organization/weaponry	Vertically organized hierarchical units using heavy weapons	Decentralized and disparate, multiple groups using light weapons
War economy	Centralized, very high participation and autarchic in world wars	Decentralized, low participation, and highly dependent on external resources
Geographical location	Northern hemisphere	Balkans, Caucasus, Central Asia, Horn of Africa, Central and West Africa

Source: Based on the discussion in Kaldor (1999).

ing groups pay for their activities through local predation and contributions from diasporic communities abroad. If there are valuable resources to commandeer or to extort (diamonds, oil, drugs), contesting groups will gravitate toward them as sources of financial support.

Table 7.4 summarizes Kaldor's characterization of the differences between old and new wars. The new wars do not begin as interstate wars in the traditional sense. Inherently, they are local or domestic wars over defining the identity of the population. These "identity wars" are difficult to contain and may very well spread to neighboring states. Warfare is of the low-intensity, guerrilla-like, avoidance-of-battles type. Atrocities and massacres of unarmed civilians are more likely to occur than are clashes between armies. The military organizational level is fairly low. Equipment, training, uniforms, and discipline are likely to be relatively absent, as are heavy weapons. The economic context is equally fragmented and characterized by low rates of output. Resource mobilization for war purposes is decentralized. Fighting groups take what they can, legally or illegally.

As a consequence of this evolution in the nature of war, Kaldor (1999) notes, the military-civilian casualty ratio has literally reversed itself. In the early twentieth century, the proportion of civilian war casualties (to total casualties) was in the neighborhood of 10–15 percent. At the end of the same century, civilian war casualties averaged roughly around

80 percent. Population displacement problems became much more severe as well. Conservative estimates of the number of refugees indicated about two and a half million people in 1975, ten and a half million in 1985, some eighteen million in 1992, and fourteen and a half million by 1995 (Kaldor 1999, 100–101).

For Kaldor (1999) the contrast between the old and new wars is rather stark. Most of the dominant characteristics of the old ways of fighting are entirely absent from the new wars, and much of what had been proscribed in the old wars is strongly encouraged in the new wars. The new wars are also geographically contained, being fought primarily in the Balkans, the Black Sea area, Central Asia, and parts of Africa. Kaldor might have added parts of the Middle East and Latin America to this list. Still, the point is that these new wars predominate in a territorial belt extending roughly from Tajikistan to Colombia. Kaldor does not appear to be arguing that the new wars necessarily will doom the old wars to extinction, only that the new wars are simply vastly different from the old wars.

Residual Thugs

In chapter 5 we discuss John Mueller's (1989) argument, and Carl Kaysen's (1990) response, that war was becoming unthinkable and therefore increasingly obsolescent as a political institution in the developed world. In a more recent book, Mueller (2004) extends his argument by developing his "remnants of war" thesis. Briefly put, his argument is that ideas rule. The idea of war—at least as a means of resolving disputes with other developed states—no longer appeals to the populations and decision-makers of developed states. As a consequence, warfare between developed states has virtually disappeared. He adds that another form of warfare—colonial or imperial warfare involving developed states against traditional empires and underdeveloped states—has also gone out of fashion because colonial possessions are no longer desired by developed states. That leaves civil wars within the less developed states and terrorism as the dominant forms of warfare.

In his 2004 book Mueller focuses primarily on civil war, which is our concern here.[17] Mueller recognizes that civil war has increased in frequency, although not exponentially and not simply because a number of new states have emerged in the past half-century. He does not give much weight to globalization pressures or to the clash of civilizations.[18] What many of these new states have are weak governments. As weak governments they are unable to control domestic predators engaged in violence and crime. Contemporary civil wars, in most cases, are simply, or quickly become, instances of uncontrolled thuggery.

Mueller (2004, 180) describes it in the following way:

> The world is not a teeming mass of frustrated, angry, hate-filled fanatics seeking to express their ethnic, religious, cultural or civilizational angst in cataclysmic violence against each other in a Hobbesian state of nature. There are small numbers of people, it is true, who are drawn to violence and yearn to experience its exhilarations and its potential profits. Some of these are, indeed, fanatics and true-believers, but most are criminals and thugs, and small, unpoliced, or badly policed bands of these people can cause vastly more devastation than their numbers would seem to imply. What is needed to keep them in check—to establish peace and order—is good government, following the path the developed world fell upon in the middle of the last millennium.

Historically, Mueller (2004) argues, developed states have gradually created strategies for controlling or policing violent and criminal bands.[19] For instance, a standing army in France emerged in the mid-fifteenth century to manage the havoc caused by disbanded soldiers from the Hundred Years' War. Some of the disbanded soldiers, in effect, were hired by the state to minimize the harmful effects of the other soldiers no longer needed to fight England (Vagts 1959). More generally, one of the principal tasks of political development was to employ the state's coercive resources to eliminate the coercive resources and threats posed by such domestic rivals as warlords, bandits, and pirates. The imposition of civil order meant the state must have a monopoly of weaponry and the use of violence. After hundreds of years of development, the more developed states can now take this domestic peace and order more or less for granted, but that was once very much not the case.[20]

New states with weak governments are unlikely to be able to control crime. As a consequence, kidnapping, extortion, banditry, looting, and armed robbery may become sufficiently prevalent as to be the "peacetime" norm in some places. When civil war breaks out, weak governments and their opponents tend to recruit criminal gangs as coercive resources either to supplant or reinforce regular troops because the irregular troops will do things regular armies may be reluctant to do. Alternatively, criminal gangs seize the opportunities created by failed states to take control of parts of the state territory. In either case their primary mission is to prey on and to intimidate unarmed civilians for their own profit. They may use ideologically based rhetoric to justify their behavior, but essentially they remain thugs engaged in brutal forms of extortion.

Mueller (2004) offers a number of examples. In the wars that followed the disintegration of Yugoslavia, a number of regular troops mutinied and deserted. Their place was taken by as many as eighty-three irregular groups operating in Croatia and Bosnia that were recruited from prisons, soccer clubs, and the underworld. It was primarily these groups who undertook the main work of ethnic cleansing. Similarly constituted groups played a central role in the 1994 Rwandan genocide, were used by the Indonesian army in East Timor, and became central players in recent civil wars in Somalia, Georgia, Chechnya, Liberia, and Sierra Leone, among other places.

In fact, Mueller (2004) finds the activities of the thugs so prevalent in contemporary civil warfare that he questions whether it is accurate to describe their behavior as war. If wars are about the use of sustained violence against an enemy for some political purpose, the irregular paramilitaries often do everything possible to avoid combat because it hinders their principal goal of making money illicitly. Even if this criminal behavior is called warfare, however, it should not be viewed (as Kaldor [1999] does) as a new type of warfare. Rather, it is an old type of warfare that has been forcibly suppressed elsewhere. It is a persistent residual, or as Mueller (2004, 116) puts it, the reduction of war to its "pathetic, if often highly destructive, remnants."

Thus we have two models that purport to speak to warfare in the less developed world but in rather different ways. Our first task is to translate the arguments into causal models using roughly the same language. This reconfiguration will sharpen what the arguments are about and how they agree or disagree. Once this translation process is accomplished, some attempt at selective synthesis can proceed.

Kaldor's model suggests that some fairly new states have been overwhelmed by imperial fragmentation, legitimacy problems, and political-economic forces. These problems led to an emphasis on identity politics, a multiplicity of lightly armed actors with and without uniforms, and a form of warfare that is often difficult to differentiate from crime. These "new war" behaviors are confined to states linked to the demise of the Soviet Union and postcolonial states, located in a band stretching from Central Asia through parts of southeastern Europe, the Middle East, Africa, and Latin America.[21]

Paul Hirst (2001) and Stathis Kalyvas (2001) join Mueller (2004) in taking issue with Kaldor's interpretation of "new wars," but each offers a different perspective. They see much less novelty in contemporary warfare in the third world. Ethnic cleansing and nationalist outbidding or scapegoatism are not practices that emerged only toward the end of the twentieth century. They were evident in the Balkans and the disintegration of the Ottoman Empire at the beginning of the twentieth century as well. Militias and bandits were also prominent in the fighting of the earlier times. Yugoslav instability is hardly anything new. The state was unstable for much of its twentieth-century history and only enjoyed some departure from that norm during the Tito regime that ended in the late 1970s/early 1980s. West African instability can often be traced back to colonial practices and the legacies of European rule. Some of the new irregular forces fighting for political dominance within various southern states, such as the Taliban, were created by external actors seeking to destabilize specific states during the Cold War.

The Cold War provided a number of impoverished states with expensive military arsenals for a period of time, courtesy of the United States and the Soviet Union, whose interests those arsenals were perceived to serve.[22] With the end of the Cold War, much of this subsidization of weak states ended. This helped to highlight the great inequalities in previously existing state wealth and governance capabilities. Without the old Cold War incentives for the superpowers to prop up weak regimes, local elites were on their own. It is not surprising that there was a proliferation of internal challenges in weak states, or that wars between adjacent weak and/or underdeveloped states continued to occur from time to time, without having much impact away from the scene of fighting.

Kalyvas (2005, 91–92) helps generalize this phenomenon by focusing on how civil wars are fought. He argues that the key variables are the relative equality of military capability between combatants and their relative access to resources. This generates a nice two-by-two table and a useful typology of civil wars, as shown in table 7.5 and as further developed in table 7.6. Domestic adversaries that have substantial resources and roughly equal resources tend to fight conventional civil wars. Both sides have regular armies and thus their combat resembles interstate wars except that it takes place within a single country. If the government has much more military capability than the other but both have good access to resources, the civil war will likely take the form of an insurgency in which the weaker side employs hit-and-run, guerrilla tactics.

TABLE 7.5 **Kalyvas's types of warfare in civil war**

		Resource Level of Incumbents	
		High	Low
Resource Distribution between the Actors	Symmetry	Conventional	Symmetric nonconventional
	Asymmetry	Irregular	*

* Presumably, incumbents with fewer resources than domestic opponents are unlikely to last long enough to fight a civil war.
Source: Based on Kalyvas (2005, 91).

TABLE 7.6 **Sources of different types of warfare**

Types of Civil Warfare	Characteristics	Nature	Examples
Conventional	Face-to-face confrontations between armies across clear frontlines	Failed military coups or secession attempts in federal states	United States, Spain, Nigeria
Irregular	Stronger incumbent fields regular troops while insurgents hide and rely on surprise, stealth, and raid	Peripheral or rural insurgencies	Mozambique, Kashmir
Symmetrical nonconventional	Irregular arms on both sides waging premodern warfare	State and state army collapse	Lebanon, Liberia

Source: Based on the discussion in Kalyvas (2005).

The third possibility is that neither side has much in the way of resources, but both sides are roughly equal in capability. This is a symmetric nonconventional war, which is most likely to occur in new states that have not yet created regular armies (as in the former Yugoslavian states) or failed states in which the regular army and government disintegrates (as in Somalia or western Africa). In the latter case, control of the state is likely to be contested by gangs of irregular soldiers, which may amount to no more than armed children in some extreme cases and often include Mueller's thugs.

The stress on symmetry and asymmetry in capabilities and resources is useful as a categorical device. Kalyvas takes the argument one step further by discussing the most likely sources of each of the three types of civil war. Conventional civil wars are most likely to be associated with failed military coups that divide the armed forces into two warring camps. Alternatively, they may stem from separatist situations in federal states in which the state attempting to break away controls some portion of the regular army. The 1967 Biafran civil war in Nigeria is one example. The American Civil War in the 1860s is another.

Irregular civil wars usually start as peripheral insurgencies in which the rebels operate initially at some distance from the capital, attempt to carve out and defend a state within a state, and also try to outlast and wear down the incumbent regime. Many of the civil wars of the past five decades have taken this form. Kalyvas's "symmetric nonconventional" wars are fairly recent in origin. Neither side employs regular armies because none have yet been created or because the incumbent army has collapsed along with the regime it once served. Groups of militias, criminals, and paramilitaries are organized to advance the interests of various warlords who may either seek to control some portion of the state or the whole state. Lebanon in the 1970s and Liberia in the 1990s fit this description well.

In a later study, Kalyvas and Balcells (2010) examine the nature of civil wars during the six-decade period from 1944 to 2004.[23] They find that 54 percent of the civil wars have been irregular, 34 percent conventional, and 12 percent nonconventional. This distribution has not been stable over time, however, and it appears that the end of the Cold War had a significant impact on the types of civil wars that have occurred. During the Cold War (from 1944 to 1990), two-thirds of the civil wars were irregular, while 28 percent were conventional, and 6 percent symmetric nonconventional. After the end of the Cold War there was a sharp drop in irregular wars, down to 26 percent of the total, and a sharp rise in symmetric nonconventional wars, up to 26 percent, with the dominant form of civil war (48 percent) being conventional wars between well-armed states and rebels. Kalyvas and Balcells attribute these shifts to the withdrawal of superpower material support for both states and rebels after the end of the Cold War, to the decline of revolutionary ideology, and along with it the decline of the relevance of military doctrines of peoples' war.

Kalyvas and Balcells (2010) emphasize that the factors shaping the nature of civil wars goes beyond the domestic situation or local threat environment to include the structure of the international system. It was the shift in system polarity associated with the end of the Cold War that led to a shift in the relative frequencies of different types of civil wars. One implication of their study is that current patterns themselves may be transitory in the face of the rise of new powers and ongoing shifts in the distribution of power in the international system. There are other considerations as well. Given the newness of many of the states involved in "new wars," it may well be that we are dealing with a transitory phenomenon. Imperial disintegration usually leads to periods of turmoil of finite duration. The new states that are created in the aftermath of an empire's breakdown may never become highly stable, but they need not remain forever plagued by Kaldor's (1999) new war syndrome. External intervention, conceivably, can alter conflict levels. It may also improve economic growth prospects, which should reverberate on the amount of ongoing conflict. Another possibility is one group among the multiplicity of actors manages to attain national hegemony and establish a new domestic order. The odds may not be great that inside or outside groups will somehow turn failed states around very quickly, but the odds are at least greater than zero.

Although new wars do involve genuine novelties, there can be no guarantee that they will crowd out conventional interstate wars into complete oblivion. New wars occurred in quite a few places in the 1990s and early 2000s, but those wars did eventually end. Nor did they spread everywhere that they might have. Thus Kaldor's new wars have definitely expanded the repertoire of ways to make war, but it is not yet clear whether they will establish themselves as the standard model for organized violence within or between states or simply constitute a passing phase in the annals of warfare.

Mueller's (2004) perspective is different. His argument, aside from the emphasis on weak governments, is not readily translatable into the six coevolving components of our general model. Alternatively, one could say that his basic model reduces to the notion that changes in ideas have driven most wars out of existence. The surviving residual is found in weak states in which political/criminal entrepreneurs, fueled more by alcohol, drugs, and Sylvester Stallone movies than by patriotism or nationalism, exploit opportunities for illegal gain. In this respect at least we can link Mueller's argument to one of the six general factors—changes in the political system.

Kaldor and Mueller would probably agree on the increasingly prominent role played by relatively undisciplined bands of armed men and children in internal warfare. The question is whether this is a newly evolved era (Kaldor's position) or a regression into the past (Mueller's position) that can be taken care of by willing regular armed forces from inside or outside the state in question.[24] Here we generally side with Kaysen (1990), whom we discussed in chapter 5, in arguing that ideas are not unimportant but that they do not drop from the sky. They emerge from and then coevolve with more material changes. The rising opposition to the idea of war in the west, for example, is significantly (but perhaps not entirely) driven by the rapidly increasing destructiveness of war between advanced industrial states.

In addition, even "weak" states cannot be taken as simply givens. We have argued that states tend to be weak in large part because they have not experienced the same historical trajectories as have older states in Europe and North America. In turn the older historical trajectories were couched firmly in war-driven, coevolutionary patterns that produced various types of strong states. The choice, therefore, is not so much between good and bad government but more a matter of generating third world pathways to political systems capable of maintaining order that do not depend on warfare and its coevolutionary implications.

Kaldor (1999) argues that the type of low-intensity conflict with which she is most concerned tends to be concentrated geographically. The low-intensity threat environment is far from a monolithic freight train racing to wreck states everywhere. The problem is more complex and more selective. In each wave some states are more likely to be targeted than are others. Some states have disintegrated and others, no doubt, will follow this path as well. Even in most of these cases, however, wars, which are primarily internal but which include some low-intensity international conflicts, do end.

Postwar circumstances rarely resemble the prewar state of affairs, but the same can be said of some high-intensity conventional wars and their postwar aftermaths of demographic decimation, population displacement, and economic deterioration. The difference is that the political organizations that fight conventional wars tend to survive, become stronger, or are reconstructed after the war ends. Many of the political organizations that attempt to defend themselves against low-intensity warfare were weak states from their conception. The weak states that fail to survive cannot necessarily be reconstructed into something stronger after the fighting ends. As in Somalia or Lebanon, it is difficult to put the pieces back together again.

Still, it is hardly clear that failed states will become the planetary norm in the twenty-first century. Some proportion of weak state political organizations will continue to disintegrate just as a few weak states may find ways to become stronger organizations. Imperial and heterogeneous constructions (India, China) may or may not continue to fall apart. If they do fall apart, a number of new weak political organizations will emerge, subject to all of the pathologies of weak states and low-intensity conflict.

Alternatively, the survival of large, underdeveloped states that seek to become more developed and more powerful leaves some significant potential for conventional warfare in the twenty-first century. States attempting to improve their status in the world system tend to clash with other states with similar objectives and with states that are threatened by their challenges of the status quo. States armed with precision-guided munitions will find themselves employing them in a mix of conventional and unconventional situations—not unlike the situation illustrated by the 2003 Iraq war and the subsequent occupation of Iraq. A number of more affluent and older states will seek to stay above the fray and costs of engaging in warfare. Low-intensity warfare will persist in parts of the global south and may spread to states hitherto unaffected. Phased north–south conflict with different foci—colonial self-determination, Marxist revolutions, Islamic fundamentalism, and apparently whatever supplants it—will also continue to evolve. These conflicts are not exclusively north–south in orientation. They are also intrasouthern contests, as exemplified most clearly by the conflicts between radical Muslim fundamentalists and secular states with a large Muslim population.

CHAPTER EIGHT

The Coevolution of War, Past and Future

War involves politically organized groups engaging in coordinated and sustained armed combat. Warfare, political organization, military organization, political economy, weapons, and threat environment coevolve. Significant changes in one or more of the six spheres tend to lead to significant changes in the other variables. None of the six is consistently the exclusive driver of the other five. Yet we think a strong case can be made that macrochanges in political economy have been a consistently important driver of other changes in war and other spheres. The movement from the predominance of hunting and gathering practices to agrarian cultivation to industrialization parallels major shifts in the scope and lethality of war and the ability of other spheres of activity to sustain this enlarged scope and lethality.

We examined arguments and evidence regarding the origins of warfare in prehistoric times in chapter 2. We developed our theoretical arguments in chapter 3. We identified and explored two early accelerations in the western (and Chinese) trajectory in chapter 4. We then turned in chapter 5 to the "modern," largely post-1500 and western, acceleration and intensification of coevolutionary changes in military affairs. In chapter 6 we took a step back and traced the evolutionary trajectory of the "west" from its Mesopotamian starting point to its latest exemplar (the United States). We argued that paradigmatic armies and navies (Lynn 1996) are the primary agents of change, propelling coevolutionary developments within the context of leading states seeking primacy in their regions. Periods of warring states in which primacy is thwarted by highly competitive states bidding up the resource mobilization for war seem to define the conditions most conducive to periods of coevolutionary acceleration.

The long-term trend in warfare and its coevolutionary implications, however, is not ever onward and upward. Industrialized states have reacted to the rapidly increasing human and economic costs of warfare by concluding that the possible benefits of warfare against other industrialized states are substantially exceeded by its likely costs. As a result the probability of major power warfare between advanced industrial states has been significantly reduced.

The transformations of warfare, however, have not been restricted to advanced industrialized states. Nonindustrialized states, which largely missed the third evolutionary acceleration, function with weak political organizations that find it difficult to mobilize resources for interstate warfare and that are especially vulnerable to internal challenges. Their principal threat environment is internal rather than external. As a result internal war is more common than interstate war in much of the global south.

Nothing that we have seen detracts from the initial coevolutionary premise that none of the six primary variables has been the exclusive driver throughout time. The ancient Egyptian case featured the interaction of the external threat environment and political economy with political organization. Changes in external threat had implications for changes in weaponry and military organization. Military organization, in turn, influenced political organization. In ancient Greece the external threat environment influenced military organization and weaponry. Military organization and weaponry interacted on each other and with political organization. In Rome, changes in the external threat environment again had implications for military organization and weaponry, and they also influenced political organization and political economy. In ancient China the coevolutionary pattern focused on an interaction between political organization and political economy, with changes in the external and internal threat environments influencing military organization and political organization. In Mesoamerica, political economy interacted with the external threat environment, with stabilizing implications for military organization and weaponry. In early modern and modern Europe, we see changes in weaponry altering military organization, which in turn had ramifications for the interactions of political organization and political economy. Consequent changes in political organization and political economy led to expanded military organizations and more lethal weaponry.

This sampling of older trajectories strongly suggests that there is no universal template for coevolutionary developments. It is conceivable that any of the six could change first. There is no guarantee that all six will change uniformly and predictably, but there is some probability that once change is initiated in one of the six variables, changes in the other five spheres are likely to follow. Even so, it is difficult to escape the idea that all six of our primary variables have not played equal roles in the evolution of warfare. We end our examination with some tentative hypotheses about the relative importance of the six explanatory foci.

If we exclude war itself as a major channel or venue through which the other coevolutionary processes work, we think the three most important causal factors have been political economy, threat environments, and political organization. As we have argued in chapter 3, the political-economic context has been consistently pervasive throughout the evolution of warfare. The nature of hunting-gathering activities brought together a number of considerations influencing preagrarian warfare. Hunting technology produced early tactics, organization, and weaponry. The nature of hunting game presumably led to initial conceptualizations of territorial monopolies that needed defense and retribution for violations. The nonsedentary nature of hunting-gathering may also have contributed to inadvertent contacts and clashes with other bands. The small populations associated with hunting-gathering also restricted the intensity of warfare in the early prehistoric era.

The emergence of agriculture facilitated increasing population density, urbanization, and states. Increasing specialization of roles led to more sharply defined, generally better trained, and larger military organizations. States had more to defend and more to gain by expanding territorial control. The interaction of increased motivation and capability led ultimately to a greater frequency and intensity of warfare, although not inexorably so. For instance, the political economy of post-Roman Europe favored decentralization that placed limits on capability and martial intensification.

Industrialization led to further increases in population density and overall population sizes. Technological changes revolutionized the damage that weapons could do, just as they ensured that warfare would increasingly affect larger proportions of society, directly and indirectly. Modern or contemporary changes in the coevolution of warfare have been dominated by revolutionary changes in the scale of participation and improvements in military lethality. For some, but not for all, it may be that the nature of the changes—as in increased economic interdependence, greater emphases on economic development, and the implications of technological lethality—have actually led to a decreased probability of warfare. Whether that holds in the future and how far such changes extend remains to be seen.

Threat environments have been highly significant to the local direction and pace biases of war trajectories. Consider Egypt before and after the coming of the Hyksos around the seventeenth century BCE. Before the Hyksos, the Egyptian threat environment was largely confined to fending off raiders from adjacent desert areas. After the Hyksos, Egyptian military practices were forced to catch up with prevailing techniques in southwest Asia. Its foreign policy ambitions expanded and competition with other eastern Mediterranean great powers ensued. Several hundred years later, the post-1200 BCE meltdown of eastern Mediterranean order contributed to the decay of the New Kingdom and the more gradual infiltration of Egypt by Libyans. One could argue, without much fear of exaggeration, that the external threat environment overwhelmed Egypt for the next two millennia or so.

The Egyptian case is not an outlier when it comes to the role of external threat environments. The absence of acute threats in Mesoamerica for much of its history contributed to very slow and limited changes in military organization, weaponry, and warfare prior to about 1500 CE. A more recent example of reduced external threat is the slowdown in weaponry development in Japan after the establishment of the Tokugawa hegemony in the sixteenth century CE. Compare these developments with the long impact of attempting to deal with nomadic raiders in the rim of cities around central Eurasia. It has been argued persuasively (Chase 2003) that the areas bordering the homelands of the archers on horseback never had the luxury of experimenting sufficiently with gunpowder weapons to develop them fully. The roughly half-millennium of years needed to develop gunpowder weapons took place only in areas with some immunity to highly effective, light cavalry raiding.

The Chinese exposure to threat from nomadic horsemen was fairly high between 300 BCE and 1700 CE. Before 300 BCE the external threat from nomads primarily on foot was much less. After 1700 CE the threat increasingly diminished as sedentary armies, armed with gunpowder weapons, finally developed the ability to suppress the threat of light cavalry. Thus China had a much different threat environment between 300 BCE and 1700 CE than did western Europe, which enjoyed some insulation from nomadic attacks, or pre-Columbian Mesoamerica, which had some nomads armed with bows but no horses. These are important differences that generate broad contexts in which some choices are made more probable than others. Varying threat environments can also give us strong clues as to why some things worked out differently in one part of the world than in others.

It is difficult, moreover, to escape the centrality of political organization to changes in warfare. By definition, warfare requires some form of military organization to fight, but fighting also requires political motivation and direction. Early on, military organizations evolved out of groups of hunters into chiefly retinues and then into warrior aristocracies. All three configurations depended on some level of political centralization, however minimal at the onset. As political centralization became more pronounced, the need for military organization internally and externally also became more pronounced. Internal rivals and external foes had to be defended against and ultimately defeated in order to survive. Consolidation of rule led to political expansion, which both required resources to carry off and resulted in greater resources for political allocation when triumphant. Whatever the various origins of the state, they tended to become war-making organizations.

Repeatedly we have seen the interaction between political centralization and war making ramp upward toward more intensified warfare and, for the winners at least, greater political centralization. A number of authors make this point albeit in different ways in terms of early chiefdom-state transitions. We have observed this pattern in terms of the ancient Old World sequence of Mesopotamia-Egypt-Assyria-Persia-Macedonia-Rome. Much the same happened in the Chinese warring states period (circa 500–200 BCE) as was to happen in the early modern warfare and military revolutions of western Europe. States became more powerful and authoritarian, armies expanded, and warfare became deadlier. The relationships among these processes were hardly coincidental. States needed larger armies to compete with other states with larger armies. They also needed to become more authoritarian to acquire the resources to pay for their expanding armies. As a consequence, more soldiers died in expanded and more frequent wars.

These escalatory spirals were not experienced universally or even constantly. The evolution of pre-1500 CE American warfare seems almost static compared to developments in Eurasia. Even the Mesopotamian-Roman sequence, however, came to a temporary escalatory halt that was not renewed for nearly a thousand years. When and where they were operative, however, the reciprocal interactions between state and warfare have been extremely powerful—so powerful that it is difficult to imagine what states will look like when they lack the "opportunity" to engage in external warfare and when they face only the threat of disintegrative internal warfare. That is the apparent fate of the majority of states in existence today.

Compared to political economy, threat environment, and political organization, military organization and weaponry tend to take on a secondary hue in the long run. The demands of military organizations have certainly stimulated and strained state capabilities, so that there is an important coevolutionary nexus between political and military organization. But unless we accept the now-discredited argument that European feudalism emerged because kings could not afford to maintain centralized armies, it is difficult to imagine military organizations as a persistent driver of the nature of political organizations operating independently of the political-economic context in which political and military organizations operate. Military organizations can and have restrained changes in political organizations. Aristocratic officer classes have often looked askance at democratic political reforms. It is one thing, however, to serve as a constraint on rapid change and another to be a persistent source of rapid change.[1]

Weaponry has at least an intermittent claim to significance. Chariots reinforced aristocratic privilege in some places and helped to create it elsewhere. Central Eurasian cavalry had to be met with cavalry, thereby precluding strong commitments to infantry and gunpowder in areas close to central Eurasia. A commitment to gunpowder and cannon, on the other hand, encouraged the development of authoritarian states in order to pay for their expense. Industrialized weaponry led to European dominance worldwide for a time. It also contributed substantially to the horrors of industrialized warfare in the twentieth century. Nuclear weapons, no doubt, contributed considerably to the low probability of major power warfare after 1945. Precisely how much it contributed (is contributing) is a topic that will undoubtedly be debated well into the future.[2]

Readers may be surprised that we have skirted this issue throughout the book. We have no doubt that nuclear weapons have influenced the nature of diplomacy and warfare since Hiroshima and Nagasaki. We think we can make a reasonable case, however, for the transformation of warfare, at least between industrialized states, without relying too greatly on the nuclear card. At the same time we view nuclear weapons as a penultimate manifestation of industrialized warfare. Thus we are not ignoring the difficult-to-estimate impact of recent weapons so much as we are subsuming it within a heightened cost-limited benefits framework.

FIGURE 8.1. Another look at the coevolutionary complex.

Weaponry thus matters, but not necessarily as much as the political-economic context and political organization that help to encourage the development of some types of weaponry while discouraging the development of others. Political and to a lesser extent military organizations had to choose to invest in chariots, cavalry, infantry, or cannon. Once their choices were made the organizations had to determine strategies for developing, acquiring, and maintaining the weapons of choice.[3] If they made the wrong choices or could not sustain the choices they had made they ran the risk of being defeated in war and perhaps subsumed into more successful political-military organizations. Weapons alone were unlikely to select which organizations thrived and which ones were destroyed, but they did contribute to such outcomes.

That brings us back to war itself. Anyone undertaking an analysis of the evolution of war is exceedingly unlikely to underestimate the causal effects and significance of war. War is often an important catalyst in changes in political organization, political economy, military organization, and weaponry. War can also bring about changes in threat environment. In this sense war may have the best single claim to centrality within the coevolutionary complex. Yet it remains both a catalyst and a vehicle for encouraging changes in other spheres. In that respect it is very much dependent on changes in the other coevolving areas.

Figure 8.1, which recasts an earlier figure, attempts to capture some of these distinctions. Capitalized processes are more significant than the noncapitalized processes. Each line should be viewed as a double-headed causal arrow, signifying the potential for reciprocal causality. We do not attempt to draw all of the connecting arrows that are prevalent. There are simply too many. In the end analysis we reiterate our commitment to the notion that all six of the variables/processes highlighted in the figure, regardless of what weights we choose to give them, tend to coevolve. They have done so for thousands of years. They are likely to continue to do so into at least the near future. Evolutionarily speaking, it is not possible or wise to forecast beyond that point, certainly with any degree of confidence.

The Future of Warfare

We have no reason to think these coevolutionary processes are coming to an end—even in places that no longer engage in much warfare. It is conceivable that places that still engage in warfare will become more pacific, just as it is not inconceivable that places that rarely engage in warfare at least close to home might become less pacific. Given our focus on threat environment, political economy, and political organization as the primary coevolutionary drivers of warfare, that is where we should first look for the most likely sources of potential future changes.

Environmental problems are undoubtedly becoming more significant. The need for water and agricultural land is increasing at the same time as they are becoming scarcer, problems are compounded by environmental degradation, and shortages in one area trigger migrations that compound problems in other areas and generate new social conflicts in the process. Shortages of petroleum and energy sources will further exacerbate conflicts. New technology to address environmental problems will be developed and new energy sources will be found, of course, but the questions are whether they will suffice to cope with the types of scarcity problems that are emerging and whether they will do so quickly enough for sustaining life and evading increased conflict.[4] If they are not sufficient, and/or if environmental deterioration continues relatively unchecked, we can anticipate a significantly altered threat environment in which key scarcities might trump transformations that have led to decreased probabilities of warfare. To the extent that the changes in scarcities and deterioration turn out to be as significant as many forecasters predict, we might expect an increase in warfare between weak political organizations in the global south.

The economic and military significance of China and India are growing. In the past, political leaders have often had difficulties in developing successful formulas for accommodating the demands of new major powers, as theorists of power transition and systemic change have emphasized.[5] Will the twenty-first century be any different? Conflict in Asia is always possible, but it is likely to take several decades of further structural change before we will know much about the possibility or probability of renewed major power warfare. Again, such a change in the future would reflect a much different threat environment than the present one. The increasing lethality of weapons and increasing economic interdependence associated with globalization might provide enough deterrent to ward off major power warfare, but the major systemic changes of the past should be a cause for concern.

There is something more that can be said about political organization as a coevolutionary factor. The current number of relatively weak states is very large. Consequently, there is little reason to anticipate that internal conflict is likely to disappear in the twenty-first century. Attempts at separatism will persist. Weak states cannot suppress minor revolts very well. Nor are they any more likely to defeat major rebellions without outside help. But does that mean all lesser-developed states will descend into never-ending civil war? The answer is probably not, as otherwise we would have already have seen such an outcome. Even places with endemic internal conflict fluctuate in the extent to which warfare is ongoing.

Nor should we be read as dismissing the possibility of widespread interstate fighting in the less industrialized world. The long war between Iraq and Iran, the continuing clashes between Pakistan and India, the ongoing Arab-Israeli conflict, and the extended fighting in the Congo, all caution pessimism on the likelihood of a cessation of warfare between states in the global south. Yet these same cases also reinforce the notion that however lethal or lasting the combat is likely to be, interstate warfare at this level is likely to remain limited in its coevolutionary implications. We do not expect warfare in the south, in most cases, to hasten the advent of stronger states, more developed economies, or new military organizations and weaponry technology. By no means is that the same thing as saying that southern warfare will have no impact on organizations and economies—only that it is unlikely to precisely mirror earlier changes in the global north.

We might hope, though, for some of the deterrent effects of the limited diffusion of high-cost industrialized warfare as seen in nuclear proliferation. Even this possibility is in doubt, though, if the possession of nuclear weapons tends to encourage conflict escalation up to some perceived ceiling before both sides seek deescalation, as in the Kargil War between India and Pakistan.[6] If the chances for misperception and miscalculation are increased, so, too, are the chances for the accidental exchange of nuclear missiles somewhere sometime.

Thus the future of warfare in the twenty-first century depends on a variety of factors. Will the threat environment turn more hostile because of increased scarcity? Will more new political organizations emerge that are highly vulnerable to domestic conflict? Will old political organizations rediscover new reasons to go to war? For that matter, will they revert to old reasons for coercive encounters with their neighbors and rivals? It is not a simple matter of projecting trends in one or more types of warfare. These wars occur within specific contexts and are influenced in coevolutionary terms by other factors that we have sought to identify. Even more difficult to forecast than the nature of warfare later in this century is how threat environment, political and military organizations, war, weaponry, and political economy will coevolve together.

Nonetheless, the historian Marc Bloch (1999, 118, quoted in Neiberg 2001, 102) once wrote:

> By examining how and why yesterday differed from the day before, [history] can reach conclusions which will enable it to foresee how tomorrow will differ from yesterday. The traces left by past events never move in a straight line, but in a curve that can be extended into the future.

Whether history per se can help us reach conclusions, we leave to others to decide. For our own efforts, we have sought to trace Bloch's curve—in our case, the arc of war—over as long a period of time as was possible. Our assumption is that behaviors are subject to evolution (coevolution) and path dependence and that warfare is no exception to these rules. Subject to various qualifications about things we cannot foresee at this time, the arc of war is neither vanishing nor expanding inexorably. Neither is it a simple matter of having moved upward to some peak before having declined in the contemporary era. War may be path dependent but it is also more complex than it sometimes seems. Different types of warfare, in particular, have exhibited different curves or arcs. Classical imperial warfare and intrastate warfare, for example, have not moved in the same direction. One has pretty much disappeared while the other still thrives. A specific type of war may become obsolete while another type becomes more prevalent. Thus the frequency of various formats changes but the basic practice persists.

War is a social practice that has persisted longer than many ancient practices. Yet its persistence appears to be uneven. A century or two from now many of our descendants may be able to say that war went the same way as other practices deemed obsolete. It is a practice that has prevailed quite widely for a long period of time, but as social conditions evolve or its costs escalate too high to be sustained, it can be replaced by other strategies for addressing conflicts of interest. It is true that different people, operating in different ecological niches and driven by different assumptions, will arrive at different calculations regarding the relative utility of war as an instrument of policy.

At the same time it would not be too surprising if war practices retain some of their attractions a century from now. In various types of situations some actors might still see war as the best policy alternative. Although there may well be alternatives to coordinated and sustained fighting to resist coercive territorial expansion, to prevent ethnic cleansing, or to maintain access to necessary resources, the mere existence of alternatives does not mean that all parties concerned will judge those alternatives to be the optimal policy choices. Nor does it mean that the alternatives to war will work as well in accomplishing preferred policy goals. Sometimes the answer to the pop musical question of what war is good for is not absolutely nothing. The only thing we can be sure of is that coevolutionary processes will continue to shape and reshape warfare and related phenomena.

Notes

Chapter One

1. We stumbled too late on Maurice Davie's (1929, ix) advice that in studying the evolution of war it is good to start at the beginning but that it is impossible to encompass the full span in one lifetime.

2. Clausewitz ([1832] 1976, 75, 89) argues that "war is thus an act of force to compel our enemy to do our will," and that "war is a pulsation of violence."

3. See Vasquez (2009, chap. 1) for a useful review of definitions of war.

4. Clausewitz ([1832] 1976, 87), for example, repeatedly emphasizes that war is a "political instrument, a continuation of political activity by other means." The anthropologist Bronislaw Malinowski (1941, 523) defined war as an "armed contest between two independent political units, by means of organized military force, in the pursuit of a tribal or national policy."

5. Aum Shinrikyo's motivations for the attack have still not been definitively established. In any case, they do not qualify as a political group and their violence was not sustained, so their actions did not constitute a war.

6. See Diamond (1992) and Gat (1999b, 2006) for further discussion of this topic.

7. Any count of wars is sensitive to coding procedures, and the twentieth century is no exception. There are six twentieth-century great power wars if we include the limited Russo-Japanese war of 1939 over Nomohan and the 1950–53 Sino-American war (if we treat China as a great power at that time), five or four if we exclude one or both. For data on patterns and trends in great power war during the last five centuries, see Levy (1983) and Levy, Walker, and Edwards (2001). See also Wright (1965) and Luard (1986). On the decline in major war, see Väyrynen (2006).

8. Gaddis (1987) and others speak about "the long peace" after World War II. That period has been far from peaceful for most of the world's peoples, however, and is more accurately described as a "long great power peace."

9. The severity data are based on battle deaths associated with Levy's (1983) great power war series and reflect additional information in Goldstein (1988,

397–98). For additional discussion of the validity of battle-related deaths as a measure of the severity of war, see Singer and Small (1972).

10. This is true both in absolute and relative terms, as the ratio of battle deaths to population—defined as the *intensity* of war—has also steadily increased (Levy 1983). This does not imply that each and every great power war was successively more severe than its predecessor. Rather, we mean that the trend line in the severity or intensity of great power warfare has increased over time. This holds true for both interstate wars between the great powers ("major-major" wars) and interstate wars involving the great powers (which include both "major-major" and "major-minor" wars). Interstate wars involving great power wars killed approximately 12.3 thousand combatants per million Europeans in the sixteenth century. The respective numbers for the seventeenth, eighteenth, nineteenth, and twentieth (through 1975) centuries were approximately 44,000, 34,000, 22,000, and 161,000. These cumulative figures derive from calculations based on information on thirty-five wars in the 1500s, twenty-nine in the 1600s, seventeen in the 1700s, twenty in the 1800s, and fifteen wars in the 1900s through 1975, as listed in Levy (1983). The five-hundred-year trend line in battle deaths, aggregated by century, is certainly positive but not linearly so. In contrast, the trend in the decline in war frequency is negative and nearly linear. We will argue that the jump in severity between the nineteenth and twentieth centuries is correlated with the coevolution of our six factors and especially the industrialization of warfare and the tendency toward more total wars. On the inverse relationship between the frequency and seriousness of interstate war involving the great powers during the last five centuries, see Morgan and Levy (1990).

11. The fact that interstate warfare occurred in South America as recently as the 1980s and 1990s, with the 1982 Falklands-Malvinas War being the most prominent, suggests that we should be cautious in forecasting the total absence of war in the near future. On the history of Latin American wars, see Scheina (2003). For different explanations for the relative paucity of warfare in Latin America, see Holsti (1996), Hurrell (1998), Mares (2001), and Centeno (2002).

12. For data and coding rules on interstate war during the last two centuries, see Singer and Small (1972) and Sarkees and Wayman (2010). For analyses of patterns in the last half-century, including the shift of warfare away from Europe, away from the great powers, and toward intrastate warfare and violence involving nonstate actors, see Singer (1991), Holsti (1996), Marshall (1999), Gurr (2000), the Human Security Centre (2005), Pettersson and Themnér (2010), Hewitt, Wilkenfeld, and Gurr (2010), and Strahan and Scheipers (2011).

13. In some cases, the groups fighting the colonial power have not yet been formally colonized, in which case the term *imperial* warfare is more appropriate. Imperial warfare is a term that is used quite loosely in various contexts, but here we mean that states are attempting to expand the size of their empires over different non-state peoples by conquest.

14. Some scholars trace the increase in the frequency of intrastate wars after the 1960s or so to the dramatic increase in the number of new states in the world system as a result of decolonization in the aftermath of World War II (from about sixty in 1945 to over 190 in the current system). In addition to the fact that more states create more opportunities for militarized conflict, new states are particularly vulnerable to internal challenges because they have not had sufficient time to consolidate state power and legitimacy and to build political institutions that provide alternatives to violence. The problem with this argument is that it cannot account for other trends in warfare. Although the expanding number of states and new states in particular is correlated with the increasing frequency of intrastate war from 1945 to 1990, it is inversely correlated with the declining frequency of intrastate war after 1990 or the pronounced decline in interstate war since 1945.

15. Terrorism is not a new strategy or form of warfare, but its modern variant possesses a number of novel characteristics that are unique to the contemporary era. However, we will not devote much attention to this topic in this book because it would divert attention from the longer perspective on warfare that we are advancing. For useful historical perspectives on changing patterns of terrorism over time, see Rapoport (2004) and Rasler and Thompson (2009). For analyses of contemporary terrorism, see Betts (2002), Pape (2005), and Bloom (2005). For counterterrorism strategies, see Cronin and Ludes (2004) and von Knop, Neisser, and van Creveld (2005).

16. One example concerns responses to the problem of how to protect the body against enemy projectiles. Two strategies involve shields and armor. Early shields were made of wicker, animal hides, or wood. Later developments utilized bronze and then iron. Early armor was often a helmet to protect the head from club blows and perhaps a cloak to help protect against arrows. Leather and metal were pressed into service at later points, gradually encompassing the whole body. Of course, the advances in protection were not simply a matter of the availability of new materials, although that was part of the story. Better shields and armor were needed to the extent that projectiles could be thrown with increasingly greater penetrating force. One example is the sequence in which simple bows gave way to compound bows, which gave way to cross bows in some places, all with increasing penetration capabilities. Thus shields, armor, and projectiles evolved over time. They also *co-evolved* because more deadly projectiles changed the incentives for developing better armor and shields (and vice versa). Where the projectile penetrating potential changed very little, armor and shields also changed little. Mesoamerican military change, or the lack thereof, is the most obvious case in point.

17. This is an old idea that goes back at least to Angel (1912), who argued, perhaps somewhat prematurely, that the industrialization of war had increased its costs to the point that war was no longer rational for advanced industrial states. Similarly, Mueller (1989) argued that the increasing destructiveness of war, even

before the development of nuclear weapons, was contributing to the obsolescence of war between advanced industrial states.

18. Arguments based on revolutionary changes in warfare are hardly new, though scholars vary on the precise number of fundamental changes and on their timing. Gabriel (2002) emphasizes these same periods as periods of "military revolution" but looks only at the first two. On military revolutions in the last seven centuries, see Krepinevich (1994), Rogers (1995), Knox and Murray (2001), and Gray (2002).

19. Most states did not survive. It has been estimated that there were as many as one thousand political units around 1000 CE and something like five hundred by 1500 CE. Fewer than fifty survived in Europe to 2000 CE. It is conceivable that there might eventually be only one state in this region at some point in the foreseeable future.

20. On the concept of total war, see Chickering (1999).

21. Briefly, the third acceleration in warfare and its coevolutionary concomitants contributed to the advent of the industrial revolution, which, in turn, fueled even faster acceleration in warfare and its concomitants. The linkage between warfare-induced coevolutionary change and the advent of industrialization is a complicated process that we will not pursue in this book

Chapter Two

1. Scholars use the term *origins of war* in different ways. We follow anthropologists, who almost always use the term to refer to the question of when war first emerged among humans. Or referring to the title and second chapter of Otterbein's (2004) book, the question is *How War Began* or "How War Originated." Although some historians follow this usage (Archer et al. 2002, introduction), one can find numerous books by historians titled "The Origins of xxx War," as illustrated by the studies in the Longman series on Origins of Modern Wars under the general editorship of Harry Hearder. These historians use the term *origins* to refer to what most political scientists would label *causes*. The military historian Donald Kagan wrote the book *On the Origins of War and the Preservation of Peace* (1995) that begins with the Peloponnesian War and says nothing about how war as a general phenomenon originated.

2. See also Ferguson (2006) for a continuing discussion of early evidence on the origins of warfare.

3. Archaeologists are also working hard to push dates of first activity back further in time (Flannery and Marcus 2003).

4. See Keeley's (1996, 5–8, 15–24) useful critique on this subject.

5. O'Connell (1995, 15–24) looks briefly at ants, while LeBlanc with Register (2003, 77–99) discuss, perhaps more profitably, chimpanzee behavior.

6. Once popular versions on this theme are Lorenz (1966) and Ardrey (1966).

7. This was the logic that led Margaret Mead (1940), in her famous essay "Warfare Is Only an Invention, Not a Biological Necessity," to reject the argument that war results from man's "pugnacious instincts." She argued that there were examples, even in the twentieth century, of the absence of war and of the absence of the very concept of war. This same logic led Mead to reject a third possibility, that war was a "sociological inevitability," the necessary result of the development of the state and the competition for land and resources.

8. We are a bit dubious that this generalization will survive unchallenged. The evidence for chimpanzee intergroup aggression, nonetheless, is quite striking (Mitani, Watts, and Amsler 2010). See also de Waal (1989).

9. Gat recommends, in particular, that one should look at chimpanzees because they are the human species' most closely related group in the animal world. See also Tiger and Fox (1971), Bygott (1972), Johnson (1972), Teleki (1973), Carpenter (1974), Wilson (1978), Hausfater and Hrdy (1984), Goodall (1986), Huntingford and Turner (1987), Van Hoof (1990), Dennen and Falger (1990), de Waal (1996), and Wrangham and Peterson (1997). See Ferguson (2000) for a direct response to some of Gat's generalizations.

10. For reviews see Ferguson (1984, 1999), Keeley (1996), and Arkush and Allen (2006). For our purposes a selective review will be sufficient here.

11. Cohen (1984) argues that wars may be more terrible today than earlier because they are more efficiently executed, but that the number of battle deaths in tribal warfare, relative to the size of the population, was often much higher than that in modern times. A more detailed critique of the primitive war conceptualization can be found in Keeley (1996, 8–15).

12. It is synthetic because we selectively combine several partial arguments that other scholars have already proposed. In doing so our argument is more comprehensive than are individual accounts.

13. See also Turney-High ([1949] 1991, 26–27).

14. However, archaeologists continue to debate the purpose of the walls that have been found to enclose these settlements.

15. One minority perspective on the emergence of agriculture is that food cultivation came about because soldiers guarding some resource monopoly needed to be fed. Rather than agricultural expansion leading to food surpluses that needed to be protected by armed guards, the causal order is reversed, with the guards protecting something like fresh water, obsidian, or salt deposits. The more general issue is whether agriculture preceded urbanization, the mainstream view, or vice versa. For some of the arguments on this question, see Mellaart (1975), Gabriel (1990, 30), and Soja (2000, 44–48).

16. The logic of this argument parallels that of the argument that warfare encouraged the emergence of industrialization. Note that the subsequent escalation of warfare in places such as Mesopotamia and Egypt can be attributed at least in

part to agriculturally induced population explosions and the availability of more armed men to serve in expanding armies. From Ferrill's (1997) vantage point, then, the emergence and escalation of warfare are not necessarily linked to the same causality patterns.

17. Compare this number with Ember's (1978) calculation that 88–90 percent of her sample of hunter-gathers engaged in warfare.

18. The Neolithic era translates into the late Stone Age immediately prior to the adoption of metal tools (initially made of copper and then bronze) and about the time of the adoption of agriculture. In the Near East, these markers would date to approximately 10,000 years ago.

19. There is also an implicit assumption about scale here. The response of a nuclear family will involve fewer people than the response of a segmented group. As scale increases, we are more likely to identify the ensuing conflict as warlike even though interfamily feuding might qualify as warlike in other respects. We should also note that we view segmentation as rudimentary political organization—not unlike the rudimentary military organization associated with hunting parties.

20. Mattingly (1992, 33) goes on to observe: "At the higher levels of confederation there is clear evidence for chiefs and elites exercising greater centralized control." That would seem to suggest that greater segmentation is correlated to some extent with greater political centralization, or that greater segmentation is likely to lead to greater political centralization.

21. One of the two unsegmented warlike groups is attributable to European-imposed disruptions in Canadian fur trading in the seventeenth century.

22. Presumably, the disappearance of big game is causally related to the increase in the number of human hunters and mouths to feed.

23. An example is found in Cheyenne oral tradition (Biolsi 1984, 154–55), which recounts how the Assiniboin and Cheyenne became traditional enemies after attempting accidentally to surround the same buffalo herd. The Assiniboin later attacked the Cheyenne camp in the night, thereby initiating an intertribal rivalry.

24. Circumscription also figures prominently in Hall and Chase-Dunn's (1997) evolutionary model of world system development. See Webster (1975) for an interpretation that looks at similar variables to Carneiro's but reaches different conclusions.

25. Anthropologists have created various continuums of organizational complexity. The most common one is the one encompassing band, tribe, chiefdom, and state. Some analysts place isolated villages between band and tribe, with chiefdoms usually being associated with multiple village systems. It should also be noted that anthropologists have become increasingly leery of the categorical accuracy and utility of these continuums (Haas 2001).

26. Earle (1997) goes on to discuss Maori and Hawaiian cases, which more closely approximate Carneiro's expectations.

27. O'Connell (1995, 58) would add that the advent of agriculture was accompanied by some probability of wild swings in productivity, thereby making political-economic activities less stable and more conflict-prone.

28. The unsegmented nature of most groups at that time would have reduced both the probability of intergroup violence and its escalation, raising questions regarding how frequently this behavior crossed the threshold of sustained and coordinated intergroup violence.

29. This raises methodological problems in inferring from evidence of weapons to the presence of war.

30. Large game animals survived in sub-Saharan Africa and North America much longer than in the Near East or East Asia. As a consequence, hunting persisted much longer in these areas with various implications for political economy and political-military organization.

31. Note that this argument runs contrary to Ferrill's (1997) view that warfare encouraged the emergence of sedentary agriculture.

32. It would be useful to place this emphasis on resource scarcity in the context of the broader literature on the origins and causes of war. Scarcity plays a central role in much of the anthropological literature (Vayda 1976; Ferguson 1984; Otterbein 2004). It also occupies a central place in Marxist-Leninist theories, which argue that the competition for resources on the "periphery" of the global system was a major source of imperialism and warfare for the great powers of the past (Lenin [1916] 1939) and for the United States in the last half century (Magdoff 1969). Until recently resource scarcity has been given relatively little attention in most of the mainstream literature in political science on interstate war, with the important exception of Choucri and North (1975). Environmental scarcity has received renewed attention, however, in the contemporary literature on war in the developing world, on "environmental security" (Ronnefeldt 1997; Homer-Dixon 1999; Diehl and Gleditsch 2000), and on civil war (Collier and Hoeffler 2004; Le Billon 2001; de Soysa 2002; Ross 2003; Ballentine and Sherman 2003; and Humphreys 2005). Scholars have given special attention to the potential for conflict over oil and water (Klare 2001; Lowi 1993). Scholars have also begun to examine the impact of demographic changes and migration on conflict (Choucri 1984; Krebs and Levy 2001; Hudson and Den Boer 2005; Greenhill 2010).

33. The theme of what is sometimes referred to as "resource unpredictability" (defined as situations in which resources suddenly become more scarce) is quite common in the anthropological literature on war. See, among many others, Vayda (1961); Ember (1982); Milner, Anderson, and Smith (1991); Shankman (1991); Ember and Ember (1992); Bamforth (1994); and Lekson (2002). The theme is also emphasized by the international relations specialist, Thayer (2004), who looks at the evolutionary origins of war from a biological evolutionary point of view.

34. Basically, Otterbein sought to assess empirically the relationship between military sophistication/efficiency and political centralization. He drew his sample from the first 628 societies listed in an ethnographic atlas attempting to amass data on every known society. Each society in the larger archive is grouped into one of sixty culture areas. As each society was extracted for the working sample using random numbers, its culture area was noted and not drawn upon again, yielding

one representative society for fifty of the sixty culture areas. The specific societies focused upon are listed in Otterbein (1970, 12–14).

35. Bands are hunting-gathering groups with a leader who has little authority. Tribes combine several local groups through some pantribal affinity. Chiefdoms have chiefs with the power to redistribute resources. States have the pangroup affinity, redistributive powers, and a government. For subsistence modes, intensive agriculture is contrasted with shifting cultivation, animal husbandry, and hunting-gathering. Warfare is defined as military organizations representing political communities fighting with weapons. Internal warfare, therefore, is excluded from the database by definition.

36. Otterbein (1970, 63–70) demonstrates that his six war causes are quite typical of the anthropology literature at the time he was writing. Yet in coding his societies he was quite sensitive to the likelihood that war causes might vary from instance to instance, but his intent was to capture the most predominant motivations. Consequently, he allowed each group to be coded for as many as the causes as was appropriate, albeit subject to a rank order with the most prevalent motivation given first place and so forth. He hypothesized that more complex groups would be associated with more causes than the less complex groups. The hypothesis was supported. For the sake of convenience, we use only the first motivation associated with each group and impose our own sense of the more/less territorial conceptualization (as in territorial expansion) on Otterbein's six causes and database.

37. Whether the evidence supports Otterbein's (2004) argument that agriculture emerged only in the pristine zones when warfare had been absent for some time is a claim that needs further investigation.

Chapter Three

1. For another view of international politics as the ongoing interaction of elements in a complex system, in which a change in one element leads to changes in other elements, see Jervis (1997). For a more technical but accessible discussion of complex adaptive systems, see Miller and Page (2007).

2. For instance, Tilly's (1975, 1990) long-standing emphasis on war making states and states making war is easily subsumed within our framework, as are many other dimensions of the military revolution of the sixteenth to seventeenth centuries (Roberts [1955] 1995). More generally, we argue that most material arguments about warfare can be translated readily into the six-factor framework.

3. In a more fine-tuned future study we might want to give climate and population growth more explicit emphasis in a model of the evolution of war.

4. One can think of other influences on other variables in our framework. Metallurgical developments (bronze, iron, steel) provide a context for changes in weaponry. Military doctrine is readily linked to military organization and to weaponry.

5. On strategic cultures of military organizations, see Builder (1989), Snyder (1990), Johnston (1995), Kier (1995), Rosen (1995), and Mahnken (2008). On the role of religion in war, see Horowitz (2009).

6. This was Carr's (1940) critique of economic liberal ideology: it served as a rationalization for the economic self-interest of the most efficient economies in the system because it was they who would benefit most from an open, free-trading system.

7. Similarly, we recognize the role of gender considerations (Goldstein 2003) but give them less priority for our present purposes.

8. On the debate over whether military doctrines are shaped by the external threat environment or internal organizational interest and cultures, see Posen (1984), Evangelista (1988), and Rosen (1991).

9. We return to the question of military revolutions in chapter 6.

10. The experience of Japan after World War II provides a good example.

11. Evolutionary change may start, accelerate, and slow down but it does not end as long as what is evolving continues to exist.

12. Here we borrow significantly from Gerhard Lenski (2005, 53–124), who develops what he calls an ecological-evolutionary theory focused on the interactions among population, ideology, technology, social organization, and biophysical and sociocultural environments as his master variables. However, he privileges technology as becoming the most important of the six after an initial development period. Within this complex Lenski postulates that there are six types of society: hunting and gathering, horticultural (agriculture without plows), agrarian (agriculture with plows), nomadic, maritime, and industrial, with most of the first five yielding ultimately to the sixth type. We prefer to emphasize different principal factors (military and political organization, weaponry, threat environment, war, and political economy). We do not privilege technology per se but our political-economy emphasis certainly overlaps considerably. We also choose to simplify, for present purposes, the basic societal types although for other questions we could certainly see some definite theoretical utility in injecting information on nomadic and maritime societies and even horticultural agriculture. Thus while we are not adopting Lenski's perspective wholesale, we borrow heavily from its insights.

13. Should we then have a fourth postindustrial dominant strategy in our theory? There is ample disagreement on this subject of postindustrialism, but we do not necessarily equate the proliferation of service jobs with the predominance of a postindustrial political-economic strategy. Whether postindustrial societies have really arrived does not seem to matter all that much to our argument. We have not seen states jumping from either hunter-gatherer or agrarian economies to postindustrial economies. Whatever transitions have occurred have been from agrarian to industrial and then perhaps to some form of postindustrial approach. Yet the logic on which we base our argument works equally well for both industrial and postindustrial situations. Since postindustrial economies would be very advanced

forms of industrial economies, whatever political-economic, organizational, and weaponry-war transformations that are applicable to industrial development should also apply, doubly so, to postindustrial development.

14. On the link between economic interdependence and peace for the last two centuries of the modern system, see Russett and Oneal (2001). A different view for some situations with acute potential for escalation is expressed in Rapkin and Thompson (2006).

15. The overall costs of warfare should be even greater in a postindustrial political-economic context than in an industrial setting.

16. The irony here is that the industrial era's technological leader, given perceived responsibilities for guarding the world economy's status quo, is apt to be the exception to the generalization about the tendency for industrialized states to drop out of coercive competition. It may not be able to afford warfare but it also cannot afford to drop out of the competition without sacrificing its hard-earned systemic position.

17. World military expenditures in 2005 totaled 1.16 trillion in constant 2005 dollars (which were worth less than 1996 dollars).

18. Downes (2008) believes that he has captured about 82 percent of the civilian deaths in this time period. He also provides low, middle, and high estimates for each war. We have aggregated the middle range estimates.

19. We are unaware of instances in which multiple agrarian societies (or hunting-gathering societies for that matter) abandoned fighting due to the perceived costs of warfare. Certainly, individual agrarian societies have from time to time "dropped out" of coercive competitions to the extent that they could do so. Examples may be found in Scandinavia, for instance, where Sweden and Denmark were once regional powers but were gradually eclipsed by the rise of Russia and Prussia in the eighteenth century. Another example is late nineteenth-century Paraguay, which lost too many males in combat to continue competing with its neighbors for a time—at least until the Chaco War in the 1930s. But these cases represent specific reactions to defeat and war costs, as opposed to categorical or generic responses.

20. Additional discussions of Smith's argument can be found in Goodwin (1991) and Doyle (1997, 231–41).

21. The literature on this question is fast expanding. See Rosecrance (1986); Doyle (1997); Mousseau (2000); Mousseau, Hegre, and Oneal (2003); Weede (2003); Rasler and Thompson (2005); Gartzke (2007); McDonald (2009); Mueller (2010); Russett (2010); and Schneider and Gleditsch (2010). The Schneider and Gleditsch article is the introduction to a special issue of *International Interactions* on the subject.

22. Gat specifically cites analyses he feels are pertinent in Small and Singer (1982), Levy (1983), and Luard (1986).

23. Daggett's estimates exclude peacetime spending on war preparations as well as veteran benefits, national debt interest, and aid for allies and thus might have been higher than they are.

24. Once again, we do not argue that interstate warfare between industrial states has been eliminated—only that its probability has declined considerably.

25. This argument is very Darwinian in tone. Darwin argued:

> The strongest and most vigorous men,—those who could best defend and hunt for their families and during later times the chiefs or head-men,—those who were provided with the best weapons and possessed the most property, such as a larger number of dogs or other animals, would have succeeded in rearing a greater average number of offspring than would the weaker, poorer and lower members of the same tribes. ([1871] 2004, vol. 1, 161)
>
> ... Now, if some one man in a tribe, more sagacious than the others, invented a new snare or weapon, or other means of attack or defense, the plainest self-interest, without the assistance of much reasoning power, would prompt the other members to imitate him. ...
>
> ... If the invention were an important one, the tribe would increase in number, spread, and supplant other tribes. (Darwin [1871] 2004, vol. 2, 368–69)

26. For counterfactual arguments about different scenarios through which the rise of Europe to global dominance in the modern era might have been aborted or derailed, and how history might have taken different paths, see Tetlock, Lebow, and Parker (2006). On methodological criteria for evaluating counterfactual arguments, see Levy (2008a).

27. The phenomenon of "failed states" (Starr 2009, Marten 2010)—political organizations that have collapsed and that are no longer characterized by any effective, central decision-making institutions—represent extreme examples of this problem.

28. This same hunting hardware (weapons) and software (such as coordination tactics) make it difficult to distinguish their applications to hunting and to warfare.

29. We see this development as a part of very early political organization.

30. This is the sense in which scholars such as Mead (1940) and Vasquez (2009) argue that war is best understood as learned behavior. This raises a definitional question regarding what is meant by "learning" and a difficult analytic question as well. If we distinguish between a model based on *adaptation* to environmental change and one based on *learning* (Levy 1994), we can ask how much of the diffusion of war behavior can be traced to adaptation to changing structural conditions (threat environment, scarcity, political economy, etc.) and how much to individual and perhaps collective learning about what strategies might help achieve certain goals. In this usage, the term *learning* implies some variation across units in the lessons learned. If actors adapt to changing environmental circumstances, they would always behave in similar ways under similar conditions. If actors learn (and if they act on the basis of what they have learned), and if different actors learn different

lessons, then actors would sometimes behave in different ways under similar conditions. If we observe war behavior, is it because actors are responding "rationally" to existing conditions, as the adaptation hypothesis suggests, or are they learning from their observation and interpretation of others' war behavior, as the learning hypothesis suggests. This is extremely difficult to determine empirically, particularly for earlier historical eras.

31. Shock weaponry consists of weapons that are hand-held instruments used to strike or bludgeon the opponent. Stone hammers, swords, and bayonets are examples. The main contrast is with projectile weaponry, which are used to launch something damaging—an arrow, spear, or bullet for instance—at an opponent from a distance. See Hassig (1988, 1992) and chapter 5 for older forms of warfare in Central America.

32. For treatments of China, see Lewis (1990, 2007), Graff and Higham (2002), Sawyer (2004), Hui (2005), and chapter 4. On India, see Gommans (2002) and Khan (2004). On Japan, see Farris (1995) and Friday (2004).

33. Even so, the nomadic attacks on Europe were much less impressive than those in areas closer to Central Asia.

34. The Ming voyages are described in Levathes (1994). The most popular scholarly source for the Japanese suppression of gunpowder weaponry is Perrin (1980), but his version is not considered very accurate (Chase 2003, 195; Lorge 2008, 62–63). Guns were not effectively banned by the government; they simply were not utilized very much in the absence of Japanese warfare. As Lorge (2008, 63) puts it, the gunpowder revolution in Japan was "rendered irrelevant by peace."

35. Throughout our analysis, we emphasize developments in land armies. Naval developments are also important, but their inclusion would complicate our ability to generalize succinctly about such matters as the shape of military trajectories.

36. Balancing strategies are one of the reasons for the repeated failure to form a unified empire. See Gulick (1955), Dehio (1962), and Levy and Thompson (2005, 2010a).

37. Here we build on Kalyvas (2005).

38. That lack of capability does not preclude the ability to wage long intrastate wars that can proceed intermittently on limited resource inputs indefinitely and without resolution. External intervention can also help prolong the duration of internal warfare.

39. The fifteen post-1945 wars involving developed states also tended to be short and roughly to the same extent (60 percent lasted fewer than six months). The main difference is that wars involving developed states tend to be short because developed states can apply their greater capabilities more decisively, as in the "shock and awe" invasion of Iraq. Guerrilla warfare by the less developed state can complicate this process by making mixed wars longer than they might otherwise have been. The conventional forces of less developed states, however, usually stop fighting because they lack sufficient capabilities to decide the disputed issue.

40. Some analysts argue that criminals prominent in some intrastate war situations are operating strictly for personal gain. That may well be but our point in including them along with paramilitary and militia forces is that decision-makers in weak states have recruited criminals to engage in activities (such as ethnic cleansing) that regular armed forces sometimes decline to do. See, for example, Mueller's (2004) chapter on Yugoslavia.

41. Whether it is reasonable to say the Middle East "chose" to exit the western military trajectory after about 600 CE, it clearly evolved along separate lines after the Islamic expansion from its European counterpart.

Chapter Four

1. In an earlier study, Gabriel (1990, 25–31) demarcates the Stone Age development of weapons as the first military revolution.

2. Gabriel (2002) focuses only on the first two revolutions.

3. The American Revolution is a clear exception to this generalization.

4. These numbers exaggerate the mobility of ancient armies. They were not expected to patrol every portion of the expanding empires nor would they necessarily move armies from one frontier to another. Instead, armies would be raised for specific campaigns or delimited theaters of operation.

5. Gabriel (2002, 4) argues that a prototype for every weapon developed up to 1500 CE was created in the 1500 BCE–100 CE era.

6. Gabriel's 1500 BCE starting point precedes the beginning of the transition to iron, which is roughly a first millennium BCE phenomenon commencing initially in the eastern Mediterranean and spreading outward in concentric circles over space and time.

7. We are dependent on Egyptian sources for information on the outcomes of the battles with the Sea Peoples. There may be some exaggeration in the extent to which the Egyptians were able to defeat the invaders. However, it is known that some Sea Peoples (Philistines) were encouraged to occupy "Palestinian" territory, thereby leading to the area to the east of Egypt being referred to as Palestine.

8. This aspect of Egyptian history and political economy is not discussed here but is examined and demonstrated in Thompson (2002).

9. In the Mycenaean age, armor had been buried with deceased warriors, but that practice was abandoned in the 700s (Bowden 1993), presumably because armor was too valuable to the living.

10. Wees (2004) contends that hoplite armor progressed through its own trajectory. In the late eighth century, armor was slowly being introduced. By the mid-seventh century, the adoption of a full set of armor had peaked. In the middle of the sixth century, some of the armor was no longer used in order to lighten the hoplite's burden.

11. The argument is also extended to the need to have citizens manning the oars in states with large navies.

12. The First Peloponnesian War is usually dated 478–460 BCE, and the second, better-known Peloponnesian War about which Thucydides wrote was 431–404 BCE.

13. Whether or not the changes were Greek in origin remains in doubt. Wees (2004, 206) thinks they were copied from Persian models.

14. The other two candidates are mounting cannon onboard ships in the fourteenth century CE and abandoning wooden ships for ironclads in the nineteenth century CE.

15. Keppie (1984) thinks it probably started with one class encompassing anyone who could muster some useful equipment; it then became more stratified at later points. At a later point, age became more important than wealth for who served in which rank. Cornell (1995, 189) thinks there were probably two classes most of the time—those with some armor and those without any.

16. There is some disagreement as to whether ancient Chinese dynasties were strictly sequential in time and space or coexisted and alternated in relative power. Either way, the Xia, Shang, Zhou sequence has survived intact.

17. Shaughnessy (1999, 307–9) credits the triumphant Zhou forces with three hundred chariots and forty-five thousand infantry.

18. Li Liu and Xingcan Chen (2003) restrict their study to pre-Zhou states, but it is conceivable that their interpretation of decentralization dynamics continued into the first millennium BCE.

19. The Zhou dynasty period is thus divided into the western Zhou dynasty before 771 and the more decentralized eastern Zhou dynasty after 770.

20. The irony here is that heavy cavalry are usually thought of as one possible response to coping with nomadic light cavalry, but in this case the heaviest cavalry were introduced first by the Hsien-pi and Xiongnu in the early 300s.

21. An atlatl is a device that assists in launching projectiles from the arm and that generates greater distance and force.

22. On the fall of the Aztecs, see, for instance, Restall (2003).

23. Indian military development also accelerated in the last half of the first millennium BCE, but we know far less about what occurred there than elsewhere.

Chapter Five

1. General treatments of the evolution of military technology over time may be found in Brodie and Brodie (1973), Dupuy (1980), McNeill (1982), van Creveld (1989), and Boot (2006).

2. Similarly, Howard (1979) emphasizes "the forgotten dimensions of strategy."

3. The concept has a very strong prescriptive element and has been used by RMA proponents in an attempt to persuade American military and political lead-

ers to accelerate the military revolution in US strategic doctrine and weapons systems. This suggests that RMAs are the products of the behavior of political organizations as well as the outcomes of impersonal technological and social forces. In fact, Shapiro (1999, quoted in Gray 2002, 44) argues that "the current proposed information-based revolution in military affairs has been the most self-conscious military revolution in history."

4. For critiques of the punctuated equilibrium model of war, see Murray (1997) and Gray (2002, 46–52). For an evolutionary perspective on future warfare, see Biddle (1998).

5. The next several sections build on Levy, Walker, and Edwards (2001).

6. The fact that the longbow did not diffuse beyond England, despite its effectiveness on the battlefield, is a puzzle. It took a long time, however, to train bowmen in the effective use of the longbow, and English bowmen needed less training because the weapon was part of English and Welsh hunting culture. On the continent, the easier-to-learn, "point-and-shoot" crossbow reigned supreme. Even after their defeat by the English, most famously and decisively at the hands of numerically inferior English forces with longbowmen at Agincourt in 1415, the French never attempted to develop their own longbow specialists.

7. The tactical preference would be to catch the wind so that one's own fleet could sail on a perpendicular vector across the bows of the opposing fleet before the opponent could bring its own guns to bear. One of the implications of such a tactic is that it required more training to be able to execute such maneuvers. It also spelled an end to what had been one-on-one melee fighting in fleet encounters.

8. Black (1991) offers a different perspective on this period.

9. Although invented in the late eighteenth century, the steam engine did not have a significant impact on land warfare for nearly a century. Steamships, however, were able to move up rivers to bombard enemy cities (as opposed to sailing ships being forced to hover near the coast) much earlier in the nineteenth century.

10. Nef (1950) suggests that another consequence of the industrial revolution was that the earlier moral and cultural restraints on war associated with the Christian and Humanist traditions were gradually eroded by the materialism and individualism of industrial society.

11. On the offensive/defensive balance, see also Jervis (1978), Van Evera (1999), and Brown et al. (2003).

12. On the influence of different conceptions of naval warfare on how naval strategists in the United States and the United Kingdom learned from experience about the effectiveness of new naval technologies, see Vacca (2009).

13. For an evolutionary interpretation of the changing nature of warfare in the interwar period, see Biddle (1998). On the role of strategy, see Mearsheimer (1988).

14. Some of the potential military consequences of this information revolution were anticipated in its early stages by Soviet military theorists after observing the

American use of precision-guided munitions, cruise missiles, and other information-based innovations in the 1960s and 1970s (Murray and Knox 2001, 3–4).

15. Although analysts conceive of the contemporary revolution in military affairs in terms of the exploitation of new information technologies by the most economically advanced states in the international system, one can make the argument that another contemporary revolution in military affairs is equally consequential. That RMA involves new political organizations—namely, nonstate actors—with new military doctrines that have made equally good use of new information systems to use old technologies like roadside bombs and improvised explosive devices to change the nature of warfare by the weak against the strong, exploiting their own invulnerability to deterrence by retaliation.

16. We have seen similar patterns in earlier historical systems.

17. Parker (1988) argues that many of these innovations could be found at an earlier time in the Spanish military, but it was the reforms of Maurice and Gustavus that served as the model that others emulated.

18. The size of armies expanded dramatically during the Thirty Years' War and then again toward the end of the seventeenth century (Parker 1988; Lynn 1995). Thompson and Rasler (1999) argue that these increases of army size, and indeed other major increases in army size over the last five centuries, were due primarily to the occurrence of global wars and not primarily to military revolutions.

19. At the same time we need to be cautious in attributing immediate, major changes to an up swelling of French patriotism in the French Revolutionary Wars. A closer examination of the numbers involved suggests that the scalar increases in the warfare of 1792–1815 were more gradual and much less popular than is often believed.

20. For arguments and evidence on the societal impacts of total wars, see Marwick (1965, 1974), Wright (1968), Stein (1978), Emsley (1979), Milward (1979), Best (1982), Bond (1986), Rasler and Thompson (1989), Porter (1994), Leebaert (2002), Black (2006), Bell (2007), and Sheehan (2008).

21. Millis (1956) gives primary emphasis to material factors and calls this the "scientific revolution" in warfare, but that concept underestimates the autonomous impact of political, social, and ideational factors.

22. Alternatively, one could say we have come full circle.

23. The United States also made a major defense effort, but in terms of defense spending/GNP and in terms of the disruptive effects of military spending on the economy and society, the Soviet Union mobilized to a much greater extent.

24. On the democratic peace, see Ray (1995); Russett and Oneal (2001); Mousseau (2000, 2003); Mousseau, Hegre, and Oneal (2003); Rasler and Thompson (2005); Gat (2006); Gartzke (2007); Gibler (forthcoming); and McDonald (2009). Whether Kant was right that economic interdependence is a significant contributor to peace is the subject of a lively debate (Mansfield and Pollins 2003; Schneider, Barbieri, and Gleditsch 2003; and Rapkin and Thompson 2006).

25. Liberman (1996) questions this standard argument, and argues that Nazi Germany was able to exploit the territories of the industrial societies that it occupied for the benefit of the German economy.

26. On the link between territorial disputes and the outbreak of war, see Vasquez and Henehan (2010).

27. This approximates Boulding's (1978) concept of "stable peace."

28. On the sources of variation in beliefs about the "lessons of history," see Jervis (1976, chap. 6) and Levy (1994).

29. Thus Mueller argues that Hitler was a necessary condition for the outbreak of World War II (and that Mussolini and Tojo also played critical roles), and he supports his argument with a careful (but ultimately unsatisfactory) counterfactual analysis. On necessary condition counterfactuals, see Goertz and Levy (2007) and Levy (2008a). For a range of views on the causes of World War II, and on Hitler's role in the process, see Robertson (1971). On the wars in Asia and in the Pacific, which Mueller does not address, see Iriye (1987).

30. Kaysen (1990) does not deal with the likelihood of preemption based on an actor's belief that its adversary was about to strike and that the utility of striking first exceeded the utility of nonaction, even if both outcomes involved net losses.

31. Warfare between industrialized states and nonindustrialized states is not subject to the same constraints.

Chapter Six

1. We focus on general tendencies and make no claim that every trajectory either looks alike or shares every possible common denominator.

2. We say *ultimately* because it is possible for a new regional hegemon to cause considerable change by fiat, but we would not expect these command changes to continue indefinitely.

3. We examined three of these trajectories in more detail in chapter 4.

4. Bids for regional hegemony are also central in Mearsheimer's (2001) theory of offensive realism.

5. This observation also reflects an appreciation for world system history (Denemark et al. 2000) and a preference for tracing the origins of long-term processes to fourth millennium BCE Sumerian urbanization, as opposed to the more traditional inclination to begin everything "western" with the first millennium BCE Greeks.

6. We do not take on all of these questions directly in this book. But at least some indirect answers are provided in these pages. Chapter 4 focuses on contrasting several different ancient trajectories. Chapters 5 and 7 examine the distinctive divergence of the western trajectory and its implications.

7. An omitted factor also describes how these changes were manifested in warfare.

8. Readers should by now recognize this combination as involving political organization, political economy, and weaponry.

9. *Trace italienne* artillery fortresses were fortified walls reconfigured to better absorb cannon fire. The reconfigurations included thickening and sloping the walls as well as building projecting blockhouses to rake attackers from the sides as they approached the walls (Lynn 1995).

10. The political costs of conscription may be particularly high in states lacking a political culture of legitimacy. This creates some incentives for such states to seek security through external alliances rather than through an expansion in the size of their armies. This argument is most commonly applied to the contemporary developing world, but it has implications for earlier eras (Barnett and Levy, 1991).

11. Again, in order to focus on the complex causal linkages involved, we limit our attention almost entirely to land warfare.

12. Hassig (1992, 178) simplifies this process in the following way. Conquest is easiest when one state enjoys a significant military advantage over the targets of its expansion. Little expansion is likely if military symmetry exists. The loss of asymmetry is likely to lead to imperial contraction. See also Wright (1965).

13. Mearsheimer (2001) makes a similar argument for the last several centuries of the modern system.

14. On theories of balancing, see Gulick (1955) and Levy and Thompson (2005, 2010a).

15. Mention of this phenomenon creates an opening for constraints such as the currently popular democratic-regime-type arguments in which the type of political system is thought to be a major constraint on certain kinds of behavior (Doyle 1983; Russett and Oneal 2001; for a review see Levy and Thompson 2010, chap. 4). Given the recent advent of democratization, our inclination is to suggest that there may be longer-term processes at work that are capable of producing outcomes for which democratization is now inaccurately given much of the credit. This question is examined more fully by Rasler and Thompson (2005) and by Sheehan (2008), who credits democratization with facilitating the increase in European state resource mobilization and lethality while also leading to a consequent popular rejection of the use of force.

16. The debate on this subject is summarized in Jervis (1989) and in Sagan and Waltz (2002).

17. On the strong/weak state idea, see Migdal (1988), Holsti (1996), Desch (1996), Centeno (2002), and Hironaka (2005). Holsti, for instance, defines weak states as ones that are unable to mobilize adequate resources, monopolize weaponry within their societies, and fail to earn the loyalties of their populations.

18. On the possibility that these norms might have destabilizing effects, see Atzili (2006/7).

19. Contrasts between the impact of warfare on state building in non-European and European areas can be found in Barnett (1992), Herbst (2003), Heydemann (2000), and Centeno (2002). We return to this subject in chapter 7.

20. Since Marcus (1998) looked at Mesopotamian developments as one of her cases, we could be said, figuratively speaking, to be extending Lynn's model back to Marcus's model.

21. See, among others, Ferguson (1984, 1990), O'Connell (1995), Keeley (1996), Kelly (2000), LeBlanc with Register (2003), and Gat (2006).

22. Low population densities would also suggest that there was less scarcity of desired values over which to fight, other things being equal.

23. A reasonable question is why focus on these cases and not some others? One answer is that it is not coincidental that most studies of ancient military history tend to focus on the same cases. For instance, Gabriel and Metz's (1991) title is *From Sumer to Rome*. Their examples focus on Sumer, Akkad, Egypt, Assyria, Persia, Greece/Macedonia, and Rome, although the presentation approach is more topically oriented. Ferrill (1997) starts with Neolithic practices and then moves to a discussion of Sumerian-Egyptian-Assyrian-Persian-Macedonian cases. Dawson (2001) focuses primarily on Sumer, Akkad, Egypt, Assyria, and Persia. Archer et al.'s (2002) first two chapters begin with Egypt and proceed to discuss Assyrian-Persian-Greek-Macedonian-Roman cases, with brief Indian and Chinese detours. Carey, Allfree, and Cairns (2005) look at Sumer, Egypt, Mycenaeans, Assyria, Persia, Greeks, Macedonia, and Rome. Of course, a justification that suggests only that other authors tend to focus on the same cases is less than compelling. Reasonable criticisms would include that authors on ancient military matters tend to read one another and/or that ancient specialists merely emphasize the cases on which we have the most information. More compelling is that the analysts who survey ancient military history often describe these armies as the most powerful of their time. Another important attribute is that these armies put together different packages of military organization and weaponry, often building and improving on the strengths of their immediate predecessor in the trajectory sequence.

24. One reason that the Macedonians were more favorable to cavalry was the Macedonian location on the northern Greek frontier and therefore greater exposure to and experience with horseback riding as a way of life.

25. See Bachrach (1972, 1973) on this Merovingian/Carolingian phenomenon. Some of the most successful medieval knights, the Normans, were initially Viking infantry and raiders who adopted the heavy cavalry model after capturing parts of western Europe.

26. We examined this question earlier in chapter 5. See, for instance, Roberts ([1955] 1995); Parker (1988); Downing (1992); Krepinevich (1994); Eltis (1995); Ayton and Price (1995); Rogers (1995); Cohen (1996); Lynn (1996); Nye and Owens (1996); Ross (1996); France (1999); Levy, Walker, and Edwards (2001); Murray and Knox (2001); and Sloan (2002).

27. *Tercios* were pike-armed infantry units into which men firing the harquebus (an early form of musket) were integrated in the early sixteenth century.

28. The Muslim commitment to light cavalry "slave soldiers" is an interesting mutation and deviation from the western Eurasian military trajectory. Despite the

fact that this strategy emerged in areas initially central to the west, it manifests the deepening cleavage between areas south and north of the Mediterranean after the development of Islam, a different threat environment, and the earlier shift of western centrality to the north. For further reading on medieval Middle Eastern military developments, see Crone (1980) and Pipes (1981).

29. Admittedly, "flirtations" that last almost a millennium represent something more than brief dalliances, except perhaps from a very long-term perspective.

30. For a different critique of the Hanson argument, see Lynn (2003, 12–27).

31. The Chinese did the same several hundred years later.

32. The United States acquired regional hegemony in North America prior to developing the world's leading army in the second half of the twentieth century. Space precludes a discussion of the distinctive US case, except to note that the theory is restricted to regional hegemony, not global hegemony. See Elman (2004).

33. This topic provides the armature for much of the modern history of European international relations and a respectable proportion of international relations theory. It is another question we do not explore in this book.

34. On differences between land powers and sea powers, the threats they pose to others, and the strategic responses they elicit, see Levy and Thompson (2010a).

Chapter Seven

1. Other factors have also played an important role in shaping the two different worlds of warfare. Political economy, for example, is the primary driver in creating agrarian-industrialization divergence in the first place.

2. We omit Asia, primarily because scholars have given it less attention in terms of the link between war making and state making (though see Stubbs's [2005] thesis on the impact of war on east and southeast Asian economic growth in the contemporary era). We strongly suspect that the patterns we attribute to other contemporary, "third world" regions apply to places such as south, central, and southeast Asia as well. Whether they apply equally to northeast Asia remains to be seen, given the presence of the powerful states of China and Japan.

3. On the death of states, see Fazal (2007).

4. US intervention in and throughout the twentieth century meant that the European external environment had changed substantially, but only after some four centuries of relatively autonomous regional competition. European regional autonomy was also shaped by the Mongol invasions and by the fact that the Mongols had not succeeded in moving farther west than Hungary in the thirteenth century.

5. This generalization does not hold in Central America where relatively weak efforts (short in duration and intensity) were made to conquer the entire region in the early nineteenth and twentieth centuries. On the wars of Latin America, see Scheina (2003), among others.

6. The populations of the West Bank and Gaza and the former population of the Golan Heights might disagree with this generalization, but their ultimate fate is still a matter of negotiation.

7. Cold War bipolarity prevented some wars from occurring and increased the duration of many that did occur, while the demise of the Cold War altered the likelihood of certain types of war and affected their duration as well. The United States would have been significantly less likely to attack Iraq in 1991 and 2003 if Iraq had still been closely tied to the Soviet Union. It may have also been somewhat less likely to insert American troops into Saudi Arabia after the Iraqi invasion of Kuwait in 1990, due to the fear of a US-Soviet confrontation, but that same fear might have led the Soviet Union to restrain Iraq in the first place. Yugoslavia might not have disintegrated into warfare among its constituent parts in the absence of the collapse of the Soviet Union and Soviet influence throughout Eastern Europe. Internal warfare in newly independent states in the Caucuses and central Asia would also have been less probable. Each of these differences, however, relates more to the disintegration of the Soviet Union than to the unipolarity of the United States. It is also easy to exaggerate the primacy of the United States in the current structural setting, but this is a topic better examined elsewhere. See Thompson (2006) and Russett (2011). For another perspective on the impact of the Cold War on internal wars, see Kalyvas and Balcells (2010).

8. The latest revision of the Correlates of War data (Sarkees and Wayman 2010), upon which we rely for our calculations, ends in 2007.

9. A different kind of regional displacement, triggered by the end of the Cold War, has taken place for civil wars. There was a shift in civil wars away from Latin America and Asia toward Eurasia and sub-Saharan Africa, with a weaker shift toward the Middle East and North Africa (Kalyvas and Balcells 2010, 423).

10. Rather than post–Cold War changes leading to an expansion in the frequency of internal warfare, it was Cold War pressures that contributed to the protraction of civil warfare, as Hironaka (2005) demonstrates.

11. These numbers are normalized or control for the changing number of states in the system by dividing the number of wars each year by the number of states in the system. Technically, interstate wars should be divided by the number of interstate dyads in the system, as opposed to the number of states, but we use the same denominator here for ease of comparison.

12. Mathematically, a large increase in the number of new states, other things being equal, should increase the frequency of internal and external warfare. If states were equally likely to engage in internal or external warfare, it is conceivable that the ratio might remain constant over time. But other things are not equal when it comes to the new states of the post-1945 era. To the extent that new states are weaker than older states in terms of mobilizational capabilities, governmental legitimacy, and popular loyalties, a fair number of internal wars might be anticipated. At the same time, weak states are less capable of engaging in interstate

warfare. Hence the ratio of internal to external warfare has increased in the past half-century or so.

13. For other treatments of "new wars," see Münkler (2005) and Duyvesteyn and Angstrom (2005).

14. See Luard (1986) for an analysis of the changing issues involved in wars over time.

15. Much of the German literature emphasizes the impact of globalization as a major factor leading to new wars. For a useful review see Brzoska (2004). For a more detailed argument, see Münkler (2005). On warlords see Marten (2011).

16. This phenomenon is addressed in the interstate war literature on the diversionary theory of war (Levy 1989).

17. In a subsequent book, Mueller (2009) addresses terrorism. He argues that terrorism is generally likely to be ineffectual, largely because he believes it represents sporadic attacks by individuals and small groups. The number and identity of the attackers rule it out as a form of warfare, which for Mueller evidently requires the participation of large groups or states on both sides. Instead he categorizes terrorism as a form of violence, not unlike crime, that has been around for a long time and is likely to persist well into the distant future. Its aim is either to apply enough violence to persuade an opponent to comply with the terrorist group's demands or to provoke the opponent into an overreaction that results in a significant number of onlookers to support the terrorist group rather than the government. Mueller regards terrorist attacks, so far, to be underarmed, too infrequent, and too limited in damaging effects to have a high probability of success. He is more concerned with the overreaction wrought by terrorist attacks.

18. Huntington (1996), in his "clash of civilizations" thesis, argues that cultural identity will become the principal focus of individual allegiance and will lead to increasing clashes between a few large areas of rough cultural homogeneity.

19. Another type of "policing war" is one in which external armies intervene in another state's domestic violence to suppress or ameliorate its effects. One might ask whether these interventions, frequently carried out by developed states against less developed states in turmoil, represent a clean break from what was once colonial or imperial warfare. But here again Mueller thinks these policing wars are not likely to be frequent given the distaste of most developed states to incur casualties and expense when their national interests do not appear to be at risk.

20. For useful theoretical analyses of the process, see Bates (2001), Wagner (2007), and North, Wallis, and Weingast (2009).

21. Dannreuther (2007, 125) makes a similar point. He distinguishes among three types of developing states. The most common type is labeled "praetorian" and represents weak states that specialize primarily in internal repression and conflict. Some developing states are "globalizing." They are being successfully integrated into the global economy and they are shifting away from internal repression. The last category is the "failed" state. These cases are praetorian states in which

the ruling elite have lost control and suffered institutional collapses, "new wars," and intervention by developed states.

22. Kalyvas and Balcells (2010) make the same point in emphasizing the changing nature of the "technology of rebellion" as a function of the changing power structure of the international system.

23. The technologies of the rebellion dimension of their civil war typology includes military technologies of both states and rebels. These are operationalized in terms of whether each side used heavy weaponry (artillery and armor) or light weapons.

24. Mueller (2004) argues that intervention by the regular military forces from developed states is more likely to be effective than is intervention by regular military forces from less developed states. The latter tend either to be too poorly armed or led to do the job, or they end up using the same criminal tactics they are supposed to be suppressing.

Chapter Eight

1. Military organizations can also be an important cause of the initiation and especially the escalation of some wars (but see Betts 1977), but that is a different question.

2. Arguing that nuclear weapons have had a revolutionary impact on international politics in general and the likelihood of a major power war in particular are Brodie (1946), Bundy (1988), Jervis (1989), and Waltz (1990). Arguing that nuclear weapons have had a minimal impact are Mueller (1989, 2010), Zagare and Kilgour (2000), and many power transition theorists (Organski and Kugler 1980; Tammen et al. 2000). Some argue that the deterrent effect of nuclear weapons allows states to behave more aggressively at the conventional level, confident that the risks of escalation are too great to be tolerated (Snyder 1965). Others emphasize the temptations to manipulate risk and the associated dangers of loss of control (Schelling 1966), which can be exacerbated by organizational pathologies (Sagan 1995). On nuclear blackmail, see Betts (1987) and on the tradition of nonuse of nuclear weapons, see Tanenwald (2007) and Paul (2009). For a useful review of the debate, see Geller (forthcoming).

3. On different state choices about nuclear weapons in the contemporary era, see Solingen (2007).

4. Some might see the environment as a logical seventh coevolutionary factor, but as we stated earlier, we prefer to include it as a source of resource scarcities within the political-economy factor or, alternatively, a source of problems for the threat environment.

5. See Tammen et al. (2000), Chan (2007), Levy (2008b), and Thompson (2009).

6. The fighting between China and the Soviet Union in 1969 may have been an earlier example of this phenomenon.

References

Adams, Colin. 2007. "War and Society." In *The Cambridge History of Greek and Roman Warfare*. Vol. 2, *Rome from the Late Republic to the Late Empire*, edited by Philip Sabin, Hans van Wees, and Michael Whitby. Cambridge: Cambridge University Press.

Algaze, Guillermo. 1993. *The Uruk World System*. Chicago: University of Chicago Press.

Alstone, Richard. 2007. "Warfare and the State: The Military and Politics." In *The Cambridge History of Greek and Roman Warfare*. Vol. 2, *Rome from the Late Republic to the Late Empire*, edited by Philip Sabin, Hans van Wees, and Michael Whitby. Cambridge: Cambridge University Press.

Angel, Norman. 1912. *The Great Illusion: A Study of the Relation of Military Power to National Advantage*. London: William Heinemann.

Anglin, Simon, Phyllis G. Jestice, Rob S. Rice, Scott M. Rusch, and John Serreti. 2002. *Fighting Techniques of the Ancient World, 3000 BC–AD 500*. New York: Thomas Dunne.

Archer, Christian, John R. Ferris, Holger H. Herwig, and Timothy H. E. Travers. 2002. *World History of Warfare*. Lincoln: University of Nebraska Press.

Ardant, Gabriel. 1975. "Financial Policy and Economic Infrastructure of Modern States and Nations." In *The Formation of National States in Western Europe*, edited by Charles Tilly. Princeton, NJ: Princeton University Press.

Ardrey, Robert. 1966. *The Territorial Imperative*. New York: Atheneum.

Arkush, Elizabeth N., and Mark W. Allen, eds. 2006. *The Archaeology of Warfare: Prehistories of Raiding and Conquest*. Gainesville: University Press of Florida.

Aron, Raymond. 1985. *Clausewitz*. Translated by Christine Booker and Norman Stone. Englewood Cliffs, NJ: Prentice-Hall.

Arquilla, John, and David Ronfeldt. 1997. *In Athena's Camp: Preparing for Conflict in the Information Age*. Santa Monica, CA: Rand.

Arrenguin-Toft, Ivan. 2001. "How the Weak Win Wars: A Theory of Asymmetric Conflict." *International Security* 26 (Summer): 93–128.

Atzili, Boaz. 2006/7. "When Good Fences Make Bad Neighbors: Fixed Borders, State Weakness, and International Conflict." *International Security* 31 (Winter): 139–73.

Ayton, Andrew, and J. L. Price, eds. 1995. *The Medieval Military Revolution: State, Society, and Military Change in Medieval and Early Modern Europe*. London: I. B. Taurus.

Bachrach, Bernard S. 1972. *Merovingian Military Organization, 481–751*. Minneapolis: University of Minnesota Press.

———. 1973. *A History of the Alans in the West*. Minneapolis: University of Minnesota Press.

———. 1993a. "Charlemagne's Cavalry: Myth and Reality." In *Armies and Politics in the Early Medieval West*, edited by Bernard S. Bachrach. Brookfield, VT: Ashgate.

———. 1993b. "Charles Martel, Mounted Shock Combat, the Stirrup, and Feudalism." In *Armies and Politics in the Early Medieval West*, edited by Bernard S. Bachrach. Brookfield, VT: Ashgate.

Bailey, Jonathan B. A. 2001. "The First World War and the Birth of Modern Warfare." In *The Dynamics of Military Revolution, 1300–2050*, edited by MacGregor Knox and Williamson Murray, 132–53. Cambridge: Cambridge University Press.

Bajpai, Kanti, P. R. Chari, Pervaiz Iqbal Cheema, Stephen P. Cohen, and Sumit Ganguly, eds. 1995. *Brasstacks and Beyond: Perception and the Management of Crisis in South Asia*. New Delhi: Manohar Books.

Ballentine, Karen, and Jake Sherman, eds. 2003. *The Political Economy of Armed Conflict: Beyond Greed and Grievance*. Boulder, CO: Lynne Rienner.

Bamforth, Douglas B. 1994. "Indigenous People, Indigenous Violence: Pre-Contact Warfare on the North American Great Plains." *Man* 29: 95–115.

Barnett, Michael N. 1992. *Confronting the Costs of War: Military Power, State, and Society in Egypt and Israel*. Princeton, NJ: Princeton University Press.

Barnett, Michael N., and Jack S. Levy. 1991. "Domestic Sources of Alliances and Alignments: The Case of Egypt, 1962–1973." *International Organization* 45 (Summer): 369–95.

Bates, Robert H. 2001. *Prosperity and Violence: The Political Economy of Development*. New York: Norton.

Bean, R. 1973. "War and the Birth of the Nation State." *Journal of Economic History* 33: 203–21.

Bell, David A. 2007. *The First Total War: Napoleon's Europe and the Birth of Warfare as We Know It*. Boston: Houghton Mifflin.

Benjamin, Daniel, and Steven Simon. 2003. *The Age of Sacred Terror*. New York: Random House.

Bensahel, Nora. 2006. "Mission Not Accomplished: What Went Wrong with Iraqi Reconstruction." *Journal of Strategic Studies* 29 (June): 453–73.

Berghahn, Volker R. 1981. *Militarism: The History of an International Debate, 1861–1979*. Cambridge: Cambridge University Press.
Best, Geoffrey. 1982. *War and Society in Revolutionary Europe, 1770–1870*. Bungay, Suffolk, UK: Fontana.
Betts, Richard K. 1977. *Soldiers, Statesmen, and Cold War Crises*. Cambridge, MA: Harvard University Press.
———. 1987. *Nuclear Blackmail and Nuclear Balance*. Washington, DC: Brookings.
———. 2002. "The Soft Underbelly of American Primacy: Tactical Advantages of Terror." *Political Science Quarterly* 117 (1): 19–36.
———. 2008. "U.S. Counterterrorism Policy: An Inventory of Unresolved Hard Choices." Columbia University, unpublished paper.
Biddle, Stephen. 1998. "The Past as Prologue: Assessing Theories of Future Warfare." *Security Studies* 8 (1): 1–74.
———. 2004a. *Afghanistan and the Future of Warfare: Implications for Army and Defense Policy*. Honolulu: University Press of the Pacific.
———. 2004b. *Military Power: Explaining Victory and Defeat in Modern Battle*. Princeton, NJ: Princeton University Press.
Biolsi, Thomas. 1984. "Ecological and Cultural Factors in Plains Indian Warfare." In *Warfare, Culture and Environment*, edited by Brian R. Ferguson, 141–68. Orlando, FL: Academic Press.
Black, Jeremy. 1991. *A Military Revolution? Military Change and European Society, 1550–1800*. Atlantic Highlands, NJ: Humanities Press International.
———. 2004. *War and the New Disorder in the 21st Century*. New York: Continuum.
———. 2006. *The Age of Total War, 1860–1945*. Westport, CT: Praeger Security.
———. 2007. *Tools of War: The Weapons That Changed the World*. London: Quercus.
Blainey, Geoffrey. 1988. *The Causes of War*. 3rd ed. New York: Free Press.
Bloch, Marc. 1999. *Strange Defeat: A Statement of Evidence Written in 1940*. New York: W. W. Norton.
Bloom, Mia. 2005. *Dying to Kill: The Allure of Suicide Terror*. New York: Columbia University Press.
Boemeke, Manfred F., Roger Chickering, and Stig Förster, eds. 1999. *Anticipating Total War: The German and American Experiences, 1871–1914*. Washington, DC: German Historical Institute; Cambridge: Cambridge University Press.
Boggs, Marion William. 1941. "Attempts to Define and Limit Aggressive Armament in Diplomacy and Strategy." *University of Missouri Studies* 16 (1): 1–113.
Bond, Brian. 1986. *War and Society in Europe, 1870–1970*. New York: Oxford University Press.
Boot, Max. 2006. *War Made New: Technology, Warfare, and the Course of History, 1500 to Today*. New York: Penguin.

Boulding, Kenneth. 1978. *Stable Peace*. Austin: University of Texas Press.

Bousquet, Antoine. 2009. *The Scientific Way of Warfare: Order and Chaos on the Battlefields of Modernity*. London: Hurst.

Bowden, Hugh. 1993. "Hoplites and Homer: Warfare, Hero Cult, and the Ideology of the Polis." In *War and Society in the Greek World*, edited by John Rich and Graham Shipley, 45–63. London: Routledge.

Brodie, Bernard. 1941. *Sea Power in the Machine Age*. Princeton, NJ: Princeton University Press.

Brodie, Bernard, ed. 1946. *The Absolute Weapon: Atomic Power and World Order*. New York: Harcourt, Brace.

Brodie, Bernard, and Fawn M. Brodie. 1973. *From Crossbow to H-Bomb*. Bloomington: Indiana University Press.

Brown, Michael E., Owen R. Coté Jr., Sean M. Lynn-Jones, and Steven E. Miller, eds. 2003. *Offense, Defense, and War*. Cambridge, MA: MIT Press.

Brzoska, Michael. 2004. "'New Wars' Discourse in Germany." *Journal of Peace Research* 41 (January): 107–17.

Buckley, John. 1999. *Air Power in the Age of Total War*. Bloomington: Indiana University Press.

Budiansky, Stephen. 2004. *Air Power: The Men, Machines, and Ideas that Revolutionized War, from Kitty Hawk to Iraq*. New York: Penguin.

Builder, Carl H. 1989. *The Masks of War: American Military Styles in Strategy and Analysis*. Baltimore, MD: Johns Hopkins University Press.

Bundy, McGeorge. 1988. *Danger and Survival: Choices about the Bomb in the First Fifty Years*. New York: Random House.

Burns, Thomas S. 1973. "The Battle of Adrianople: A Reconsideration." *Historia* 22: 336–45.

Buzan, Barry. 1987. *An Introduction to Strategic Studies: Military Technology and International Relations*. Basingstoke, UK: Macmillan.

Bygott, J. D. 1972. "Cannibalism among Wild Chimpanzees." *Nature* 238: 410–11.

Campbell, Brian. 1999. "The Roman Empire." In *War and Society in the Ancient and Medieval Worlds: Asia, the Mediterranean, Europe, and Mesoamerica*, edited by Kurt Raaflaub and Nathan Rosenstein, 217–40. Cambridge, MA: Harvard University Press.

Carey, Brian T., Joshua B. Allfree, and John Cairns. 2005. *Warfare in the Ancient World*. South Yorkshire, UK: Pen and Sword.

Carneiro, Robert L. 1970. "A Theory of the Origin of the State." *Science* 169: 733–38.

———. 1990. "Chiefdom-Level Warfare as Exemplified in Fiji and the Cauca Valley." In *The Anthropology of War*, edited by Jonathan Haas, 190–211. Cambridge: Cambridge University Press.

Carpenter, C. R. 1974. "Aggressive Behavioral Systems." In *Primate Aggression, Territoriality, and Xenophobia*, edited by R. L. Holloway. New York: Academic Press.

Carr, Edward Hallett. 1940. *The Twenty Years' Crisis, 1919–1939: An Introduction to the Study of International Relations.* London: Macmillan.

Casson, Lionel. 1991. *The Ancient Mariners: Seafarers and Sea Fighters of the Mediterranean in Ancient Times.* 2nd ed. Princeton, NJ: Princeton University Press.

Centeno, Miguel A. 2002. *Blood and Debt: War and the Nation-State in Latin America.* University Park: Pennsylvania State University Press.

Chagnon, Napoleon. 1990. "Reproductive and Somatic Conflicts of Interest in the Genesis of Violence and Warfare among Tribesmen." In *The Anthropology of War*, edited by Jonathan Haas, 77–104. Cambridge: Cambridge University Press.

Chaliand, Gérard, and Arnaud Blin. 2007. *The History of Terrorism: From Antiquity to al Qaeda.* Berkeley: University of California Press.

Chan, Steve. 2007. *China, the US and the Power-Transition Theory: A Critique.* London: Routledge.

Chandler, David. 1966. *The Campaigns of Napoleon.* New York: Macmillan.

Chaniotis, Angelos. 2005. *War in the Hellenistic Worlds: A Social and Cultural History.* Oxford: Blackwell.

Chapman, John. 1999. "The Origins of Warfare in the Prehistory of Central and Eastern Europe." In *Ancient Warfare: Archaeological Perspectives*, edited by John Carman and Anthony Harding. Phoenix Mill, Gloucestershire, UK: Sutton Publishing.

Chase, Kenneth. 2003. *Firearms: A Global History to 1700.* Cambridge: Cambridge University Press.

Chase-Dunn, Christopher, and Thomas Hall. 1997. *Rise and Demise: Comparing World Systems.* Boulder, CO: Westview Press.

Chickering, Roger. 1999. "Total War: The Use and Abuse of a Concept." In *Anticipating Total War: The German and American Experiences, 1871–1914*, edited by Manfred R. Boemeke, Roger Chickering, and Stig Förster, 13–28. New York: Cambridge University Press.

Chickering, Roger, and Stig Förster, eds. 2000. *Great War, Total War: Combat and Mobilization on the Western Front, 1914–1918.* Washington, DC: German Historical Institute; Cambridge: Cambridge University Press.

Choucri, Nazli, ed. 1984. *Multidisciplinary Perspectives on Population and Conflict.* Syracuse, NY: Syracuse University Press.

Choucri, Nazli, and Robert North. 1975. *Nations in Conflict: National Growth and International Violence.* San Francisco: W. H. Freeman.

Cioffi-Revilla, Claudio. 2000. "Ancient Warfare: Origins and Systems." In *Handbook of War Studies II*, edited by Manus I. Midlarsky, 59–89. Ann Arbor: University of Michigan Press.

Cipolla, Carlo M. 1965. *Guns, Sails, and Empires: Technological Innovations and the Early Phases of European Expansion, 1400–1700.* New York: Minerva.

Claessen, Henri J. M., and Peter Skalnik. 1978. "The Early State: Theories and Hypotheses." In *The Early State*, edited by Henri J. M. Claessen and Peter Skalnik. The Hague: Mouton.

Clark, John F. 2002. *The African Stakes in the Congo War.* New York: Palgrave Macmillan.

Clausewitz, Carl von. [1832] 1976. *On War.* Edited and translated by Michael Howard and Peter Paret. Princeton, NJ: Princeton University Press.

Cohen, Arthur A. 1991. "The Sino-Soviet Border Crisis of 1969." In *Avoiding War: Problems of Crisis Management,* edited by Alexander L. George, 269–96. Boulder, CO: Westview Press.

Cohen, Eliot A. 1996. "A Revolution in Warfare." *Foreign Affairs* 75 (March/April): 37–54.

Cohen, Ronald. 1984. "Warfare and State Formation: Wars Make States and States Make War." In *Warfare, Culture, and Environment,* edited by Brian R. Ferguson, 329–58. Orlando, FL: Academic Press.

Collier, Paul, and Anke Hoeffler. 2004. "Greed and Grievance in Civil War." *Oxford Economic Papers* 56 (4): 563–95.

Cornell, T. J. 1995. *The Beginnings of Rome: Italy and Rome for the Bronze Age to the Punic Wars (c. 1000–264 BC).* London: Routledge.

Cotterell, Arthur. 2005. *Chariot: From Chariot to Tank, the Astounding Rise and Fall of the World's First War Machine.* Woodstock, NY: Overlook.

Crone, Patricia. 1980. *Slaves on Horses: The Evolution of the Islamic Polity.* Cambridge: Cambridge University Press.

Cronin, Audrey Kurth, and James M. Ludes, eds. 2004. *Attacking Terrorism: Elements of a Grand Strategy.* Washington, DC: Georgetown University Press.

Daase, Christopher. 1999. *Kleine Krieg—Große Wirkung: Wie Unkonventionelle Kriegführung die Internationale Politik Verändert.* Baden-Baden: Nomos Verlagsgesellscaft.

———. 2007. "Clausewitz and Small Wars." In *Clausewitz in the Twenty-First Century,* edited by Hew Strachan and Andreas Herberg-Rothe, 182–95. Oxford: Oxford University Press.

Daggett, Stephen. 2010. "Costs of Major U.S. Wars." Congressional Research Service, Report for Congress, RS22926, 6/29/2010.

Dannreuther, Roland. 2007. *International Security: The Contemporary Agenda.* Oxford: Polity.

Darnell, John, and Collen Manasa. 2007. *Tutankhamun's Armies: Battle and Conquest during Ancient Egypt's Late 18th Dynasty.* Hoboken, NJ: Wiley.

Darwin, Charles. [1871] 2004. *The Descent of Man, and Selection in Relation to Sex.* London: Penguin.

Davie, Maurice R. 1929. *The Evolution of War: A Study of Its Role in Early Societies.* New Haven, CT: Yale University Press.

Dawson, Doyne. 2001. *The First Armies.* London: Cassell.

Dehio, Ludwig. 1962. *The Precarious Balance: Four Centuries of the European Power Struggle.* New York: Random House/Vintage.

Delbruck, Hans. 1975. *History of the Art of War.* 4 vols. Translated by Walter J. Renfroe. Lincoln: University of Nebraska Press.

Denemark, Robert A., Jonathan Friedman, Barry K. Gills, and George Modelski, eds. 2000. *World System History: The Social Sciences of Long-Term Change.* London: Routledge.

Dennen, J. van der, and V. Falger, eds. 1990. *Sociobiology and Conflict.* London: Chapman.

Desch, Michael C. 1996. "War and Strong States, Peace and Weak States?" *International Organization* 50 (Spring): 237–68.

de Soysa, Indra. 2002. "Paradise Is a Bazaar? Greed, Creed, and Governance in Civil War, 1989–1999." *Journal of Peace Research* 39 (4): 395–416.

de Waal, Frans. 1989. *Peacemaking among Primates.* Cambridge, MA: Harvard University Press.

———. 1996. *Good Natured: The Origins of Right and Wrong in Humans and Other Animals.* Cambridge, MA: Harvard University Press.

de Waal, Frans, and Frans Lanting. 1997. *Bonobo: The Forgotten Ape.* Berkeley: University of California Press.

Diamond, Jared. 1992. *The Rise and Fall of the Third Chimpanzee: Evolution and Human Life.* London: Vintage.

———. 1997. *Guns, Germs, and Steel: The Fates of Human Societies.* New York: W. W. Norton.

Diamond, Larry. 2005. *Squandered Victory: The American Occupation and the Bungled Effort to Bring Democracy to Iraq.* New York: Times Books/Henry Holt.

Di Cosmo, Nicola. 2002. *Ancient China and Its Enemies: The Rise of Nomadic Power in East Asian History.* Cambridge: Cambridge University Press.

Diehl, Paul F., and Nils Petter Gleditsch, eds. 2000. *Environmental Conflict: An Anthology.* Boulder, CO: Westview Press.

Downes, Alexander B. 2008. *Targeting Civilians in War.* Ithaca, NY: Cornell University Press.

Downing, Brian M. 1992. *The Military Revolution and Political Change: Origins of Democracy and Autocracy in Early Modern Europe.* Princeton, NJ: Princeton University Press.

Doyle, Michael. 1983. "Kant, Liberal Legacies, and Foreign Affairs, Part II." *Philosophy & Public Affairs* 12 (Fall): 323–53.

———. 1997. *Ways of War and Peace.* New York: Norton.

Drews, Robert. 1993. *The End of the Bronze Age: Changes in Warfare and the Catastrophe ca. 1200 B.C.* Princeton, NJ: Princeton University Press.

Dreyer, Edward L. 2002. "Continuity and Change." In *A Military History of China*, edited by David A. Graff and Robin Higham. Boulder, CO: Westview Press.

Duffy, Christopher. 1985. *Siege Warfare.* Vol. 2, *The Fortress in the Age of Vauban and Frederick the Great, 1660–1789.* London: Routledge and Kegan Paul.

Dupuy, R. Ernest, and Trevor N. Dupuy. 1977. *The Encyclopedia of Military History.* New York: Harper and Row.

Dupuy, Trevor N. 1980. *The Evolution of Weapons and Warfare.* Indianapolis, IN: Bobbs-Merrill.

Duyvesteyn, Isabelle, and Jan Angstrom, eds. 2005. *Rethinking the Nature of War*. London: Frank Cass.

Earle, Timothy. 1997. *How Chiefs Come to Power: The Political Economy in Prehistory*. Stanford, CA: Stanford University Press.

Eckhardt, William. 1992. *Civilizations, Empires, and Wars: A Quantitative History of War*. Jefferson, NC: McFarland.

Eckstein, Arthur M. 2006. *Mediterranean Anarchy, Interstate War, and the Rise of Rome*. Berkeley: University of California Press.

Eldredge, Niles, and S. J. Gould. 1972. "Punctuated Equilibria: An Alternative to Phyletic Gradualism." In *Models in Paleobiology*, edited by T. J. M. Schopf, 82–115. San Francisco: Freeman Cooper.

Ellis, Peter B. 1998. *Celt and Roman*. New York: St. Martin's Press.

Elman, Colin. 2004. "Extending Offensive Realism: The Louisiana Purchase and America's Rise to Regional Hegemony." *American Political Science Review* 98 (4): 563–76.

Eltis, David E. 1995. *The Military Revolution in Sixteenth-Century Europe*. New York: Barnes and Noble.

Ember, Carol R. 1978. "Myths about Hunter-Gatherers." *Ethnology* 17: 639–48.

Ember, Carol R., and Melvin Ember. 1992. "Resource Unpredictability, Mistrust, and War." *Journal of Conflict Resolution* 36: 242–62.

Ember, Melvin. 1982. "Statistical Evidence for an Ecological Explanation of Warfare." *American Anthropologist* 84: 645–49.

Emsley, Clive. 1979. *British Society and the French Wars, 1793–1815*. London: Macmillan.

Evangelista, Matthew. 1988. *Innovation and the Arms Race: How the United States and the Soviet Union Develop New Military Technologies*. Ithaca, NY: Cornell University Press.

Falger, Vincent S. E. 2001. "Evolutionary World Politics Enriched: The Biological Foundations of International Relations." In *Evolutionary Interpretations of World Politics*, edited by William R. Thompson, 30–51. New York: Routledge.

Farris, William W. 1995. *Heavenly Warriors: The Evolution of Japan's Military, 500–1300*. Cambridge, MA: Harvard University Press.

Farrokh, Kareh. 2007. *Shadows in the Desert: Ancient Persia at War*. Oxford: Osprey.

Fazal, Tanisha M. 2007. *State Death: The Politics and Geography of Conquest, Occupation, and Annexation*. Princeton, NJ: Princeton University Press.

Fearon, James D. 1995. "Rationalist Explanations for War." *International Organization* 49 (Summer): 379–414.

———. 2007. "Iraq's Civil War." *Foreign Affairs* 86 (March/April): 2–15.

Fearon, James D., and David D. Laitin. 2001. "Mass Violence in the Long Half-Century: 1945–1999." Unpublished paper. Palo Alto, CA: Center for Advanced Study in the Behavioral Sciences.

Ferejohn, John A., and Frances McCall Rosenbluth. 2010. *War and State Building in Medieval Japan*. Stanford, CA: Stanford University Press.

Ferguson, R. Brian. 1984. "Introduction: Studying War." In *Warfare, Culture, and Environment*, edited by R. Brian Ferguson, 1–81. Orlando, FL: Academic Press.

———. 1990. "Explaining War." In *The Anthropology of War*, edited by Jonathan Haas, 26–55. Cambridge: Cambridge University Press.

———. 1999. "A Paradigm for the Study of War and Society." In *War and Society in the Ancient and Medieval Worlds: Asia, the Mediterranean, Europe, and Mesoamerica*, edited by Kurt Raaflaub and Nathan Rosenstein, 389–437. Washington, DC: Center for Hellenic Studies.

———. 2000. "The Causes and Origins of 'Primitive Warfare': On Evolved Motivations for War." *Anthropological Quarterly* 73: 159–64.

———. 2002. "The History of War: Fact vs. Fiction." In *Must We Fight?*, edited by William L. Ury. San Francisco, CA: Jossey-Bass.

———. 2006. "Archaeology, Cultural Anthropology, and the Origins and Intensification of War." In *The Archaeology of Warfare: Prehistories of Raiding and Conquest*, edited by Elizabeth N. Arkush and Mark W. Allen, 469–523. Gainesville: University Press of Florida.

Ferguson, R. Brian, and Neil C. Whitehead, eds. 1992. *War in the Tribal Zone: Expanding State and Indigenous Warfare*. Santa Fe, NM: School of American Research Press.

Ferrill, Arther. 1997. *The Origins of War: From the Stone Age to Alexander the Great*. 2nd ed. Boulder, CO: Westview Press.

Finer, Samuel E. 1975. "State and Nation Building in Europe: The Role of the Military." In *The Formation of National States in Western Europe*, edited by Charles Tilly, 84–163. Princeton, NJ: Princeton University Press.

Flannery, Kent V., and Joyce Marcus. 2003. "The Origin of War: New ^{14}C Dates from Ancient Mexico." *Proceedings of the National Academy of Science* USA 100 (20): 11801–5.

Förster, Stig, and Jörg Nagler, eds. 1997. *On the Road to Total War: The American Civil War and the German Wars of Unification, 1861–1871*. Washington, DC: German Historical Institute; Cambridge: Cambridge University Press.

France, John. 1999. *Western Warfare in the Age of the Crusades, 1000–1300*. Ithaca, NY: Cornell University Press.

Freeman, Christopher, and Francisco Louca. 2001. *As Time Goes By: From the Industrial Revolutions to the Information Revolution*. Oxford: Oxford University Press.

Freeman, Christopher, and Carlotta Perez. 1988. "Structural Crises of Adjustment: Business Cycles and Investment Behavior." In *Technical Change and Economic Theory*, edited by Giovanni Dosi, Christopher Freeman, Richard Nelson, Gerald Silverberg, and Luc Soete. London: Pinter.

Friday, Karl F. 2004. *Samurai, Warfare, and the State in Early Medieval Japan*. London: Routledge.

Friedman, George, and Meredith Freidman. 1996. *The Future of War: Power, Technology, and American World Dominance in the Twenty-First Century*. New York: St. Martin's Press.

Fuller, J. F. C. 1954–56. *A Military History of the Western World*. 3 vols. New York: Funk and Wagnalls.

———. 1961. *The Conduct of War, 1789–1961*. London: Eyre and Spottiswoode.

Gabriel, Richard A. 1990. *The Culture of War: Invention and Early Development*. New York: Greenwood Press.

———. 2002. *The Great Armies of Antiquity*. Westport, CT: Praeger.

Gabriel, Richard A., and Karen S. Metz. 1991. *From Sumer to Rome: The Military Capabilities of Ancient Armies*. New York: Greenwood.

Gabrielsen, Vincent. 2007. "Warfare and the State." In *The Cambridge History of Greek and Roman Warfare*. Vol. 1, *Greece, the Hellenistic World, and the Rise of Rome*, edited by Philip Sabin, Hans van Wees, and Michael Whitby. Cambridge: Cambridge University Press.

Gaddis, John Lewis. 1987. *The Long Peace*. New York: Oxford University Press.

Ganguly, Sumit. 2002. *Conflict Unending: India-Pakistan Tensions since 1947*. New Delhi: Oxford University Press.

Gartzke, Erik. 2007. "The Capitalist Peace." *American Journal of Political Science* 51 (January): 106–91.

Gat, Azar. 1999a. "The Pattern of Fighting in Simple, Small-scale, Prestate Societies." *Journal of Anthropological Research* 55: 563–83.

———. 1999b. "Social Organization, Group Conflict, and the Demise of the Neanderthals." *Mankind Quarterly* 39: 437–54.

———. 2000a. "The Human Motivational Complex: Evolutionary Theory and the Causes of Hunter-Gatherer Fighting. Part I: Primary Somatic and Reproductive Causes." *Anthropological Quarterly* 73: 20–34.

———. 2000b. "The Human Motivational Complex: Evolutionary Theory and the Causes of Hunter-Gatherer Fighting. Part II: Proximate, Subordinate and Derivative Causes." *Anthropological Quarterly* 73: 74–88.

———. 2000c. "The Causes and Origins of 'Primitive Warfare': Reply to Ferguson." *Anthropological Quarterly* 73: 165–68.

———. 2005. "The Democratic Peace Theory Reframed: The Impact of Modernity." *World Politics* 58 (October): 73–100.

———. 2006. *War in Human Civilization*. New York: Oxford University Press.

———. 2009. *Victorious and Vulnerable: Why Democracy Won in the 20th Century and How it Is Still Imperiled*. Lanham, MD: Rowman and Littlefield.

Geller, Daniel S. forthcoming. "Nuclear Weapons and War." In *What Do We Know about War II?*. 2nd ed., edited by John A. Vasquez. Lanham, MD: Rowman and Littlefield.

Gerges, Fawaz A. 2005. *The Far Enemy: Why Jihad Went Global*. Cambridge: Cambridge University Press.

Gibler, Douglas M. forthcoming. "The Implications of a Territorial Peace." In *What Do We Know about War II?*, edited by A. Vasquez. Lanham, MD: Rowman and Littlefield.

Gilbert, Felix, ed. 1975. *The Historical Essays of Otto Hintze*. New York: Oxford University Press.

Gilbert, Martin, ed. 1967. *Churchill*. Englewood Cliffs, NJ: Prentice-Hall, 1967.

Gilpin, Robert. 1981. *War and Change in World Politics*. New York: Cambridge University Press.

Gleditsch, Nils Petter. 2008. "The Liberal Moment Fifteen Years On." *International Studies Quarterly* 52 (December): 691–712.

Glete, Jan. 2000. *Warfare at Sea, 1500–1650: Maritime Conflicts and the Transformation of Europe*. London: Routledge.

Gnirs, Andrea M. 1999. "Ancient Egypt." In *War and Society in the Ancient and Medieval Worlds: Asia, the Mediterranean Europe, and Mesoamerica*, edited by Kurt Raaflaub and Nathan Rosenstein, 71–104. Washington, DC: Center for Hellenic Studies.

Goertz, Gary, and Jack S. Levy, eds. 2007. *Explaining War and Peace: Case Studies and Necessary Condition Counterfactuals*. New York: Routledge.

Goldstein, Joshua S. 1988. *Long Cycles*. New Haven, CT: Yale University Press.

———. 2003. *War and Gender: How Gender Shapes the War System and Vice Versa*. Cambridge: Cambridge University Press.

Goldstone, Jack S. 1993. *Revolution and Rebellion in the Early Modern World*. Berkeley: University of California Press.

Goldsworthy, Adrian. 2003. *The Complete Roman Army*. London: Thames and Hudson.

———. 2007. "War." In *The Cambridge History of Greek and Roman Warfare*. Vol. 2, *Rome from the Late Republic to the Late Empire*, edited by Philip Sabin, Hans van Wees, and Michael Whitby. Cambridge: Cambridge University Press.

Gommans, Jos. 2002. *Mughal Warfare*. London: Routledge.

Goodall, Jane. 1986. *The Chimpanzees of Gombe*. Cambridge, MA: Belknap Press.

Goodwin, Crauford D. W. 1991 "National Security in Classical Political Economy." In *Economics and National Security*, edited by Crauford D. W. Goodwin, 23–25. Durham, NC: Duke University Press.

Gordon, Michael R., and General Bernard E. Trainor. 2006. *Cobra II: The Inside Story of the Invasion and Occupation of Iraq*. New York: Pantheon Books.

Graff, David A. 2002a. *Medieval Chinese Warfare, 300–900*. London: Routledge.

———. 2002b. State Making and State Breaking." In *A Military History of China*, edited by David A. Graff and Robin Higham. Boulder, CO: Westview Press.

Graff, David A., and Robin Higham, eds. 2002. *A Military History of China*. Boulder, CO: Westview Press.

Gray, Colin S. 2002. *Strategy for Chaos: Revolutions in Military Affairs and the Evidence of History*. London: Frank Cass.

———. 2005. *Another Bloody Century: Future Warfare*. London: Weidenfeld and Nicholson.

Greenhalgh, P. A. L. 1973. *Early Greek Warfare: Horsemen and Chariots in the Homeric and Archaic Age*. Cambridge: Cambridge University Press.

Greenhill, Kelly M. 2010. *Weapons of Mass Migration: Forced Displacement, Coercion, and Foreign Policy*. Ithaca, NY: Cornell University Press.

Grousset, Rene. 1970. *The Empire of the Steppes: A History of Central Asia*. Translated by N. Walford. New Brunswick, NJ: Rutgers University Press.

Guerlac, Henry. 1986. "Vauban: The Impact of Science on War." In *Makers of Modern Strategy*, edited by Peter Paret, 64–90. Princeton, NJ: Princeton University Press.

Guilane, Jean, and Jean Zammit. 2005. *Origins of War: Violence in Prehistory*. Translated by Melanie Hersey. Malden, MA: Blackwell.

Guilmartin, John F. 1988. "Ideology and Conflict: The Wars of the Ottoman Empire, 1453–1606." *Journal of Interdisciplinary History* 18 (Spring): 721–47.

Guilmartin, John F. 1995. "The Military Revolution: Origins and First Tests Abroad." In *The Military Revolution Debate: Readings on the Military Transformation of of Early Modern Europe*, edited by C. J. Rogers, 299–333. Boulder, CO: Westview Press.

Gulick, Edward. 1955. *Europe's Classical Balance of Power*. New York: W. W. Norton.

Gunaratna, Rohan. 2002. *Inside Al Qaeda: Global Networks of Terror*. New York: Berkeley Books.

Gurr, Ted Robert. 2000. *People versus States: Minorities at Risk in the New Century*. Washington, DC: United States Institute of Peace.

Haas, Jonathan. 1990. "Warfare and the Evolution of Tribal Polities in the Prehistoric Southwest." In *The Anthropology of War*, edited by Jonathan Haas, 171–89. Cambridge: Cambridge University Press.

———. 1999. "The Origins of War and Ethnic Violence." In *Ancient Warfare: Archaeological Perspectives*, edited by John Carman and Anthony Harding. Gloucestershire, UK: Sutton Publishing.

———. 2001. "Cultural Evolution and Political Centralization." In *From Leaders to Rulers*, edited by Jonathan Haas. New York: Kluwer Academic.

Hall, Jonathan M. 2007. *A History of the Archaic Greek World, ca. 1200–479 BCE*. Oxford: Blackwell.

Hall, Thomas, and Christopher Chase-Dunn. 1997. *Rise and Demise: Comparing World Systems*. Boulder, CO: Westview Press.

Hamblin, William J. 2006. *Warfare in the Ancient Near East to 1600 BC: Holy Warriors at the Dawn of History*. London: Routledge.

Hammond, Allen. 1998. *Which World? Scenarios for the 21st Century*. Washington, DC: Island Press.

Hanson, Victor D. 1991. "Hoplite Technology in Phalanx Battle." In *Hoplites: The Classical Greek Battle Experience*, edited by Victor D. Hanson. London: Routledge.

———. 2001. *Carnage and Culture: Landmark Battles in the Rise of the West*. New York: Anchor Books.

Harari, Yuval Noah. 2008. *The Ultimate Experience: Battlefield Revelations and the Making of Modern War Culture, 1450–2000*. New York: Palgrave-Macmillan.

Harbom, Lotta, and Ralph Sundberg, eds. 2009. *States in Armed Conflict 2008*. Uppsala, Sweden: Uppsala University, Department of Peace and Conflict.

Harris, William V. 1985. *War and Imperialism in Republican Rome, 327–70 BC*. Oxford: Clarendon Press.

Hassig, Ross. 1988. *Aztec Warfare: Imperial Expansion and Political Control*. Norman: University of Oklahoma Press.

———. 1992. *War and Society in Ancient Mesoamerica*. Berkeley: University of California Press.

Hausfater, Glen, and Sarah B. Hrdy, eds. 1984. *Infanticide: Comparative and Evolutionary Perspectives*. New York: Aldine.

Herbst, Jeffrey. 2003. "States and War in Africa." In *The Nation State in Question*, edited by T. V. Paul, G. John Ikenberry, and John A. Hall. Princeton, NJ: Princeton University Press.

Herwig, Holger. 2001. "The Battlefleet Revolution, 1885–1914." In *The Dynamics of Military Revolution, 1300–2050*, edited by MacGregor Knox and Williamson Murray, 114–31. Cambridge: Cambridge University Press.

Hewitt, J. Joseph, Jonathan Wilkenfeld, and Ted R. Gurr. 2010. *Peace and Conflict 2010*. Boulder, CO: Paradigm.

Heydemann, Steven. 2000. "War, Institutions, and Social Change in the Middle East." In *War, Institutions, and Social Change in the Middle East*, edited by Steven Heydemann. Berkeley: University of California Press.

Hironaka, Ann. 2005. *Neverending Wars: The International Community, Weak States, and the Perpetuation of Civil War*. Cambridge, MA: Harvard University Press.

Hirst, Paul. 2001. *War and Peace in the 21st Century*. Cambridge: Polity.

Holsti, Kalevi J. 1996. *The State, War, and the State of War*. New York: Cambridge University Press.

Homer-Dixon, Thomas F. 1999. *Environment, Scarcity, and Violence*. Princeton, NJ: Princeton University Press.

Hopkins, Keith. 1977. *Conquerors and Slaves*. Cambridge: Cambridge University Press.

Horowitz, Michael C. 2009. "Long Time Going: Religion and the Duration of Crusading." *International Security* 34 (Fall): 162–93.

———. 2010. *The Diffusion of Military Power: Causes and Consequences for International Politics*. Princeton, NJ: Princeton University Press.

Howard, Michael. 1976. *War in European History*. Oxford: Oxford University Press.
———. 1983. *Clausewitz*. Oxford: Oxford University Press.
———. 2001. "Mistake to Declare This a 'War.'" *RUSI* 146 (December).
Hudson, Valerie M., and Andrea M. Den Boer. 2005. *Bare Branches: The Security Implications of Asia's Surplus Male Population*. Cambridge, MA: MIT Press.
Hui, Victoria Tin-bor. 2005. *War and State Formation in Ancient China and Early Modern Europe*. Cambridge: Cambridge University Press.
Human Security Centre. 2005. *Human Security Report 2005: War and Peace in the 21st Century*. New York: Oxford University Press.
Humphreys, N. Macartan. 2005. "Natural Resources, Conflict, and Conflict Resolution." *Journal of Conflict Resolution* 49 (4): 508–37.
Humphries, Mark. 2007. "International Relations." In *The Cambridge History of Greek and Roman Warfare*. Vol. 2, *Rome from the Late Republic to the Late Empire*, edited by Philip Sabin, Hans van Wees, and Michael Whitby. Cambridge: Cambridge University Press.
Huntingford, F., and A. Turner. 1987. *Animal Conflict*. London: Chapman and Hill.
Huntington, Samuel P. 1957. *The Soldier and the State: The Theory and Politics of Civil-Military Relations*. New York: Vintage.
———. 1996. *The Clash of Civilizations and the Remaking of World Order*. New York: Simon and Schuster.
Hurrell, Andrew. 1998. "An Emerging Security Community in South America?" In *Security Communities*, edited by Emanuel Adler and Michael Barnett, 228–64. Cambridge: Cambridge University Press.
Iklé, Fred C. 1971. *Every War Must End*. New York: Columbia University Press.
Iqbal, Zaryab. 2010. *War and the Health of Nations*. Stanford, CA: Stanford University Press.
Iriye, Akira. 1987. *The Origins of the Second World War in Asia and the Pacific*. New York: Longman.
Jervis, Robert. 1978. "Cooperation under the Security Dilemma." *World Politics* 30 (January): 167–213.
———. 1989. *The Meaning of the Nuclear Revolution*. Princeton, NJ: Princeton University Press.
———. 1997. *System Effects: Complexity in Political and Social Life*. Princeton, NJ: Princeton University Press.
Johnson, Roger N. 1972. *Aggression in Men and Animals*. Philadelphia: Saunders.
Johnston, Alastair Iain. 1995. "Thinking about Strategic Culture." *International Security* 19 (Spring): 32–64.
Joll, James. 1984. *The Origins of the First World War*. London: Longman.
Jones, Archer. 1987. *The Art of War in the Western World*. Urbana: University of Illinois Press.

Kaldor, Mary. 1999. *New and Old Wars: Organized Violence in a Global Era*. Cambridge: Polity Press.

Kalyvas, Stathis N. 2001. "'New' and 'Old' Civil Wars: A Valid Distinction?" *World Politics* 54 (October): 99–118.

———. 2005. "Warfare in Civil Wars." In *Rethinking the Nature of War*, edited by Isabelle Duyvesteyn and Jan Angstrom, 88–134. London: Frank Cass.

———. 2006. *The Logic of Violence in Civil War*. New York: Cambridge University Press.

Kalyvas, Stathis N., and Laia Balcells. 2010. "The International System and Technologies of Rebellion: How the Cold War Shaped Internal Conflict." *American Political Science Review* 104 (September): 415–29.

Kaplan, Robert D. 2000. *The Coming Anarchy*. New York: Random House.

Katzenstein, Peter J., ed. 1996. *The Culture of National Security: Norms and Identity in World Politics*. New York: Columbia University Press.

Kaysen, Carl. 1990. "Is War Obsolete?" *International Security* 14 (Spring): 42–64.

Keegan, John. 1993. *A History of Warfare*. New York: Vintage.

———. 2004. *The Iraq War*. New York: Knopf.

Keeley, Lawrence H. 1996. *War before Civilization: The Myth of the Peaceful Savage*. New York: Oxford University Press.

Kelly, Raymond C. 2000. *Warless Societies and the Origin of War*. Ann Arbor: University of Michigan Press.

Kennedy, Paul. 1987. *The Rise and Fall of the Great Powers: Economic Change and Military Conflict from 1500 to 2000*. New York: Random House.

Kepel, Gilles. 2002. *Jihad: The Trail of Political Islam*. Cambridge, MA: Harvard University Press.

———. 2004. *The War for Muslim Minds: Islam and the West*. Translated by Pascale Ghazaleh. Cambridge, MA: Harvard University Press.

Keppie, Lawrence. 1984. *The Making of the Roman Army: From Republic to Empire*. Totowa, NJ: Barnes and Noble.

Khan, Iqtidar A. 2004. *Gunpowder and Firearms: Warfare in Medieval India*. New Delhi: Oxford University Press.

Kier, Elizabeth. 1995. "Culture and Military Doctrine: France between the Wars." *International Security* 19 (Spring): 65–93.

Kirch, Patrick V. 1984. *The Evolution of Polynesian Chieftains*. Cambridge: Cambridge University Press.

Klare, Michael T. 2001. *Resource Wars: The New Landscape of Global Conflict*. New York: Metropolitan Books.

Knop, Katherina von, Henrich Neisser, and Martin van Creveld, eds. 2005. *Countering Modern Terrorism: History, Current Issues, and Future Threats*. Bielefeld, Germany: W. Bertelsmann Verlag.

Knorr, Klaus. 1966. *On the Uses of Military Power in the Nuclear Age*. Princeton, NJ: Princeton University Press.

Knox, MacGregor, and Williamson Murray, eds. 2001. *The Dynamics of Military Revolution, 1300–2050*. Cambridge: Cambridge University Press.

Korotayev, Andrey, Artemy Malkov, and Daria Khaltourina. 2006. *Introduction to Social Macrodynamics: Secular Cycles and Millennial Trends*. Moscow: URSS.

Krebs, Ronald R., and Jack S. Levy. 2001. "Demographic Change and the Sources of International Conflict." In *Demography and National Security*, edited by Myron Weiner and Sharon Stanton Russell, 62–105. New York: Berghahn Books, 2001.

Krepinevich, Andrew F. 1994. "From Cavalry to Computer: The Pattern of Military Revolutions." *National Interest* (Fall): 30–42.

Kupchan, Charles. A. 1994. *The Vulnerability of Empire*. Ithaca, NY: Cornell University Press.

Kyle, Keith. 1991. *Suez*. New York: St. Martin's Press.

Le Billon, Phillippe. 2001. "The Political Ecology of War: Natural Resources and Armed Conflicts." *Political Geography* 20: 561–84.

LeBlanc, Steven A. 1999. *Prehistoric Warfare in the American Southwest*. Salt Lake City: University of Utah Press.

LeBlanc, Steven A., with Katherine E. Register. 2003. *Constant Battles: The Myth of the Peaceful, Noble Savage*. New York: St. Martin's Press.

Lee, A. D. 2007a. "Warfare and the State." In *The Cambridge History of Greek and Roman Warfare*. Vol. 2, *Rome from the Late Republic to the Late Empire*, edited by Philip Sabin, Hans van Wees, and Michael Whitby. Cambridge: Cambridge University Press.

———. 2007b. *War in Late Antiquity: A Social History*. Malden, MA: Blackwell.

Leebaert, Derek. 2002. *The Fifty-Year Wound: The True Price of America's Cold War Victory*. Boston: Little, Brown.

Lekson, Stephen H. 2002. "War in the Southwest, War in the World." *American Antiquity* 67 (3): 607–24.

Lenin, V. I. [1916] 1939. *Imperialism: The Highest Stage of Capitalism*. New York: International Publishers.

Lenski, Gerhard. 2005. *Ecological-Evolutionary Theory: Principles and Applications*. Boulder, CO: Paradigm Publishers.

Levathes, Louise. 1994. *When China Ruled the Seas: The Treasure Fleet of the Dragon Throne, 1405–1433*. New York: Simon and Schuster.

Levy, Jack S. 1983. *War in the Modern Great Power System, 1495–1975*. Lexington: University Press of Kentucky.

———. 1984. "The Offensive/Defensive Balance of Military Technology: A Theoretical and Historical Analysis." *International Studies Quarterly* 28 (June): 219–38.

———. 1989. "The Diversionary Theory of War: A Critique." In *Handbook of War Studies*, edited by Manus I. Midlarsky, 259–88. London: Unwin-Hyman.

———. 1994. "Learning and Foreign Policy: Sweeping a Conceptual Minefield." *International Organization* 48 (Spring): 279–312.

———. 1999. "The Rise and Decline of the Anglo-Dutch Rivalry, 1609–1689." In *Great Power Rivalries*, edited by William R. Thompson, 172–200. Columbia: University of South Carolina Press.

———. 2008a. "Counterfactuals and Case Studies." In *Oxford Handbook of Political Methodology*, edited by Janet Box-Steffensmeier, Henry Brady, and David Collier, 627–44. New York: Oxford University Press.

———. 2008b. "Power Transition Theory and the Rise of China." In *China's Ascent: Power, Security, and the Future of International Politics*, edited by Robert S. Ross and Zhu Feng, 11–33. Ithaca, NY: Cornell University Press.

———. 2008c. "Preventive War and Democratic Politics." *International Studies Quarterly* 52 (March): 1–24.

Levy, Jack S., and William R. Thompson. 2005. "Hegemonic Threats and Great Power Balancing in Europe, 1495–2000." *Security Studies* 14 (January–March): 1–30.

———. 2010a. "Balancing on Land and at Sea: Do States Ally against the Leading Global Power?" *International Security* 35 (Summer): 7–43.

———. 2010b. *The Causes of War*. Oxford: Wiley-Blackwell.

Levy, Jack S., Thomas C. Walker, and Martin S. Edwards. 2001. "Continuity and Change in the Evolution of War." In *War in a Changing World*, edited by Zeev Maoz and Azar Gat, 15–48. Ann Arbor: University of Michigan Press.

Lewis, Herbert S. 1981. "Warfare and the Origin of the State: Another Formulation." In *The State of the State*, edited by Henri J. M. Claessen and Peter Skalnik. The Hague: Mouton.

Lewis, Mark E. 1990. *Sanctioned Violence in Early China*. Albany: State University of New York Press.

———. 2007. *The Early Chinese Empires: Qin and Han*. Cambridge, MA: Harvard University Press.

Liberman, Peter. 1996. *Does Conquest Pay? The Exploitation of Occupied Industrial Societies*. Princeton, NJ: Princeton University Press.

Li Liu. 2004. *The Chinese Neolithic: Trajectories to Early States*. Cambridge: Cambridge University Press.

Li Liu, and Xingcan Chen. 2003. *State Formation in Early China*. London: Duckworth.

Lorenz, Konrad. 1966. *On Aggression*. New York: Harcourt, Brace.

Lorge, Peter A. 2008. *The Asian Military Revolution: From Gunpowder to the Bomb*. Cambridge: Cambridge University Press.

Lowi, Miriam R. 1993. *Water and Power: The Politics of a Scarce Resource in the Jordan River Basin*. New York: Cambridge University Press.

Luard, Evan. 1986. *War in International Society*. London: I. B. Tauris.

Luft, Gal. 2002. "The Palestinian H-Bomb: Terror's Winning Strategy." *Foreign Affairs* 81 (4): 2–7.

Lynn, John A. 1995. "The *Trace Italienne* and the Growth of Armies: The French Case." In *The Military Revolution Debate*, edited by Clifford J. Rogers 169–99. Boulder, CO: Westview Press.

———. 1996. "The Evolution of Army Style in the Modern West, 800–2000." *International History Review* 18 (August): 505–45.

———. 1997. *Giant of the Grand Siècle: The French Army, 1610–1715*. Cambridge: Cambridge University Press.

———. 2003. *Battle: A History of Combat and Culture*. Boulder, CO: Westview Press.

Magdoff, Harry. 1969. The *Age of Imperialism: The Economics of U.S. Foreign Policy*. New York: Monthly Review Press.

Mack, Andrew. 1975. "Why Big Nations Lose Small Wars: The Politics of Asymmetric Conflict." *World Politics* 27 (January): 175–200.

Mahnken, Thomas G. 2008. *Technology and the American Way of War Since 1945*. New York: Columbia University Press.

Malinowski, Bronislaw. 1941. "An Anthropological Analysis of War." *American Journal of Sociology* 46 (January): 521–50.

Malthus, Thomas Robert. [1798] 1992. *An Essay on the Principle of Population*. New York: Cambridge University Press.

Mann, James. 2004. *Rise of the Vulcans: The History of Bush's War Cabinet*. New York: Viking.

Mansfield, Edward D., and Brian M. Pollins, eds. 2003. *Economic Interdependence and International Conflict: New Perspectives on an Enduring Debate*. Ann Arbor: University of Michigan Press.

Marcus, Joyce. 1998. "The Peaks and Valleys of Ancient States: An Extension of the Dynamic Model." In *Archaic States*, edited by Gary M. Feinman and Joyce Marcus. Santa Fe, NM: School of American Research Press.

Mares, David. 2001. *Violent Peace*. New York: Columbia University Press.

Marshall, Monty G. 1999. *Third World War*. Lanham, MD: Rowman and Littlefield.

Marten, Kimberly J. 2010. "Failing States and Conflict." In *The International Studies Encyclopedia*, edited by Robert A. Denemark. Hoboken, NJ: Wiley-Blackwell.

———. 2011. "Warlords." In *The Changing Character of War*, edited by Hew Strachan and Sybille Scheipers, 302–14. New York: Oxford University Press.

Martin, Lisa L. 1997. "Legislative Influence and International Engagement." In *Liberalization and Foreign Policy*, edited by Miles Kahler, 67–104. New York: Columbia University Press.

Marwick, Arthur. 1965. *The Deluge: British Society and the First World War*. New York: W. W. Norton.

———. 1974. *War and Social Change in the Twentieth Century: A Comparative Study of Britain, France, Germany, Russia, and the United States*. New York: St. Martin's Press.

Mattingly, D. J. 1992. "War and Peace in Roman North Africa: Observations and Models of State-Tribe Interaction." In *War in the Tribal Zone: Expanding States and Indigenous Warfare*, edited by R. Brian Ferguson and Neil L. Whitehead, 31–60. Santa Fe, NM: School of American Research Press.

May, Ernest. 1961. *Imperial Democracy*. New York: Harper and Row.

May, Timothy. 2007. *The Mongol Art of War: Chinggis Khan and the Mongol Military System*. Yardley, PA: Westholme.

McCauley, Clark. 1990. "Conference Overview." In *The Anthropology of War*, edited by Jonathan Haas, 1–25. Cambridge: Cambridge University Press.

McDermott, Bridget. 2004. *Warfare in Ancient Egypt*. Thrupp, UK: Sutton.

McDonald, Patrick J. 2009. *The Invisible Hand of Peace: Capitalism, the War Machine, and International Relations Theory*. Cambridge: Cambridge University Press.

McIntosh, Jane. 2006. *Handbook to Life in Prehistoric Europe*. New York: Facts on File Press.

McNeill, William H. 1963. *The Rise of the West*. Chicago: University of Chicago Press.

———. 1977. *Plagues and Peoples*. New York: Doubleday.

———. 1982. *The Pursuit of Power*. Chicago: University of Chicago Press.

Mead, Margaret. 1940. "Warfare Is Only an Invention, Not a Biological Necessity." *Asia* 40: 402–5.

Mearsheimer, John J. 1988. *Liddell Hart and the Weight of History*. Ithaca, NY: Cornell University Press.

———. 2001. *The Tragedy of Great Power Politics*. New York: Norton.

Mellaart, James. 1975. *The Neolithic of the Near East*. New York: Charles Scribner's.

Merom, Gil. 2003. *How Democracies Lose Small Wars*. New York: Cambridge University Press.

Migdal, Joel S. 1988. *Strong Societies and Weak States: State-Society Relations and State Capabilities in the Third World*. Princeton, NJ: Princeton University Press.

Miller, Benjamin. 2007. *States, Nations, and the Great Powers: The Sources of Regional War and Peace*. New York: Cambridge University Press.

Miller, John H., and Scott E. Page. 2007. *Complex Adaptive Systems: An Introduction to Computational Models of Social Life*. Princeton, NJ: Princeton University Press.

Millis, Walter. 1956. *Arms and Men*. New York: Mentor.

Milner, George R., Eve Anderson, and Virginia C. Smith. 1991. "Warfare in Late Prehistoric West-Central Illinois." *American Antiquity* 56 (4): 581–603.

Milward, Alan S. 1979. *War, Economy, and Society, 1939–1945*. Berkeley: University of California Press.

Mitani, John C., David P. Watts, and Sylvia J. Amsler. 2010. "Lethal Intergroup Aggression Leads to Territorial Expansion in Wild Chimpanzees." *Current Biology* 20 (12): R507–R508.

Monks, Sarah. 2000. "The Aegean." In *Bronze Age Warfare*, edited by Richard Osgood and Sarah Monks with Judith Toms. Thrupp, UK: Sutton.

Morgan, T. Clifton, and Jack S. Levy. 1990. "Base Stealers versus Power Hitters: A Nation-State Level Analysis of the Frequency and Seriousness of War." In *Prisoners of War?*, edited by Charles S. Gochman and Alan Ned Sabrosky, 43–56. Lexington, MA: Lexington Books.

Morillo, Stephen, Jeremy Black, and Paul Lococo. 2009. *War in World History: Society, Technology and War from Ancient Times to the Present*. 2 vols. Boston: McGraw Hill.

Mousseau, Michael. 2000. "Market Prosperity, Democratic Consolidation, and Democratic Peace." *Journal of Peace Research* 44 (August): 472–507.

———. 2003. "The Nexus of Market Society, Liberal Preferences, and Democratic Peace: Interdisciplinary Theory and Evidence." *International Studies Quarterly* 47: 453–70.

Mousseau, Michael, Havard Hegre, and John R. Oneal. 2003. "How the Wealth of Nations Conditions the Liberal Peace." *European Journal of International Relations* 9 (2): 277–316.

Mueller, John. 1989. *Retreat from Doomsday: The Obsolescence of Major War*. New York: Basic Books.

———. 1995. *Quiet Cataclysm: Reflections on the Recent Transformation of World Politics*. New York: HarperCollins.

———. 2004. *The Remnants of War*. Ithaca, NY: Cornell University Press.

———. 2009. *Atomic Obsession: Nuclear Alarmism from Hiroshima to Al-Qaeda*. New York: Oxford University Press.

———. 2010. "Capitalism, Peace, and the Historical Movement of Ideas." *International Interactions* 36 (2): 169–84.

Münkler, Herfried. 2005. *The New Wars*. Translated by Patrick Camiller. Cambridge: Polity.

Murray, Williamson. 1997. "Thinking about Revolutions in Military Affairs." *Joint Force Quarterly* 16 (Summer): 69–76.

———. 2001. "May 1940: Contingency and Frailty of the German RMA." In *The Dynamics of Military Revolution, 1300–2050*, edited by MacGregor Knox and Williamson Murray, 154–74. Cambridge: Cambridge University Press.

Murray, Williamson, and MacGregor Knox. 2001. "Thinking about Revolutions in Warfare." In *The Dynamics of Military Revolution, 1300–2050*, edited by MacGregor Knox and Williamson Murray, 1–14. Cambridge: Cambridge University Press.

Murray, Williamson, and Robert H. Scales Jr. 2003. *The Iraq War: A Military History*. Cambridge, MA: Harvard University Press.

Nef, John V. 1950. *War and Human Progress*. New York: W. W. Norton.

Neiberg, Michael S. 2001. *Warfare in World History*. London: Routledge.

Newcombe, W. W. 1960. "Toward an Understanding of War." In *Essays in the Science of Culture in Honor of Leslie A. White*, edited by G. Dole and Robert Carneiro. New York: Thomas Crowell.

Nexon, Daniel H. 2009. *The Struggle for Power in Early Modern Europe: Religious Conflict, Dynastic Empires, and International Change.* Princeton: Princeton University Press.

Nicholson, Michael. 1996. *Causes and Consequences in International Relations Theory.* London: Pinter.

Nicolle, David. 1995. *Medieval Warfare Source Book.* Vol. 1, *Warfare in Western Christendom.* London: Arms and Armour Press.

———. 1996. *Medieval Warfare Source Book.* Vol. 2, *Christian Europe and Its Neighbours.* London: Arms and Armour Press.

North, Douglass C. 1981. *Structure and Change in Economic History.* New York: W. W. Norton.

North, Douglass C., John Joseph Wallis, and Barry R. Weingast. 2009. *Violence and Social Orders: A Conceptual Framework for Interpreting Recorded Human History.* New York: Cambridge University Press.

Nye, Joseph S., Jr., and William A. Owens. 1996. "America's Information Edge." *Foreign Affairs* 75 (March/April): 20–36.

O'Connell, Robert L. 1995. *Ride of the Second Horseman: The Birth and Death of War.* New York: Oxford University Press.

O'Hanlon, Michael. 2000. *Technological Change and the Future of War.* Washington, DC: Brookings.

Oman, Charles. [1898] 1991. *History of the Art of War in the Middle Ages.* Vol. 1, *A.D. 378–1278.* London: Greenhill Press; Novato, CA: Presidio Press.

Organski, A. F. K., and Jacek Kugler. 1980. *The War Ledger.* Chicago: University of Chicago Press.

Osgood, Robert E. 1967. "The Expansion of Force." In *Force, Order, and Justice,* by Robert E. Osgood and Robert W. Tucker, 41–120. Baltimore, MD: Johns Hopkins University Press.

Otterbein, Keith. 1970. *The Evolution of War: A Cross-Cultural Study.* New Haven, CT: HRAF Press.

———. 2004. *How War Began.* College Station: Texas A&M University Press.

Owens, William A., with Ed Offley. 2000. *Lifting the Fog of War.* New York: Farrar, Straus, Giroux.

Palmer, M. A. J. 1997. "The Military Revolution Afloat: The Era of the Anglo-Dutch Wars and the Transition to Modern Warfare at Sea." *War in History* 4: 123–49.

Papayoanou, Paul A. 1999. *Power Ties: Economic Interdependence, Balancing, and War.* Ann Arbor: University of Michigan Press.

Pape, Robert A. 1996. *Bombing to Win: Air Power and Coercion in War.* Ithaca, NY: Cornell University Press.

———. 2003. "The Strategic Logic of Suicide Terrorism." *American Political Science Review* 97: 343–61.

———. 2005. *Dying to Win: The Strategic Logic of Suicide Terrorism.* New York: Random House.

Paret, Peter. 1976. *Clausewitz and the State*. New York: Oxford University Press.
———. 1983. "Revolutions in Warfare: An Earlier Generation of Interpreters." In *National Security and International Security*, edited by Bernard Brodie, Michael D. Intriligator, and Roman Kolkowicz. Cambridge, MA: Oelgschlager, Gunn and Hain.
———. 1986. "Napoleon and the Revolution in War." In *Makers of Modern Strategy: From Machiavelli to the Nuclear Era*, edited by Peter Paret, 123–42. Princeton, NJ: Princeton University Press.
Parker, Geoffrey. 1988. *The Military Revolution: Military Innovation and the Rise of the West, 1500–1800*. New York: Cambridge University Press.
Paul, T. V. 1994. *Asymmetric Conflicts: War Initiation by Weaker Powers*. New York: Cambridge University Press.
———. 2009. *The Tradition of Non-Use of Nuclear Weapons*. Stanford, CA: Stanford University Press.
Payne, James L. 2004. *A History of Force: Exploring the Worldwide Movement against Habits of Coercion, Bloodshed, and Mayhem*. Sandpoint, ID: Lytton.
Peers, C. J. 2006. *Soldiers of the Dragon: Chinese Armies, 1500 BC–AD 1840*. Oxford: Osprey.
Perrin, Noel. 1980. *Giving Up the Gun: Japan's Reversion to the Sword, 1543–1849*. Boulder, CO: Shambhala.
Pettersson, Therése, and Lotta Themnér, eds. 2010. *States in Armed Conflict 2009*. Uppsala University, Department of Peace and Conflict Research, Research Report 92.
Pinker, Steven. 2011. *The Better Angels of Our Nature: The Decline of Violence and Its Psychological Roots*. New York: Viking.
Pipes, Daniel. 1981. *Slave Soldiers and Islam: The Genesis of a Military System*. New Haven, CT: Yale University Press.
Polybius. 1967. *The Histories*. Cambridge, MA: Harvard University Press.
Porter, Bruce D. 1994. *War and the Rise of the State: The Military Foundations of Modern Politics*. New York: Free Press.
Posen, Barry R. 1984. *The Sources of Military Doctrine*. Ithaca, NY: Cornell University Press.
———. 1993. "Nationalism, the Mass Army, and Military Power." *International Security* 18 (Fall): 80–124.
Powell, Robert. 1999. *In the Shadow of Power: States and Strategies in International Politics*. Princeton, NJ: Princeton University Press.
Preston, Richard A., and Sydney F. Wise. 1979. *Men in Arms*. 4th ed. New York: Holt, Rinehart, and Winston.
Prestowich, Michael. 1996. *Armies and Warfare in the Middle Ages: The English Experience*. New Haven, CT: Yale University Press.
Prunier, Gérard. 2009. *Africa's World War: Congo, the Rwandan Genocide, and the Making of a Continental Catastrophe*. New York: Oxford University Press.

Raaflaub, Kurt, and Nathan Rosenstein, eds. 1999. *War and Society in the Ancient and Medieval Worlds.* Washington, DC: Center for Hellenic Studies.

Rankov, Boris. 2007. "Military Forces." In *The Cambridge History of Greek and Roman Warfare.* Vol. 2, *Rome from the Late Republic to the Late Empire*, edited by Philip Sabin, Hans van Wees, and Michael Whitby. Cambridge: Cambridge University Press.

Rapkin, David P., and William R. Thompson. 2006. "Economic Interdependence and the Emergence of China and India in the 21st Century." In *Strategic Asia 2006–07: Trade, Interdependence and Security*, edited by Ashley Tellis and Michael Wills, 333–64. Seattle, WA: National Bureau of Asian Research.

Rapoport, David C. 2004. "The Four Waves of Modern Terrorism." In *Attacking Terrorism: Elements of a Grand Strategy*, edited by Audrey K. Cronin and James M. Ludes. Washington, DC: Georgetown University Press.

Rasler, Karen A., and William R. Thompson. 1983. "Global Wars, Public Debts and the Long Cycle." *World Politics* 35 (July): 489–516.

———. 1989. *War and State Making.* Boston: Unwin Hyman.

———. 2005. *Puzzles of the Democratic Peace: Theory, Geopolitics, and the Transformation of World Politics.* New York: Palgrave-Macmillan.

———. 2009. "Looking for Waves of Terrorism." *Journal of Terrorism and Political Violence* 21: 28–41.

Rathbone, Dominic. 2007. "Warfare and the State: Military Finance and Supply." In *The Cambridge History of Greek and Roman Warfare.* Vol. 2, *Rome from the Late Republic to the Late Empire*, edited by Philip Sabin, Hans van Wees, and Michael Whitby. Cambridge: Cambridge University Press.

Ray, James Lee. 1995. *Democracy and International Conflict.* Columbia: University of South Carolina Press.

Reiter, Dan. 2009. *How Wars End.* Princeton, NJ: Princeton University Press.

Restall, Matthew. 2003. *Seven Myths of the Spanish Conquest.* Oxford: Oxford University Press.

Reuter, Timothy. 1999. "Carolingian and Ottonian Warfare." In *Medieval Warfare: A History*, edited by Maurice Keen. Oxford: Oxford University Press.

Rich, John, and Graham Shipley. 1993a. *War and Society in the Greek World.* New York: Routledge.

———. 1993b. *War and Society in the Roman World.* New York: Routledge.

Ritter, Gerhard. 1970. *The Sword and the Scepter*, 4 vols. Translated by Heins Norden. Coral Gables, FL: University of Miami Press.

Roberts, Michael. [1955] 1995. "The Military Revolution, 1560–1660." In *The Military Revolution Debate: Readings on the Military Transformation of Early Modern Europe*, edited by Clifford J. Rogers, 13–35. Boulder, CO: Westview Press.

Robertson, Esmonde D. 1971. *The Origins of the Second World War.* London: Macmillan.

Robinson, Ronald, and John Gallagher. 1950. "The Imperialism of Free Trade." *Economic History Review*, second series, 6: 1–15.

Rogers, Clifford J. 1993. "The Military Revolutions of the Hundred Years' War." *Journal of Military History* 57: 241–78.

Rogers, Clifford J., ed. 1995. *The Military Revolution Debate: Readings on the Military Transformation of Early Modern Europe*. Boulder, CO: Westview Press.

Ronnefeldt, Carsten F. 1997. "Three Generations of Environment and Security Research." *Journal of Peace Research* 34 (4): 473–82.

Ropp, Theodore. 1959. *War in the Modern World*. Durham, NC: Duke University Press.

Rose, Susan. 2002. *Medieval Naval Warfare, 1000–1500*. London: Routledge.

Rosecrance, Richard. 1986. *The Rise of the Trading State: Commerce and Conquest in the Modern World*. New York: Basic Books.

Rosen, Stephen P. 1991. *Winning the Next War: Innovation and the Modern Military*. Ithaca, NY: Cornell University Press.

———. 1995. "Military Effectiveness: Why Society Matters." *International Security* 19 (Spring): 5–31.

———. 2005. *War and Human Nature*. Princeton, NJ: Princeton University Press.

Rosenstein, Nathan. 1999. "Republican Rome." In *War and Society in the Ancient and Medieval Worlds: Asia, the Mediterranean, Europe, and Mesoamerica*, edited by Kurt Raaflaub and Nathan Rosenstein, 193–216. Washington, DC: Center for Hellenic Studies.

———. 2009. "War, State Formation, and the Evolution of Military Institutions in Ancient China and Rome." In *Rome and China: Comparative Perspectives on Ancient World Empires*, edited by Walter Scheidel. Oxford: Oxford University Press.

Ross, Michael L. 2003. "Natural Resources and Civil Conflict: Evidence from Case Studies." *International Organization* 58 (Winter): 35–67.

Ross, Steven T. 1996. *From Flintlock to Rifle-Infantry Tactics, 1740–1866*. London: Frank Cass.

Rothenberg, Gunther E. 1986. "Maurice of Nassau, Gustavus Adolphus, Raimondo Montecucolli, and the 'Military Revolution' of the Seventeenth Century." In *Makers of Modern Strategy: From Machiavelli to the Nuclear Age*, edited by Peter Paret, 11–31. Princeton, NJ: Princeton University Press.

Russett, Bruce. 2010. "Capitalism or Democracy? Not So Fast." *International Interactions* 36 (2): 198–205.

———. 2011. *Hegemony and Democracy*. London: Routledge.

Russett, Bruce, and John R. Oneal. 2001. *Triangulating Peace: Democracy, Interdependence, and International Organization*. New York: W. W. Norton.

Sagan, Scott D. 1995. *The Limits of Safety: Organizations, Accidents, and Nuclear Weapons*. Princeton, NJ: Princeton University Press.

Sagan, Scott D., and Kenneth N. Waltz. 2002. *The Spread of Nuclear Weapons: A Debate Renewed*. New York: W. W. Norton.

Sage, Michael M. 1996. *Warfare in Ancient Greece*. London: Routledge.
Santosusso, A. 2004. *Barbarians, Marauders, and Infidels: The Ways of Medieval Warfare*. Boulder, CO: Westview Press.
Sarkees, Meredith Reid. 2000. "The Correlates of War Data on War: An Update to 1997." *Conflict Management and Peace Science* 18 (1): 123–44.
Sarkees, Meredith Reid, and Frank Whelon Wayman. 2010. *Resort to War, 1816–2007*. Washington, DC: Congressional Quarterly Press.
Sarkees, Meredith Reid, Frank Weylon Wayman, and J. David Singer. 2003. "Inter-State, Intra-State, and Extra-State Wars: A Comprehensive Look at their Distribution over Time, 1816–1997." *International Studies Quarterly* 47 (March): 49–70.
Sawyer, Ralph D. 2004. *Fire and Water: The Art of Incendiary and Aquatic Warfare in China*. Boulder, CO: Westview Press.
Schanzer, Jonathan. 2004. *Al Qaeda's Armies*. New York: Specialist Press International.
Scheina, Robert L. 2003. *Latin America's Wars*. 2 vols. Washington, DC: Brassey's.
Schelling, Thomas C. 1966. *Arms and Influence*. New Haven, CT: Yale University Press.
Schneider, Gerald, Katherine Barbieri, and Nils Petter Gleditsch, eds. 2003. *Globalization and Armed Conflict*. Lanham, MD: Rowman and Littlefield.
Schneider, Gerald, and Nils Petter Gleditsch. 2010. "The Capitalist Peace: The Origins and Prospects of a Liberal Idea." *International Interactions* 36 (2): 107–14.
Schultz, Kenneth A., and Barry R. Weingast. 2003. "The Democratic Advantage: Institutional Foundations of Financial Power in International Competition." *International Organization* 57 (Winter): 3–42.
Schwartz, Stephen I. 1998. "Introduction." In Atomic Audit: The Costs and Consequences of U.S. Nuclear Weapons since 1940, edited by Stephen I. Schwartz, 1–32. Washington, DC; Brookings Institution.
Sekunde, Nicholas, and Philip de Souza. 2007. "Military Forces." In *The Cambridge History of Greek and Roman Warfare*. Vol. 1, *Greece, the Hellenistic World, and the Rise of Rome*, edited by Philip Sabin, Hans van Wees, and Michael Whitby. Cambridge: Cambridge University Press.
Serrati, John. 2007. "Warfare and the State." In *The Cambridge History of Greek and Roman Warfare*. Vol. 1, *Greece, the Hellenistic World, and the Rise of Rome*, edited by Philip Sabin, Hans van Wees, and Michael Whitby. Cambridge: Cambridge University Press.
Shankman, Paul. 1991. "Culture Context, Cultural Ecology, and Dani Warfare." *Man* 26: 299–321.
Shapiro, Jeremy. 1999. "Information and War: Is It a Revolution?" In *Strategic Appraisal: The Changing Role of Information in Warfare*, edited by Zalmay M. Khalilzad and John P. White, 113–53. Santa Monica, CA: Rand.

Shaughnessy, Edward L. 1999. "Western Zhou History." In *The Cambridge History of Ancient China: From the Origins of Civilization to 221 BC*, edited by Michael Loewe and Edward L. Shaughnessy, 292–351. Cambridge: Cambridge University Press.

Sheehan, James J. 2008. *Where Have All the Soldiers Gone? The Transformation of Modern Europe*. Boston: Houghton Mifflin.

Sicking, Louis. 2010. "Naval Warfare in Europe, c. 1330–c. 1680." In *European Warfare, 1350–1750*, edited by Frank Tallett and D. J. B. Trim. Cambridge: Cambridge University Press.

Singer, J. David. 1991. "Peace in the Global System: Displacement, Interregnum, and Transformation." In *The Long Postwar Peace: Contending Explanations and Projections*, edited by Charles W. Kegley Jr., 56–84. New York: Harper Collins.

Singer, J. David, and Melvin Small. 1972. *The Wages of War, 1816–1965*. New York: Wiley.

Sloan, Elinor C. 2002. *The Revolution in Military Affairs*. Montreal: McGill-Queen's University Press.

Small, Melvin, and J. David Singer. 1982. *Resort to Arms: International and Civil Wars, 1816–1980*. Beverly Hills, CA: Sage.

Smith, Adam. [1776] 1991. *The Wealth of Nations*. New York: Knopf.

Snyder, Glenn H. 1965. "The Balance of Power and the Balance of Terror." In *Balance of Power*, edited by Paul Seabury. San Francisco: Chandler.

Snyder, Jack. 1984. *The Ideology of the Offensive*. Ithaca, NY: Cornell University Press.

———. 1990. "The Concept of Strategic Culture: Caveat Emptor." In *Strategic Power: USA/USSR*, edited by Carl Jacobsen. New York: St. Martin's Press.

———. 1991. *Myths of Empire: Domestic Politics and International Ambition*. Ithaca, NY: Cornell University Press.

———. 2002. "Anarchy and Culture: Insights from the Anthropology of War." *International Organization* 56 (Winter): 7–45.

Soja, Edward W. 2000. *Postmetropolis: Critical Studies of Cities and Regions*. New York: Wiley-Blackwell.

Solingen, Etel. 2007. *Nuclear Logics: Contrasting Paths in East Asia and the Middle East*. Princeton, NJ: Princeton University Press.

Southern, Pat. 2006. *The Roman Army: A Social and Institutional History*. Santa Barbara, CA: ABC CLIO.

Spalinger, Anthony J. 2005. *War in Ancient Egypt*. Malden, MA: Blackwell.

Stack-O'Connor, Alisa. 2007. "Lions, Tigers, and Freedom Birds: How and Why the Liberation Tigers of Tamil Eelam Employs Women." *Terrorism and Political Violence* 19: 43–63.

Starr, Harvey, ed. 2009. *Dealing with Failed States: Crossing Analytic Boundaries*. Oxford: Taylor and Francis.

Stein, Arthur A. 1978. *The Nation at War*. Baltimore, MD: Johns Hopkins University Press.

Stein, Gil. 1999. *Rethinking World Systems: Diasporas, Colonies, and Interaction in Uruk Mesopotamia*. Tucson: University of Arizona Press.

Sterling, Brent L. 2009. *Do Good Fences Make Good Neighbors? What History Teaches Us about Strategic Barriers and International Security*. Washington, DC: Georgetown University Press.

Stillman, Nigel, and Nigel Tallis. 1984. *Armies of the Ancient Near East, 3,000 BC to 559 BC*. Worthing, Sussex, UK: Wargames Research Group.

Strachan, Hew, and Andreas Herberg-Rothe, eds. 2007. *Clausewitz in the Twenty-First Century*. Oxford: Oxford University Press.

Strachan, Hew, and Sybille Scheipers, eds. 2011. *The Changing Character of War*. New York: Oxford University Press.

Streich, Philip A. 2010. "The Failure of the Balance of Power: Warring States Japan, 1467–1590." Ph.D. diss., Rutgers University.

Stubbs, Richard. 2005. *Rethinking Asia's Economic Miracle: The Political Economy of War, Prosperity, and Crisis*. New York: Palgrave.

Sullivan, Brian R. 1998. "The Future Nature of Conflict: A Critique of 'The American Revolution in Military Affairs' in the Era of Jointery." *Defense Analysis* 14 (August): 91–100.

Tallett, Frank. 1992. *War and Society in Early Modern Europe, 1494–1715*. New York: Routledge.

Tammen, Ronald L., et al. 2000. *Power Transitions: Strategies for the 21st Century*. New York: Chatham House Publishers.

Tannenwald, Nina. 2007. *The Nuclear Taboo: The United States and the Non-Use of Nuclear Weapons since 1945*. New York: Cambridge University Press.

Teleki, Geza. 1973. *The Predatory Behavior of Wild Chimpanzees*. Lewisburg, PA: Bucknell University Press.

Tetlock, Philip E., Richard Ned Lebow, and Geoffrey Parker, eds. 2006. *Unmaking the West: "What If?" Scenarios that Rewrite World History*. Ann Arbor: University of Michigan Press.

Thayer, Bradley A. 2004. *Darwin and International Relations: On the Evolutionary Origins of War and Ethnic Conflict*. Lexington: University Press of Kentucky.

Thompson, John N. 1994. *The Coevolutionary Process*. Chicago: University of Chicago Press.

Thompson, William R. 1988. *On Global War*. Columbia: University of South Carolina Press.

———. 1999a. *Great Power Rivalries*. Columbia: University of South Carolina Press.

———, ed. 1999b. "The Military Superiority Thesis and the Ascendance of Western Eurasia in the World System." *Journal of World History* 10: 143–78.

———. 2000. *The Emergence of the Global Political Economy*. London: University College Press/Routledge.

———. 2002. "Testing a Cyclical Instability Theory in the Ancient Near East." *Comparative Civilizations Review* 46 (Spring): 34–78.

———. 2006. "Emerging Violence, Global War, and Terrorism." In *Kondratieff Waves, Warfare and World Security*, edited by Tessaleno Devezas and Yuri Yakovets. Amsterdam: IOS Press.

———, ed. 2009. *Systemic Transitions: Past, Present, and Future*. New York: Palgrave-Macmillan.

Thompson, William R., and David Dreyer. 2011. *Handbook of Interstate Rivalry, 1494–2010*. Washington, DC: Congressional Quarterly Press.

Thompson, William R., and Karen A. Rasler. 1999. "War, the Military Revolution(s) Controversy, and Army Expansion: A Test of Two Explanations of Historical Influences on European State Making." *Comparative Political Studies* 32 (February): 3–31.

Tiger, L., and R. Fox. 1971. *The Imperial Animal*. New York: Rinehart and Winston.

Tilly, Charles. 1975. "Reflections on the History of European State Making." In *The Formation of National States in Western Europe*, edited by Charles Tilly, 3–83. Princeton, NJ: Princeton University Press.

———. 1990. *Coercion, Capital, and European States, AD 990–1990*. Cambridge, MA: Basil Blackwell.

Turchin, Peter, and Sergey Nefedov. 2009. *Secular Cycles*. Princeton, NJ: Princeton University Press.

Turney-High, Harry H. [1949] 1991. *Primitive War: Its Practice and Concepts*. Columbia: University of South Carolina Press.

Underhill, Anne P. 2006. "Warfare and the Development of States in China." In *The Archaeology of Warfare: Prehistories of Raiding and Conquest*, edited by Elizabeth N. Arkush and Mark Waller, 253–85. Gainesville: University Press of Florida.

Vacca, William Alexander. 2009. "Learning about Military Effectiveness: Examining Theories of Learning during the Russo-Japanese War." Ph.D. diss., Rutgers University.

Vagts, Alfred. 1959. *A History of Militarism*. Rev. ed. New York: Free Press.

Van Creveld, Martin. 1989. *Technology and War: From 2000 BC to the Present*. New York: Free Press.

———. 1991. *The Transformation of War*. New York: Free Press.

Van Evera, Stephen. 1984. "The Cult of the Offensive and the Origins of the First World War." *International Security* 9 (Summer): 58–108.

———. 1990/91. "Primed for Peace." *International Security*, 15 (Winter): 7–57.

———. 1994. "Hypotheses on Nationalism and War." *International Security* 18 (Spring): 5–39.

Van Hoof, Jaram. 1990. "Intergroup Competition and Conflict in Animals and Men." In *Sociobiology and Conflict*, edited by J. van der Dennen and V. Falger. London: Chapman.

Vasquez, John A. 2009. *The War Puzzle Revisited*. New York: Cambridge University Press.

Vasquez, John A., and Marie T. Henehan. 2011. *Territory, War, and Peace*. London: Routledge.

Vayda, Andrew. 1976. *War in Ecological Perspective*. New York: Plenum.

Vayda, Andrew P. 1961. "Expansion and Warfare Among Swidden Agriculturalists." *American Anthropologist* 63: 346–58.

Väyrynen, Raimo. 2006. *The Waning of Major War: Theories and Debates*. London: Routledge.

Viner, Jacob. 1948. "Power versus Plenty as Objectives of Foreign Policy in the Seventeenth and Eighteenth Centuries." *World Politics* 1 (October): 1–29.

Vyvyan, J. M. K. 1968. "The Approach of the War of 1914." In *The New Cambridge Modern History*. Vol. 12, *The Shifting Balance of World Forces, 1898–1945*, edited by C. L. Mowat, 140–70. Cambridge: Cambridge, University Press.

Wade, Nicholas. 2006. *Before the Dawn: Recovering the Lost History of Our Ancestors*. New York: Penguin.

Wagner, R. Harrison. 2007. *War and the State: The Theory of International Politics*. Ann Arbor: University of Michigan Press.

Waltz, Kenneth N. 1990. "Nuclear Myths and Political Realities." *American Political Science Review* 84 (September): 731–45.

Walzer, Michael. 2007. *Just and Unjust Wars*. New York: Basic Books.

Webster, David. 1975. "Warfare and the Evolution of the State: A Reconsideration." *American Antiquity* 40: 464–70.

———. 1999. "Ancient Maya Warfare." In *War and Society in the Ancient and Medieval Worlds*, edited by K. Raaflaub and N. Rosenstein, 333–60. Cambridge, MA: Harvard University Press.

Weede, Erich. 2003. "Globalization, Creative Destruction, and the Prospects of a Capitalist Peace." In *Globalization and Armed Conflict*, edited by Gerald Schneider, Katherine Barbieri, and Nils Petter Gleditsch. Lanham, MD: Rowman and Littlefield.

Wees, Hans van. 2004. *Greek Warfare: Myths and Realities*. London: Duckworth.

White, Lynn T., Jr. 1962. *Medieval Technology and Social Change*. Oxford: Oxford University Press.

Whitehead, Neil. 1990. "The Snake Warriors—Sons of the Tiger's Teeth: A Descriptive Analysis of Carib Warfare ca. 1500–1820." In *The Anthropology of War*, edited by Jonathan Haas, 146–70. Cambridge: Cambridge University Press.

Wilson, Charles. 1978. *Profit and Power: A Study of England and the Dutch Wars*. The Hague: Martinus Nijhoff.

Wilson, E. O. 1978. *On Human Nature*. Cambridge, MA: Harvard University Press.

Wink, Andre. 2004. *Al-Hind: The Making of the Indo-Islamic World*. Vol. 3. Leiden: E. J. Brill.

Wrangham, Richard. 2006. "Why Apes and Humans Kill." In *Conflict*, edited by Martin Jones and A. C. Fabian, 43–62. Cambridge: Cambridge University Press.

Wrangham, Richard, and Dale Peterson. 1996. *Demonic Males: Apes and the Origins of Human Violence*. London: Bloomsbury.

Wright, David C. 2002. "The Northern Frontier." In *A Military History of China*, edited by David A. Graff and Robin Higham, 57–79. Boulder, CO: Westview Press.

Wright, Gordon. 1968. *The Ordeal of Total War*. Prospect Heights, IL: Waveland Press.

Wright, Quincy. 1965. *A Study of War*. Chicago: University of Chicago Press.

Yates, Robin D. S. 1999. "Early China." In *War and Society in the Ancient and Medieval Worlds: Asia, the Mediterranean, Europe and Mesoamerica*, edited by Kurt Raaflaub and Nathan Rosenstein, 7–45. Cambridge, MA: Harvard University Press.

Zacher, Mark W. 2001. "The Territorial Integrity Norm: International Boundaries and the Use of Force." *International Organization* 55 (Spring): 215–50.

Zagare, Frank C., and D. Marc Kilgour. 2000. *Perfect Deterrence*. Cambridge: Cambridge University Press.

Index

accelerations in warfare, 121; coevolution, 151–52; differentiated transformations, 186, 208; first acceleration, 15, 17, 87–90, 121–22; hegemonic aspirations, 177; industrialization, 222n21; paradigmatic innovation, 177; revolutions in warfare (Gabriel), 87; second acceleration, 15, 17, 90, 93, 121–22; third acceleration, 15, 17; warring states, 155; western trajectory, 77
Adams, Colin, 107
adaptation, 229n30
Adolphus, Gustavus, 138, 234n17
Adrianople, battle of, 175
aggregate-contract style, 160–61
Agincourt, 233n6
agrarian-pastoral division of labor, 46–47
agrarian strategy, 14
agrarian style warfare emergence, 90
agriculture-urbanization relationship, 223n15
Akkad, 90
Alan heavy cavalry, 181
Alexander the Great, 59, 105, 174–75
Alexandrian conquest, 105–6
Algaze, Guillermo, 173
Allen, Mark W., 223n10
Alstone, Richard, 107
Amsler, Sylvia J., 223n8
ancient army mobility, 231n4
Andean trajectory, 157
Anderson, Eric, 225n33
Angel, Norman, 221n17
Anglin, Simon, 172
archaeological/anthropological analysis of conflict, 22

Archer, Christian, 19, 51, 54, 172, 222n1, 237n23
arc of war, 51
Ardant, Gabriel, 150, 168
Ardrey, Robert, 223n6
Arkush, Elizabeth N., 223n10
armor, 221n16
Arquilla, John, 127
artillery revolution (fifteenth century), 131
Asian culture, 183
Athenian democratization and galley rower recruitment, 103–4
atlatl, 119, 232n21
Atzili, Boaz, 236n18
Aum Shinrikyo, 4, 219n5
Ayton, Andrew, 237n26
Aztecs, 119–20

Bachrach, Bernard S., 175, 237n25
Bailey, Jonathan B., 134
balancing strategies, 230n36
Balcells, Laia, 203, 239n7, 239n9, 241n22
Ballentine, Karen, 225n32
bands, 226n35
Bamforth, Douglas B., 225n33
Barbieri, Katherine, 234n24
Barnett, Michael N., 191, 236n10, 236n19
Bates, Robert H., 240n20
battle carts and chariots, 89
battleship revolution, 134
Bean, R., 60
Bell, David A., 234n20
Berghahn, Volker R., 141
Best, Geoffrey, 234n20
Betts, Richard K., 221n15, 241n1, 241n2

Biddle, Stephen, 233n4, 233n13
Biolsi, Thomas, 224n23
Black, Jeremy, 54, 127, 129, 142, 163, 233n8, 234n20
blitzkrieg, 135, 151
Bloch, Marc, 216
Bloom, Mia, 221n15
Boemeke, Manfred F., 134
Boggs, Marion, 134
Bond, Brian, 234n20
Boot, Max, 232n1
Boulding, Kenneth, 235n27
Bowden, Hugh, 107, 231n9
Brodie, Bernard, 129, 134, 232n1, 241n2
Brodie, Fawn M., 129, 134, 232n1
bronze and iron penetration comparison, 90–91
Brown, Michael E., 233n11
Brzoska, Michael, 240n15
Builder, Carl H., 227n5
Bundy, McGeorge, 241n2
Burns, Thomas S., 175
Buzan, Barry, 140
Bygott, J. D., 223n9

Caesar, Julius, 59
Campbell, Brian, 107
capability symmetry and conquest/contraction, 236n12
Carneiro, Robert, 34, 35, 47, 78, 224n24
Carolingian expansion, 175
Carpenter, C. R., 223n9
Carr, Edward Hallett, 227n6
Casson, Lionel, 102, 103
Centeno, Miguel A., 189, 191, 220n11, 236n17, 236n19
Chan, Steve, 241n5
Chandler, David, 140
Chaniotis, Angelos, 103, 107
Chapman, John, 37
Charlemagne, 163
Chase, Kenneth, 56, 179, 183, 230n34
Chase-Dunn, Christopher, 224n24
Chavin/Moche trajectory, 42–44
Chickering, Roger, 134, 222n20
chiefdom distinctions (single vs. multiple), 35
chimpanzee aggression, 223n8, 223n9; compared to bonobo behavior, 24–25
China trajectory, 79, 157; chariots, 113; co-evolution, 112–17; early years, 42–44; threat environment, 112, 123; warring states era, 115
Choucri, Nazli, 225n32
Churchill, Winston, 140
Cioffi-Revilla, Claudio, 5, 21, 47, 51, 62–65, 78
Cipolla, Carlo M., 132
circumscription thesis, 34, 51, 224n24; costs and legitimacy, 236n10; warfare exceptions, 36
Claessen, Henri J. M., 40
Clark, John F., 190
clash of civilizations thesis, 240n18
Clausewitz, Carl von, 126, 150, 219n2, 219n4
coercive advantage and regional hegemony, 184
coevolution of war thesis, 13–14, 55–63, 124, 164; acceleration, 85–86, 183–84; climate, 57; coercive advantage, 183; constraints, 166; culture, 58–59; individuals, 59; military organization, 13–14, 212; military revolutions, 17, 55, 61; perspective, 10–12; politico-economic complexity, 13–15, 55–56; political organization, 13–14, 55; population, 57–58; primary driver, 208–9; severity, 137–44; strong states, 167; threat environment, 13–14, 55–56; war, 55, 213–14; weak states, 167; weaponry, 13–14, 55, 123–24
Cohen, Eliot, 129, 133–34
Cohen, Ronald, 33, 36, 38, 46–47, 60, 223n11, 237n26
cohort, 109
Collier, Paul, 225n32
complex adaptive systems, 226n1
composite bow, 180
Congress of Vienna, 9
Cornell, T. J., 107, 232n15
Cortés, Hernán, 120
Cotterell, Arthur, 89
counterfactual arguments, 229n26
Crecy (1346), 6
Crone, Patricia, 238n28
Cronin, Audrey Kurth, 221n15
crossbow, 181, 233n6
"cult of the offensive," 134

Daggett, Stephen, 73–74, 228n23
Dannreuther, Roland, 240n21
Darnell, John, 94
Darwin, Charles, 229n25
Darwinian perspective, 12

Davie, Maurice, 219n1
Dawson, Doyne, 237n23
Dehio, Ludwig, 230n36
Delbruck, Hans, 54
democratic peace, 234n24, 236n15; industrialization, 72–75
Den Boer, Andrea M., 225n32
Denemark, Robert, 235n5
Dennen, J. van der, 223n9
Desch, Michael, 83, 192, 236n17
de Souza, Philip, 107
de Soysa, Indra, 225n32
DeWaal, Frans, 24, 223n8, 223n9
Diamond, Larry, 219n6
Di Cosmo, Nicola, 112
Diehl, Paul F., 225n32
diversionary theory of war, 240n16
double origination of war thesis, 38–39
Downes, Alexander, 69, 73, 98, 228n18
Downing, Brian M., 237n26
Doyle, Michael, 150, 228n20, 228n21, 236n15
Dreyer, David, 114, 167
Duffy, Christopher, 133
Dupuy, Ernest, 6, 132
Dupuy, Trevor, 6, 132, 232n1
Duyvesteyn, Isabelle, 240n13
dynamic of consolidation and dissolution model, 155–57

Earle, Timothy, 36, 224n26
East Asian military trajectory, 77. *See also* China trajectory
Eastern North American warfare, 44–45
Eckhardt, William, 6
Eckstein, Arthur M., 110
ecological-evolutionary theory, 227n12
economic interdependence and peace, 228n14
economic liberal ideology critique, 227n6
economic strategies, 56, 65–66; coercive competition, 228n19
Edwards, Martin S., 60, 219n7, 233n5, 237n26
Egyptian coevolutionary trajectory, 93–97, 157; threat environment, 122–23
Eldredge, Niles, 129
Ellis, Peter B., 182
Elman, Colin, 238n32
Eltis, David E., 237n26
embedded ideas, 59
Ember, Carol R., 224n17, 225n33
Ember, Melvin, 225n33

empire and army size, 91–92
Emsley, Clive, 234n20
environmental security, 225n32
European trajectory, 79; chemical explosions and technological change, 136; trading system as engine of growth, 139
Evangelista, Matthew, 227n8
evolution: biology, 12; pace acceleration, 15–16
evolutionary perspective, 10–13
evolution of war model, 76–77
extrastate war, 9

failed states, 205, 229n27, 240n21
Falger, Vincent, 11, 223n9
Farris, Willaim W., 230n32
Farrokh, Kareh, 77
Fazal, Tanisha M., 238n3
Fearon, James D., 151, 193
Ferejohn, John A., 80
Ferguson, Brian, 20–23, 222n2, 223n9, 223n19, 223n19, 225n32, 237n21
Ferrill, Arther, 5, 28–29, 60, 78, 98–99, 104–5, 107, 172, 224n16, 225n31, 237n23
feudal style, 160–61
firepower revolution, 134
first intermediate (Egypt), 94
Flannery, Kent V., 222n3
Foch, Ferdinand, 140
food storage and warfare expansion, 37
force de frappe, 69
Forster, Stig, 134
Fox, R., 223n9
France, John, 237n26
Frederick the Great, 133
Friday, Karl F., 230n32
Friedman, George, 135–36
Friedman, Meredith, 135–36
From Sumer to Rome (Gabriel and Metz), 237n23
frontiers: chronic warfare, 179; warfare severity, 37
Fuller, J. F. C., 134

Gabriel, Richard, 77, 87–91, 121, 172–73, 178, 222n18, 223n15, 231n1, 231n2, 231n5, 231n6, 237n23
Gabrielsen, Vincent, 107
Gaddis, John, 219n7
Gallagher, John, 165
Gartzke, Erik, 228n21, 234n24

Gat, Azar, 5, 12, 25, 26, 72–75, 139, 219n6, 223n9, 228n22, 234n24, 237n21
Geller, Daniel S., 241n2
Genghiz Khan, 12
Gibler, Douglas M., 145, 234n24
Gilbert, Felix, 140, 168
Gilpin, Robert, 165
Gleditsch, Nils Petter, 10, 225n32, 228n21, 234n24
Glete, Jan, 132
global hegemony and direct territorial conquest, 165
globalizing weak state, 240n21
Gnirs, Andrea M., 94, 96
Goertz, Gary, 235n29
Goldstein, Joshua S., 219n9, 227n7
Goldsworthy, Adrian, 107
Gommans, Jos, 230n32
Goodall, Jane, 223n9
Goodwin, Crauford D., 228n20
Gould, Steven J., 129
Graff, David A., 113–15, 230n32
Gray, Colin S., 127, 129, 135, 140, 222n18, 233n3, 233n4
great power warfare and increasing severity, 130–44
Great Wall (China), 112
Greece (ancient) trajectory, 97–108; chariots, 97–98; coevolution, 105–8; naval warfare 102; naval warships, 103; threat environment, 123
greek fire, 103
Greenhalgh, P. A. L., 107
Greenhill, Kelly M., 225n32
group segmentation, 29–34, 51; dowries, 32–33; political organization relationship, 224n20; sense of group identity, 30–31
Grousset, Rene, 165
Guerlac, Henry, 133
Guilmartin, John F., 132
Gulick, Edward, 230n36, 236n14
Gunpowder revolution (fifteenth to sixteenth centuries), 131
Gurr, Ted R., 10, 220n12

Haas, Jonathan, 5, 44–45, 60, 78, 224n25
Hall, Jonathan, 107
Hall, Thomas, 224n24
Hamblin, William, 23, 77, 94
Hanson, Victor D., 107, 179, 238n29
Harbom, Lotta, 10
Harris, William V., 107, 110
Hassig, Ross, 37, 77, 117–18, 230n31, 236n12
Hausfater, Glen, 223n9
Hearder, Harry, 222n1
heavy cavalry introduction, 232n20
hegemonic decline and resource overextension, 165
Hegre, Havard, 228n21, 234n24
Henehan, Marie, 235n26
Herbst, Jeffrey, 189, 191, 236n19
Herwig, Holger, 134
Hewitt, J. Joseph, 10, 220n12
Heydemann, Steven, 189, 191, 236n19
Hideyoshi, Toyotomi, 14
Higham, Robin, 230n32
Hintze, Otto, 168
Hironaka, Ann, 83, 167, 186, 187–88, 192, 236n17, 239n10
Hiroshima, 135
Hirst, Paul, 201
History of Warfare, A (Keegan), 4
Hitler, Adolf, 143, 146, 148, 235n29
Hobbes, Thomas, 24
Hoeffler, Anke, 225n32
Holsti, Kalevi J., 192, 220n11, 220n12, 236n17
Homer-Dixon, Thomas F., 225n32
homo sapiens bellicosity, 25–26; Neandertal interaction, 4–5
Hopkins, Keith, 110
hoplite formation, 98–102, 105, 174; armor, 231n10
Horowitz, Michael C., 227n5
Howard, Michael, 139, 232n2
Hrdy, Sarah B., 233n9
Hudson, Valerie M., 225n32
Hui, Victoria Tin-bor, 230n32
Human Security Centre (Canada), 10, 220n12
Humphreys, N. Macartan, 225n32
Humphries, Mark, 107
Huntingford, F., 223n9
hunting and basic military formations, 28; homicidal skills, 51; warfare, 38
hunting-gathering strategy, 14; warfare, 88
Huntington, Samuel, 141, 240n18
Hurrell, Andrew, 220n11
Hyksos, 95–97, 180–81, 210

ideational conflict and political economy, 58
identity wars, 197

Ikle, Fred C., 150
Iliad (Homer), 97, 100
imperial warfare, 220n13
incentives for warmaking, 28
Indian trajectory, 79
industrial production strategy, 14
industrialization and coercive competition, 228n16; warfare probability, 229n24
information revolution, 135
infantry revolution (fourteenth century), 131
innovation, 105
internal-external warfare ratio, 192–94
intermediate periods (Egypt), 95
intrastate war, 9
Iriye, Akira, 235n29
iron transition and agrarian productivity, 92

Japan and monopolization of firearms, 14, 80, 230n34; trajectory, 79
Jebel Sahaba mass burial, 21–22
Jervis, Robert, 135, 146, 226n1, 235n28, 236b16, 241n2
Johnson, Roger N., 223n9
Johnston, Alastair I., 227n5
Joll, James, 145
Jones, Archer, 54, 129, 172

Kagan, Donald, 222n1
Kaldor, Mary, 85, 194–98, 200–201, 204–5
Kalyvas, Stathis, 83, 201–3, 230n37, 239n7, 239n9, 241n22
Katzenstein, Peter J., 58
Kaysen, Carl, 72, 82, 146–50, 198, 204, 235n30
Keegan, John, 4–5, 58, 179, 182–83
Keeley, Lawrence, 222n4, 223n10, 223n11, 237n21
Kelley, Raymond, 21–22, 29–33, 37, 47, 51–52, 78, 237n21
Kennedy, Paul, 82, 150, 165
Keppie, Lawrence, 107, 232n15
Khaltourina, Daria, 57
Khan, Iqtidar A., 230n32
Kier, Elizabeth, 227n5
Kilgour, Marc, 241n2
Kirch, Patrick, 46
Klare, Michael T., 225n32
Knorr, Klaus, 144, 145
Knox, MacGregor, 60, 127, 222n18, 234n14, 237n26
Korotayev, Andrey, 57

Krebs, Ronald R., 225n32
Krepinevich, Andrew F., 127–28, 131–35, 151, 222n18, 237n26
Kugler, Jacek, 241n2
Kupchan, Charles A., 165

Laitin, David, 193
land powers and seapowers, 238n34
land warfare revolution (nineteenth century), 132
Lanting, Frans, 24
large game distribution and war, 39, 225n30
Latin American warfare, 220
learning, 229n30
Le Billion, Phillippe, 225n32
LeBlanc, Steven, 46, 222n5, 237n21
Lebow, R. Ned, 229n26
Lee, A. D., 107
Leebaert, Derek, 234n20
Lekson, Stephen H., 225n33
Lenin, V. I., 225n32
Lenski, Gerhard, 227n12
lessons of history and beliefs, 235n28
Levathes, Louise, 230n34
leveé en masse, 133
Levy, Jack S., 3, 59, 60, 131–32, 134, 150, 219n7, 219n9, 220n10, 225n32, 228n22, 229n26, 229n30, 230n36, 233n5, 235n28, 235n29, 236n10, 236n14, 236n15, 238n34, 240n16, 241n5
Lewis, Herbert, 36–37
Lewis, Mark, 113–16, 230n32
Liberman, Peter, 235n25
Libyan invasions (Egypt), 96
Li Liu, 112, 114, 232n18
Lococo, Paul, 54
longbow, 131, 233n6
long peace, 219n8
Lorenz, Konrad, 25–26, 223n6
Lorge, Peter A., 14, 230n34
Lowi, Miriam R., 225n32
Luard, Evan, 219n7, 228n22, 240n14
Ludes, James M., 221n15
Lynn, John, 16, 58, 80, 131, 155–63, 169, 172, 176, 207, 234n18, 236n9, 237n20, 237n26, 238n29

Macedoninan military revolution, 104–5; threat environment, 104
Magdoff, Harry, 225n32

Mahnken, Thomas G., 227n5
major power rivalries, 167
Malinowski, Bronislaw, 219n4
Malkov, Artemy, 57
Malthus, Thomas, 57
Malthusian perspective on growth dynamics, 76
managerial revolution, 141
Manasa, Collen, 94
maniple formation, 109, 175
Mansfield, Edward D., 234n24
Marathon (490 BCE), 6
marcher lords, 180
Marcus, Joyce, 155–59, 163, 222n3, 237n20
Mares, David, 220n11
Marne, Battle of the (1915), 6
Marshall, Monty G., 220n12
Martin, Lisa L., 139
Marwick, Arthur, 234n20
mass reserve style, 160–62
Mattingly, D. J., 30, 224n20
Maurice (of Nassau), 138, 234n17
McDermott, Bridget, 94
McDonald, Patrick J., 228n21, 234n24
McIntosh, Jane, 23
McNeill, William H., 129, 134, 180, 232n1
Mead, Margaret, 31, 223n7, 229n30
Mearsheimer, John J., 233n13, 236n13
mechanization of war, 134
medieval-stipendiary style, 160–61
Megiddo (1469 BCE), 6
melee format, 100; naval fighting, 233n7
Mellaart, James, 223n15
Mesoamerican coevolution, 117–18, 120–21; threat environment, 123; trajectory, 77, 79, 122, 157
Mesopotamian trajectory, 42–44
metallurgical developments, 226n4
Metz, Karen S., 172, 178, 237n23
Middle Kingdom (Egypt), 94–95
Migdal, Joel S., 236n17
military doctrines, 226n4, 227n8
military revolutions, 127–29, 135, 140, 151, 153, 158, 222n18, 227n8; early modern Europe, 17, 178; effects, 60–61; evolutionary context, 89; late medieval, 178; nanotechnology, 137; probability of war diminishment, 17; sailing ships with cannon, 132; Stone Age developments, 231n1

military styles, 156–57
military technical revolutions (MTRs), 128
military threshold, 23
Miller, Benjamin, 145
Miller, John H., 226n1
Millis, Walter, 134, 140–41, 234n21
Milward, Alan S., 234n20
Ming abandonment of naval lead, 80; voyages, 230n34
Mitani, John C., 223n8
Monks, Sarah, 107
Morgan, T. Clifton, 220n10
Morillo, Stephen, 54
Mousseau, Michael, 228n21, 234n24
Mueller, John, 85, 144–46, 148, 194, 198–201, 204, 221n17, 228n21, 235n29, 240n17, 241n2, 241n24
Munkler, Herfried, 85, 240n13, 240n15
Murray, Williamson, 60, 127–28, 131, 135, 140, 151, 222n18, 233n, 234n14, 237n26
Mussolini, Benito, 143, 148, 235n29
Mycenaean early Bronze Age, 97, 99, 106

Nagler, Jorg, 134
Napoleon (Bonaparte), 6, 59, 133
Napoleonic Wars and military technology, 140
Naqada I (Egypt), 94
nation in arms, 140
Near Eastern trajectory (ancient), 77
necessary condition counterfactuals, 235n29
Nef, John V., 233n10
Nefedov, Sergey, 57
Neiberg, Michael S., 216
Neisser, Henreich, 221n15
New Kingdom (Egypt), 94–96, 174
new major powers, 215
new states and internal warfare, 83, 221n14
new wars, 18, 194, 196–98, 200–204, 240n13; globalization, 240n15
Nicolle, David, 172
noble savage image of warfare, 24
nomadic threat, 210–11; cavalry, 179; gunpowder, 179, 183
North, Douglass C., 138, 240n20
North, Robert, 225n32
nuclear proliferation, 216
nuclear revolution, 135, 144, 241n2
nuclear weapons, 212; deterrence, 241n2; spending (U.S.), 69
Nye, Joseph, 127, 129, 135, 237n26

obsolescence of war, 145–46, 198
O'Connell, Robert L., 46, 222n5, 224n27, 237n21
offensive/defensive balance, 131, 133–34, 233n11
offensive realism, 235n4
Offley, Ed, 127
O'Hanlon, Michael, 127
Old Kingdom (Egypt), 94–95
old wars, 195, 197
Olmecs, 117–19
Oman, Charles, 175
Oneal, John, 228n14, 228n21, 234n24, 236n15
On the Origins of War and the Preservation of Peace (Kagan), 222n1
Operation Overlord (1944), 6
organizational complexity and political centralization, 47; sedentary agriculture, 47
Organski, A. F. K., 241n2
Osgood, Robert, 138, 140, 141
Otterbein, Keith, 4, 33, 38–40, 42–44, 47, 51, 78, 222n1, 225n32, 225n34, 226n36, 226n37
Owens, William A., 127, 129, 135, 237n26

Page, Scott E., 226n1
Palmer, M. A. J., 132
Pape, Robert A., 221n15
paradigmatic armies, 80, 156, 159; regional hegemony, 17; warfare acceleration, 16
paradigmatic shift model, 155–57, 159
Paret, Peter, 129
Parker, Geoffrey, 127, 129, 131, 132, 139, 229n26, 234n17, 234n18, 237n26
patriotism, French Revolutionary Wars, 234n19
Paul, T. V., 241n2
Payne, James L., 7
Peers, C .J., 77, 113–16
Peloponnesian Wars, 101–3, 105, 232n12
Perrin, Noel, 230n34
Peterson, Dale, 24, 223n9
Petterson, Therese, 220n12
phalanx, 11, 40, 81, 88, 99–100, 105, 175, 179–80, 182; Etruscan, 108; Macedonian, 104, 174; Roman, 108–9
Pinker, Steven, 7, 10
Pipes, Daniel, 238n28
poison gas, 166

policing wars, 240n19
political centralization agriculture, 47–48; military organization, 49; military sophistication/efficiency, 225n34; village fortifications, 50; warfare, 39; weaponry/body armor/shields, 50
political-economical complexity and organizational/weaponry, 71; theory, 67–68
political-economic evolution, 67; effects, 66; resource scarcity, 56–57, 225n32; war, 70
political organization centrality, 211; complexity continuums, 224n25; early stages, 40
Pollins, Brian, 234n24
popular-conscript style, 160–62
population density and scarcity, 237n22
population growth and military specialization, 35; shock tactics, 35–36
Porter, Bruce D., 137, 139, 141–43, 234n20
Posen, Barry R., 227n8
postindustrial dominant strategy, 227–28n13
Powell, Robert, 151
praetorian weak states, 240n21
pre-dynastic (Egypt), 94
preemption, 235n30
Preston, Richard, 129, 140
Prestowich, Michael, 129
Price, J. L., 237n26
projectile weaponry, 230n31
primitive war, 27–28, 223n11
pristine state evolutionary trajectories, 42–44
professionalization of military power, 141
Prunier, Gerard, 190
punctuated equilibrium model of warfare, 129, 233n4

Qin/Han dynasties (China), 114–16

Raaflaub, Kurt, 101, 102
railroad development, 133
Rankov, Boris, 107
Rapkin, David P., 228n14, 234n24
Rapoport, David C., 83, 221n15
Rasler, Karen, 138, 150, 168, 221n15, 228n21, 234n18, 234n20, 234n24, 236n15
Rathbone, Dominic, 107
rationalization of military power, 138
Ray, James Lee, 234n24
regional displacement of warfare, 192–93, 239n9

regional evolutionary trajectories, 16
regional hegemony, 176; bellicosity advantage, 164
Register, Katherine, 222n5, 237n21
Reiter, Dan, 151
remnants of war thesis, 198–200, 204
reproduction and survival emphasis, 12
resource unpredictability, 225n33
Restall, Matthew, 232n22
Retreat from Doomsday (Mueller), 145
Reuter, Timothy, 175
revolution of sail and shot, 132, 134
Ritter, Gerhard, 141
RMA (revolution in military affairs), 127–28, 135, 232n3; nonstate actors, 234n15
Roberts, Michael, 127, 129, 138–39, 141, 150, 158, 226n2, 237n26
Robertson, Esmonde D., 235n29
Robinson, Ronald, 165
Rogers, Clifford J., 60, 127, 129, 222n18, 237n26
Rome, 110–11; naval warfare, 109; slaves and fall of Roman Empire, 110; threat environment, 109; trajectory, 107–12
Ronfeldt, David, 127
Ronnefeldt, Carsten F., 225n32
Ropp, Theodore, 140
Rose, Susan, 103
Rosecrance, Richard, 228n21
Rosen, Stephen P., 227n5, 227n8
Rosenbluth, Frances McCall, 80
Rosenstein, Nathan, 101–2, 107, 109–10
Ross, Michael l, 237n26
Ross, Steven T., 225n32
Rothenberg, Gunther E., 129
Rousseau, Jean-Jacques, 24
Russett, Bruce M., 228n14, 228n21, 234n24, 236n15, 239n7

Sagan, Scott, 236n16, 241n2
Sage, Michael M., 107
Santosusso, A., 165
Sargon, 121, 173–74, 180
Sarkees, Meredith, 10, 84, 220n12, 239n8
Sawyer, Ralph D., 183, 230n32
Scales, Robert H., 135
Scheina, Robert L., 220n11, 238n5
Scheipers, Sybille, 220n12
Schelling, Thomas C., 135, 146, 241n2
Schneider, Gerald, 228n21, 234n24

Schwartz Stephen I., 69
Sea Peoples, 96, 98, 231n7
Second Intermediate (Egypt), 94–95
secular cycle, 57–58
sedentary agriculture and military organization, 49–50; origins of war, 51; village fortifications, 50; weaponry, 50
Sekunde, Nicholas, 107
selection, 11, 77
selective pacification, 68, 70; asymmetry, 82; rising costs of war, 71–72
Serrati, John, 107
Shang dynasty (China), 113–14
Shankman, Paul, 225n33
Shapiro, Jeremy, 152, 233n3
Sherman, Jake, 225n32
Shaughnessy, Edward L., 232n17
Sheehan, James J., 234n20, 236n15
shields, 221n16
shield wall, 99, 182
shock and awe, 230n39
shock tactics, 50; shock weaponry, 230n31
Sicking, Louis, 132
Singer, J. David, 192, 220n9, 220n12, 228n22
Skalnik, Peter, 40
slave soldiers, 237n28
Sloan, Elinor C., 237n26
Small, Melvin, 220n9, 220n12, 228n22
Smith, Adam, 70, 72, 225n33
Snyder, Jack, 59, 134, 165, 227n5
sociological inevitability, 223n7
Soja, Edward W., 223n15
Solingen, Etel, 241n3
Southern, Pat, 107
Southwest North America and warfare, 44–45
Spalinger, Anthony J., 77, 94, 96
stable peace, 235n27
Stallone, Sylvester, 204
state-commission style, 160–61
state-strength dilemma, 167
Starr, Harvey, 229n27
Stein, Arthur, 173, 234n20
stirrup, 181
Strachan, Hew, 220n12
stalemate of the trenches, 135
strategic culture, 58; military organization, 227n5
strategies, 11
stratification in military expenditures, 68

INDEX 281

strong/weak states, 236n17
strong states and war making tendencies, 16
Stubbs, Richard, 238n2
subrationally unthinkable, 145
Sumer: decline, 93; threat environment, 90; warfare, 88, 90
Sundberg, Ralph, 10
symmetrical capabilities and warfare, 83

Tammen, Ronald L., 241n2, 241n5
Tanenwald, Nina, 241n2
technology of rebellion, 241n22, 241n23
telegraph development, 133
Teleki, Geza, 223n9
Teotihuacán, 119
Tercios, 176, 237n27
territorial conquest value, 145, 235n25
territorially inclined causes of war, 48
Tetlock, Philip E., 229n26
terrorism, 221n15; warfare, 240n17
Thayer, Bradley, 12, 225n33
Themner, Lotta, 220n12
Thompson, John N., 12
Thompson, William R., 3, 59, 132, 138–39, 150, 167–68, 221n15, 228n14, 228n21, 230n36, 231n8, 234n18, 234n20, 234n24, 236n14, 236n15, 238n34, 239n7, 241n5
threat environment, 79–80, 210; early modern Europe, 188–91; new states, 190–92; political organization, 186
Three Kingdoms/Ts'in, 114, 116
thuggery residual, 194, 198
Tiger, L., 223n9
Tilly, Charles, 60, 138–39, 226n2
Tojo, Hideki, 148, 235n29
Toltecs, 119
trace italienne, 131–32, 137, 176, 236n9
tribe, 226n35
Turchin, Peter, 57
Turner, A., 223n9
Turney-High, Harry, 27, 223n13

Ubaid resource acquisition network, 173
Underhill, Anne P., 112, 113
Urukian expansion, 173

Vacca, William A., 233n12
Vagts, Alfred, 141, 199
van Creveld, Martin, 83, 221n15, 232n1
Van Evera, Stephen, 134, 145, 233n11

Van Hoof, Jaram, 223n9
variety, 11
Vasquez, John A., 150, 219n3, 229n30, 235n26
Vauban, Sebastien Le Prestre de, 133
Vayda, Andrew, 225n32, 225n33
Väyrynen, Raimo, 219n7
Viner, Jacob, 139
volunteer-technical style, 160–62, 177
Vyvan, J. M. K., 134

Wade, Nicholas, 5
Wagner, R. Harrison, 151, 240n20
Walker, Thomas C., 60, 219n7, 233n5, 237n26
Wallis, John J., 240n20
Waltz, Kenneth N., 236n16, 241n2
war/aggression gene, 25
warfare: agricultural emergence, 29, 38–39, 223–24n16, 226n37; ancient ritualistic conflict, 27; asymmetry, 83–84; benefits and costs, 70–72; carrying capacity, 57–58; capability symmetry, 201–3; casualties due to acceleration, 16; civilian deaths, 73; Cold War bipolarity, 239n7; Cold War pressures and internal warfare protraction, 239n10; commercialization, 139; costs, 15, 72–74, 82, 146; definitions, 3–4, 219n4, 226n35; democratization, 140; diffusion, 79 diminished probability, 15, 17–18; duration, 150–51, 203n38; duration and development, 83–84; early evidence, 21–22; environmental stress, 44–46; escalation, 79; extrastate frequency, 10; foraging societies, 30; frequency, 7–8; gender, 227n7; genetic explanations, 24–27; group segmentation, 32; industrialization, 142–43, 149, 153, 221n17; intensity, 220n10; interstate frequency, 9–10; intrastate frequency, 10; leadership and political leadership, 38; learned behavior, 229n30; limited, 149; modern warfare, 134; moral/cultural restraints, 233n10; organized complexity, 47; political development model, 62–65; political-economic complexity, 82; popularization, 140; pugnacious instincts, 223n7; regional hegemony, 16; religion, 227n5; scientific revolution, 234n21; secondary developers, 41; severity, 7–8, 137, 220n10; steam, 233n9;

warfare (*cont.*)
  total; 69, 134, 141–42; warrior aristocracy, 40–41; weapon lethality, 17
"Warfare Is Only an Invention, Not a Biological Necessity" (Mead), 223n7
war-making–state-making, 60, 226n2, 236n19, 238n2
"war of all against all" image, 24
war origins, 12–13, 16–17, 78, 222n1; agrarian-pastoral divisions, 13, 51; circumscription, 13; complexity-scarcity interaction, 13; contact hypothesis, 20; environmental problems, 214–15; environmental stress, 51; explanation strategies, 23; future, 214; group segmentation, 13, 17, 78; hunting skills, 13, 16, 78; learned behavior problem, 19; military organization, 16, 78; paucity of evidence problem, 19; political centralization, 51; population growth/density 13, 52–53; prehistory, 120; weaponry, 16, 78
warring states, 114, 155
wars of kings, 140
wars of peoples, 140
Waterloo (1815), 6
Watts, David P., 223n8
Wayman, Frank, 10, 84, 220n12, 239n8
weak states, 205, 215, 236n17; nonwestern trajectories, 78; trap, 167–68; war making, 16, 83, 187–88
weaponry, 212–13; emergence, 28–29
Webster, David, 224n24
Weede, Erich, 228n21
Wees, Hans van, 100, 103, 107, 232n13
Weingast, Barry R., 240n20

western trajectory, 77, 80–87, 169, 177; accelerations, 81, 183; bifurcation of warfare propensities, 17, chariot era, 177; constraints on war, 77; feudal era, 177, 181; heavy cavalry, 175–76; ideological justification, 182; infantry intensification, 177–79; Middle East, 231n41; nonwestern influences, 180–82; superiority, 158; third acceleration, 16, 82
Western way of war, 179–83
White, Lynn T., Jr., 175
Whitehead, Neil, 20
Wilkenfeld, Jonathan, 10, 220n12
Wilson, Charles, 139, 223n9
Wise, Sidney, 129, 140
World trajectory, 83
World War I, and winners/losers distinction, 142–43
World War II, and end of Eurocentric world system, 15
Wrangham, Richard, 24, 25, 223n9
Wright, David C., 114
Wright, Gordon, 234n20
Wright, Quincy, 131, 219n7, 236n12

Xia dynasty, 112
Xingcan Chen, 112, 232n18
Xiongnu nomads, 115–16

Yates, Robin D., 114

Zacher, Mark W., 18, 167
Zagare, Frank C., 241n2
Zapotec trajectory, 42–44
Zhou dynasty, 112–14, 232n19

www.ingramcontent.com/pod-product-compliance
Lightning Source LLC
Chambersburg PA
CBHW050859300426
44111CB00010B/1300